THE
DEAD
MAC
SCROLLS

THE MACINTOSH BIBLE GUIDE TO

SAVING THOUSANDS
ON MAC REPAIRS

THE
DEAD
MAC
SCROLLS

HOW TO FIX HUNDREDS
OF HARDWARE PROBLEMS
WITHOUT GOING BANKRUPT

LARRY PINA

GOLDSTEIN & BLAIR
BOX 7635
BERKELEY CA 94707

Additional copies of *The Dead Mac Scrolls* are available from Goldstein & Blair, Box 7635, Berkeley CA 94707, 510/524-4000. Single copies cost $32 plus $4 for shipping and tax (if any) to US addresses. (For information on other products and shipping rates to foreign addresses, see the order pages in the back of the book.) We offer quantity discounts to computer stores, other retailers and wholesalers (except bookstores and book wholesalers), user groups, businesses, schools and individuals. Distribution to the book trade is through Publishers Group West, Box 8843, Emeryville CA 94662, 510/658-3453 (toll-free: 800/788-3123).

Goldstein & Blair donates at least 10% of its pretax profits to organizations working for social justice.

Technical editing: Jean Sorensen, Chuck Meyer
Copy-editing: Virginia Rich, John Kadyk
Proofreading: John Kadyk, Jan Brenner, Karen Faria
Index: Robyn Brode
Word processing: Adam Pollock, Jan Brenner
Cover: Trevor Irvin   Cover concept: Arthur Naiman
Inside design: Arthur Naiman, Karen Faria
Page layout (using Nisus 3.06): Larry Pina, Karen Faria
Fonts: Optima (from Adobe), Utility City (from Dubl-Click)
Printing: Michelle Selby, Consolidated Printers, Berkeley CA

Library of Congress Cataloging-in-Publication Data

Pina, Larry
      The dead Mac scrolls : the Macintosh Bible guide to saving
   thousands on Mac repairs / Larry Pina.
            p.   cm.
      Includes index.
      ISBN 0-940235-25-0 : $32.00
      1. Macintosh (Computer)--Maintenance and repair I. Title
   TK7889.M33P54 1992
   621.39'16--dc20   91-42658
                                                        CIP

printed in the United States of America   printing # 1 2 3 4 5 6 7 8 9

CONTENTS

Trademark notice

Because a major purpose of this book is to describe and comment on various hardware and software products, many such products are identified by their tradenames. In most—if not all—cases, these designations are claimed as legally protected trademarks by the companies that make the products. It is not our intent to use any of these names generically, and the reader is cautioned to investigate a claimed trademark before using it for any purpose except to refer to the product to which it is attached.

In particular: *Apple* and *Macintosh* are registered trademarks of Apple Computer, Inc. *The Macintosh Bible* is a trademark of Goldstein & Blair, which is not affiliated with Apple Computer, Inc.

Disclaimer

We've got to make a disclaimer that common sense requires: Although we've tried to check all the information in this book to make sure it's accurate, we can't guarantee that it is.

We can't be—and aren't—responsible for any damage or loss to your data or your equipment, or injury to yourself, that results directly or indirectly from your use of this book. We make no warranty, express or implied, about the contents of this book, its merchantability or its fitness for any particular purpose. The exclusion of implied warranties is not permitted by some states. The above exclusion may not apply to you. This warranty provides you specific legal rights. There may be other rights that you may have which vary from state to state.

Introduction

This book is like a family medical guide, except that it covers the Macintosh family of computer equipment. Reading it won't grant you a doctor's degree, but it will enable you to recognize common symptoms and correctly diagnose hardware problems.

The purpose of this book is to save you money. By looking up symptoms *before* you call for service, you can get a good idea of what's wrong and how much repairs should cost.

How to use this book

Every page describes a unique symptom, with text and illustrations (if you can't find the symptom you're looking for, check the *Symptom index* at the back of the book). Then there's a diagnosis of the problem (generally to the component level) and a suggested solution. Finally, each page provides three different cost estimates for effecting repairs:

The approximate cost of repairing it yourself assumes that you have access to tools and test equipment *and* that you already have the skills to use them. This applies to electronics instructors and their students, electrical engineers and their students, and independent service providers who've stayed away from Macintosh because of the lack of reliable troubleshooting information.

The wholesale part prices quoted in this section were taken (in no particular order) from the 1991 catalogs of the companies listed under *Parts vendors and service providers* at the end of this book. No attempt was made to find the lowest price; once I found the part I was looking for, that's the price I used. Since they're wholesale prices, there's often a minimum order quantity to get the price quoted.

The approximate third-party repair cost estimates what you'd pay for component-level repairs by an independent service provider. (If you can't find one in your area, check the *Parts vendors and service providers* list.)

The retail part prices quoted in this section are based on a common trade practice: The minimum parts charge is usually $5 and beyond that, the shop charges twice its own cost.

The $65 hourly labor rate is based on the various classified advertisements which run in the back of Mac magazines and occasionally in user group newsletters. Labor rates vary, though, and you don't always get what you pay for.

The approximate dealer repair cost reflects the cost of module or sub-assembly replacement. The prices quoted here were kindly provided by a local Apple dealer. Since you're paying for a whole new board or drive (instead of component-level repairs) dealer repair costs are *much* more expensive than third-party shops'. Still, sometimes it's worth spending the extra money.

For most people, the most cost-effective approach is to deal with a third-party repair shop—one that's willing to make guaranteed component-level repairs at a reasonable price. Dealing knowledgeably with a qualified service provider (rather than placing yourself at the mercy of an authorized board-swapper) is guaranteed to save you money, and that's what this book is all about.

How this book differs from a service manual

Service manuals are usually written while the equipment is in the design stage. This book, written after *years* of field experience, is more like a collection of service *bulletins*. It doesn't include schematics, complete parts lists and lengthy discussions of circuit theory. Instead, it describes known circuit failures and reveals proven solutions. And the material can be understood by anyone who wants to save money on Mac repairs, not just repair technicians.

Since it takes *years* for real failure data to accumulate, the older Macs are given the most coverage (because we know more about them) and the newer Macs are given the least coverage (because we know less about them). The Mac Classic and Classic II, the LC, IIsi, PowerBooks and Quadras aren't covered at all in this edition, since, as this is being written, every one of those Macs ever sold is still under warranty. Whatever failures they may have incurred have been handled for free by Apple dealers. Even after their one-year warranties expire, many of them will continue to be covered by AppleCare.

Failure histories don't mean that equipment manufacturers make inferior products; they make fine products, but nothing lasts forever. People get ill, computer equipment breaks. The real problem is the high cost of repairs—but with *The Dead Mac Scrolls,* costs can be kept to a minimum. Even if you only refer to it once, it should save you hundreds of dollars.

Guides for do-it-yourselfers

The Dead Mac Scrolls is a reference book, not a do-it-yourself repair guide. While most people are interested in getting as much as they can out of their computers, very few are interested in becoming repair technicians. As long as we can get good service at a fair price, most of us prefer to pay someone else to do the work.

If you take exception to that statement, you may enjoy one of my other Macintosh repair books:

Macintosh Repair & Upgrade Secrets, 350 pages, published in 1990 under the Hayden label by Sams (now Macmillan) teaches basic electronics (safety rules, how to solder, how to use test equipment, etc.) as applied to the Macintosh. Written for beginners, this book contains detailed take-apart instructions for the Mac 128K, 512K, 512Ke, Plus and SE, the Lisa and the Mac XL. Focusing primarily on analog board repairs and video adjustments, it comes with black-and-white Test Pattern Generator software for video alignment. The appendix includes a complete parts list for Mac Plus and Mac SE power supplies. $32.95

Macintosh Printer Secrets, 450 pages, also published in 1990 under the Hayden label, teaches introductory computer science in the context of the ImageWriter printer. Written for beginners, it contains detailed take-apart instructions for the ImageWriter I (standard and wide models) and the ImageWriter II. It focuses primarily on serial interface problems, mechanical repairs and maintenance adjustments, and comes with Test Character Generator printer-alignment software. $34.95

Macintosh II Repair and Upgrade Secrets, 250 pages, published in 1991 by Brady Publishing, teaches basic electronics as applied to a Macintosh II-and-monitor system. Written for beginners, this book covers the II/IIx/IIfx, the IIcx/IIci, IIsi, the Apple High-Resolution Monochrome monitor and AppleColor High-Resolution RGB monitor. Devoted primarily to logic board repairs and video adjustment instructions, it comes with Color Test Pattern Generator video-alignment software. $39.95

LaserWriter Repair and Upgrade Secrets, 250 pages, (as yet unpublished) will cover the LaserWriter, LaserWriter Plus, and the LaserWriters IISC, IINT and IINTX. Primarily focusing on logic board repairs, maintenance and step-by-step fuser repair instructions, it will come with Laser Test Character Generator diagnostic software.

The latest versions of Color Test Pattern Generator and Laser Test Character Generator are also available from Goldstein & Blair on the *Dead Mac Scrolls Disk*—see the end pages of this book.

Other Macintosh repair books to look for include:

Gene B. Williams' *Chilton's Guide to Macintosh Repair and Maintenance,* 212 pages, published in 1986 by Chilton Book Company. Written for beginners, this book covers the 128K and 512K Macs and the ImageWriter I. It explains how to take early Macs apart and swap boards, is nicely illustrated and well worth having. $12.50

Sams COMPUTERFACTS folder, product number CP8/08941, 29 pages, published in 1985 by Howard W. Sams & Company. Written for bench technicians, this file folder covers the ImageWriter I. It contains a complete logic board schematic (with clearly-marked reference voltages), a handy semiconductor cross-reference and a comprehensive set of logic charts. Focusing primarily on logic board repairs, this industry-standard package provides component-level troubleshooting information not found in *Macintosh Printer Secrets.* $24.95

Sams COMPUTERFACTS folder, product number CP27/09005, 37 pages, published in 1987 by Howard W. Sams & Company covers the ImageWriter II. Written for bench technicians, this file folder contains a complete logic board schematic (with clearly-marked reference voltages), a handy semiconductor cross-reference and a comprehensive set of logic charts. Focusing primarily on logic board repairs, this industry-standard package provides component-level troubleshooting information not found in *Macintosh Printer Secrets.* $24.95

Finally, up-to-date parts and test equipment information can be obtained by calling the vendors in the *Parts vendors and service providers* list at the end of this book. Most of them offer free quarterly catalogs, but it takes some time to get on the mailing list.

CHAPTER 1
EARLY MACS

Symptoms: On startup, a herringbone pattern appears on the display. Otherwise, the computer is usable.

Probable diagnosis: The problem is on the analog board.

Solution: Replace the flyback transformer (Apple part 157-0026-B) at board reference T1 with a later type (157-0042-C).

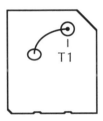

Approximate cost of repairing it yourself:		**$21.00**
1 flyback transformer	21.00	**1 hour**
Approximate third-party repair cost:		**$107.00**
1 flyback transformer	42.00	
1 hour labor	65.00	
Approximate dealer repair cost:		**$253.33**
1 new analog board	183.33	
1 hour labor	70.00	

Symptoms: An ozone (air-pollution/car exhaust) smell lingers about the computer. Otherwise, it seems OK.

Probable diagnosis: The problem is on the analog board.

Solution: Replace the flyback transformer (Apple part 157-0026-B) at board reference T1 with a later type (157-0042-C).

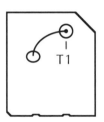

Approximate cost of repairing it yourself:		*$21.00*
1 flyback transformer	21.00	*1 hour*
Approximate third-party repair cost:		*$107.00*
1 flyback transformer	42.00	
1 hour labor	65.00	
Approximate dealer repair cost:		*$253.33*
1 new analog board	183.33	
1 hour labor	70.00	

Symptoms: On startup, the computer *momentarily* makes a loud whistle noise (like a teakettle). Otherwise, it seems OK.

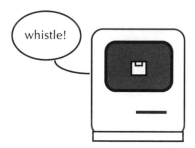

Probable diagnosis: The problem is on the analog board.

Solution: Replace the tunable coil (marked *Width)* at board reference L2 with a later type made of Litz wire.

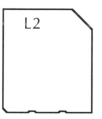

Approximate cost of repairing it yourself:		*$12.00*
1 width coil	12.00	*1 hour*
Approximate third-party repair cost:		*$89.00*
1 width coil	24.00	
1 hour labor	65.00	
Approximate dealer repair cost:		*$253.33*
1 new analog board	183.33	
1 hour labor	70.00	

Symptoms: Occasionally, the computer makes a high-pitched whining noise (like a mosquito). Otherwise, it seems OK.

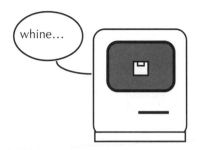

Probable diagnosis: The problem is on the analog board.

Solution: Replace the flyback transformer (Apple part 157-0026-B) at board reference T1 with a later type (157-0042-C).

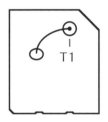

Approximate cost of repairing it yourself:		***$21.00***
1 flyback transformer	21.00	***1 hour***
Approximate third-party repair cost:		***$107.00***
1 flyback transformer	42.00	
1 hour labor	65.00	
Approximate dealer repair cost:		***$253.33***
1 new analog board	183.33	
1 hour labor	70.00	

Symptoms: There is a normal startup bong, but the display is dark or severely distorted. The computer makes a high-pitched whining noise (like a mosquito). After a few minutes, there is a burning smell.

Probable diagnosis: The problem is on the analog board.

Solution: Replace the flyback transformer at board reference T1 and check/replace the BU406 transistor (horizontal output) at board reference Q1 (may be burned). If possible, replace with a heavy-duty BU406D transistor.

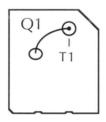

Approximate cost of repairing it yourself:		***$26.00***
1 flyback transformer	21.00	***1 hour***
1 BU406D transistor	5.00	
Approximate third-party repair cost:		***$117.00***
1 flyback transformer	42.00	
1 BU406D transistor	10.00	
1 hour labor	65.00	
Approximate dealer repair cost:		***$253.33***
1 new analog board	183.33	
1 hour labor	70.00	

Symptoms: There is a normal startup bong, but the display is dark. The computer makes a high-pitched whining noise (like a mosquito). After a few minutes, there is a burning smell.

Probable diagnosis: The problem is on the analog board.

Solution: Replace the flyback transformer at board reference T1 and check/replace the BU406 transistor at board reference Q1.

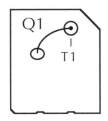

Approximate cost of repairing it yourself:		***$26.00***
1 flyback transformer	21.00	***1 hour***
1 BU406D transistor	5.00	
Approximate third-party repair cost:		***$107.00***
miscellaneous parts	42.00	
1 hour labor	65.00	
Approximate dealer repair cost:		***$253.33***
1 new analog board	183.33	
1 hour labor	70.00	

Symptoms: There is no startup bong. The display is dark. A loud AC hum is coming through the speaker. The internal 800K disk drive is making an unusual vibration noise.

Probable diagnosis: The problem is on the analog board.

Solution: With the power off, check resistance across CR5. If the reading indicates 44/45Ω (not 3.6K/∞), replace the flyback transformer (Apple part 157-0026-B) at board reference T1.

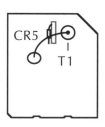

Approximate cost of repairing it yourself:		**$21.00**
1 flyback transformer	21.00	**1 hour**
Approximate third-party repair cost:		**$107.00**
1 flyback transformer	42.00	
1 hour labor	65.00	
Approximate dealer repair cost:		**$253.33**
1 new analog board	183.33	
1 hour labor	70.00	

Symptoms: There's no startup bong. There's no video. The display is dark. The computer makes a *very loud* screeching noise.

Probable diagnosis: The problem is on the analog board.

Solution: With the power off, check resistance across CR5. If the reading indicates 44/45Ω (not 3.6K/∞), replace the flyback transformer (Apple part# 157-0026-B) at board reference T1.

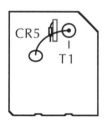

Approximate cost of repairing it yourself:		*$21.00*
1 flyback transformer	21.00	*1 hour*
Approximate third-party repair cost:		*$107.00*
1 flyback transformer	42.00	
1 hour labor	65.00	
Approximate dealer repair cost:		*$253.33*
1 new analog board	183.33	
1 hour labor	70.00	

Symptoms: There's no startup bong. The display is dark. The computer makes a dreadful groaning noise.

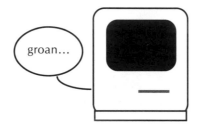

Probable diagnosis: The problem is on the analog board.

Solution: With the power off, check in-circuit resistance across CR5. If the reading indicates 44/45Ω (not 3.6K/∞), replace the flyback transformer (Apple part 157-0026-B) at board reference T1. If the reading is normal (3.6K/∞), see the next entry.

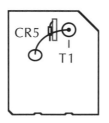

Approximate cost of repairing it yourself:		**$21.00**
1 flyback transformer	21.00	*1 hour*
Approximate third-party repair cost:		**$107.00**
1 flyback transformer	42.00	
1 hour labor	65.00	
Approximate dealer repair cost:		**$253.33**
1 new analog board	183.33	
1 hour labor	70.00	

Symptoms: The Mac does absolutely nothing. There is no startup bong. There are no unusual noises. The display is dark.

Probable diagnosis: The problem is on the analog board.

Solution: With the power off, check the in-circuit resistance across CR5. If the reading indicates 11/12Ω (not 3.6K/∞), replace the flyback transformer (Apple part 157-0026-B) at board reference T1. If the resistance across CR5 is normal (3.6K/∞), see the next entry.

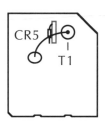

Approximate cost of repairing it yourself:		***$21.00***
1 flyback transformer	21.00	***1 hour***
Approximate third-party repair cost:		***$107.00***
1 flyback transformer	42.00	
1 hour labor	65.00	
Approximate dealer repair cost:		***$253.33***
1 new analog board	183.33	
1 hour labor	70.00	

Symptoms: The Mac does absolutely nothing. There is no startup bong. There are no unusual noises. The display is dark.

Typical history: The resistance across CR5 suggests that the flyback transformer at board reference T1 is fine.

Probable diagnosis: The problem is on the analog board.

Solution: With the power off, check the in-circuit resistance across CR21 (IR31DQ, R-Schottky Barrier, 40V, 6A). If the reading indicates 0Ω/0Ω (not 52Ω/53Ω), replace CR21 with a heavy-duty MBR360 rectifier. If the in-circuit reading is normal (52Ω/53Ω), see the next entry.

CR21

Approximate cost of repairing it yourself:		*$5.00*
1 MBR360 Schottky rectifier	5.00	*1 hour*
Approximate third-party repair cost:		*$75.00*
1 MBR360 Schottky rectifier	10.00	
1 hour labor	65.00	
Approximate dealer repair cost:		*$253.33*
1 new analog board	183.33	
1 hour labor	70.00	

Symptoms: The Mac does absolutely nothing. There is no startup bong. There are no unusual noises. The display is dark.

Typical history: The resistance across CR5 suggests that the flyback transformer at board reference T1 is fine. The resistance across CR21 suggests that CR21 is fine.

Probable diagnosis: The problem is on the analog board.

Solution: Check/replace resistor R46 (22Ω, 1W, 5%); resistors R47, R49 and R50 (1.5Ω, ¼-watt, 5%); transistor Q9 (2N3906); silicon controlled rectifier Q10 (CR400Y) and other small parts in the switching power supply at the bottom of the analog board.

Approximate cost of repairing it yourself:		$24.00
miscellaneous parts	24.00	1 hour
Approximate third-party repair cost:		$113.00
miscellaneous parts	48.00	
1 hour labor	65.00	
Approximate dealer repair cost:		$253.33
1 new analog board	183.33	
1 hour labor	70.00	

Symptoms: On powerup, the computer makes a *flup flup flup* noise. There's no bong. The display is dark. The computer is unusable.

Typical history: The problem occurred out of the blue, not right after upgrade or service work.

Probable diagnosis: The problem is on the analog board.

Solution: With the power off, check the in-circuit resistance across the barrel rectifier at board reference CR20 (IR31DQ, R-Schottky Barrier, 40V, 6A). If the reading indicates $0\Omega/0\Omega$ (not $31\Omega/30\Omega$), replace CR20 with a heavy-duty MBR1045 (TO-220) rectifier. If the reading is normal ($31\Omega/30\Omega$), see the next entry.

Approximate cost of repairing it yourself:		*$5.00*
1 MBR1045 Schottky rectifier	5.00	*1 hour*
Approximate third-party repair cost:		*$75.00*
1 MBR1045 Schottky rectifier	10.00	
1 hour labor	65.00	
Approximate dealer repair cost:		*$253.33*
1 new analog board	183.33	
1 hour labor	70.00	

Symptoms: On powerup, the computer makes a *flup flup flup* noise. There's no bong. The display is dark. The computer is unusable.

Typical history: The problem occurred out of the blue, not shortly after installation of a memory upgrade. The in-circuit resistance across CR20 suggests that CR20 is OK.

Probable diagnosis: The problem is on the analog board.

Solution: Check/replace leaky electrolytic capacitors C24 and C29 (2,200µ, 10V) and also C25, C26 and C31 (1,000µ, 10V).

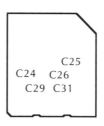

Approximate cost of repairing it yourself:		***$3.00***
1 electrolytic capacitor	3.00	***1 hour***
Approximate third-party repair cost:		***$71.00***
1 electrolytic capacitor	6.00	
1 hour labor	65.00	
Approximate dealer repair cost:		***$253.33***
1 new analog board	183.33	
1 hour labor	70.00	

Symptoms: There's no startup bong. The computer makes a low-pitched *flup flup flup* noise. The display is dark.

Typical history: The problem occurred after completion of upgrade or service work (right after you put everything back together).

Probable diagnosis: The power/video cable is disconnected.

Solution: Check/reconnect both ends of the power/video cable. If that's not it, check the blue wire (pin 6 to pin 6) for continuity. If that doesn't do it, see the next entry.

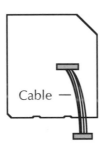

Cable —

Approximate cost of repairing it yourself:		*15 min.*
Approximate third-party repair cost:		**$65.00**
1 hour labor	65.00	
Approximate dealer repair cost:		**$253.33**
1 new analog board	183.33	
1 hour labor	70.00	

Symptoms: There's no startup bong. The computer makes a low-pitched *flup flup flup* noise. The display is dark.

Typical history: The problem occurred after completion of upgrade or service work (right after you put everything back together).

Probable diagnosis: The analog board is out of adjustment. The voltage is too high.

Solution: Turn variable resistor R56 (labeled *Voltage*) fully counterclockwise. Restart the computer and adjust R56 for 5.0V DC as measured from pin 6 of the power video cable to chassis ground. Also see the prior entry.

Voltage

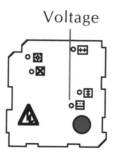

Approximate cost of repairing it yourself:		*15 min.*
Approximate third-party repair cost:		*$65.00*
1 hour labor	65.00	
Approximate dealer repair cost:		*$253.33*
1 new analog board	183.33	
1 hour labor	70.00	

Symptoms: An upgraded 512Ke works fine, but once it heats up, it can't be shut down and restarted. When you try a hot restart, there's no bong, and the Mac makes a *flup flup flup* noise. If you let the Mac cool down overnight, it restarts normally the next morning and works fine until the next time you try a hot restart.

Typical history: The problem occurred shortly after installing a Dove/MacSnap 524 or 548 memory upgrade.

Probable diagnosis: The problem is on the analog board.

Solution: Replace the OEM barrel rectifier at board reference CR21 (IR31DQ, R-Schottky Barrier, 40V, 6A) with a heavy-duty MBR 360 (TO-220) rectifier.

Approximate cost of repairing it yourself:		**$5.00**
1 MBR 360 Schottky rectifier	5.00	**1 hour**
Approximate third-party repair cost:		**$75.00**
1 MBR 360 Schottky rectifier	10.00	
1 hour labor	65.00	
Approximate dealer repair cost:		**$253.33**
1 new analog board	183.33	
1 hour labor	70.00	

Symptoms: On powerup, the computer makes a *bong... flup, bong... flup* noise. The display never comes up. The computer is unusable.

Probable diagnosis: The problem is on the analog board.

Solution: Replace the silicon rectifier (1N4001, R-SI, 600V, 1A) at board reference CR29.

CR29

Approximate cost of repairing it yourself:		*25¢*
1 1N4001 silicon rectifier	.25	*1 hour*
Approximate third-party repair cost:		*$70.00*
1 1N4001 rectifier	5.00	
1 hour labor	65.00	
Approximate dealer repair cost:		*$253.33*
1 new analog board	183.33	
1 hour labor	70.00	

Symptoms: The right side of the display wiggles (like a worm). The center wiggles less. The left side is fairly stable.

Typical history: At some point, the flyback transformer on this computer was replaced, but the BU406 (horizontal-output) transistor was not replaced, even though there was evidence of overheating on the heat sink.

Probable diagnosis: The problem is on the analog board.

Solution: Replace the BU406 transistor (horizontal output) at board reference Q1. Also see the next entry.

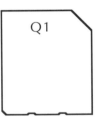

Approximate cost of repairing it yourself:		**$5.00**
1 BU406D transistor	5.00	**1 hour**
Approximate third-party repair cost:		**$75.00**
1 BU406D transistor	10.00	
1 hour labor	65.00	
Approximate dealer repair cost:		**$253.33**
1 new analog board	183.33	
1 hour labor	70.00	

Symptoms: The right side of the display wiggles (like a worm). There is a loud sizzling noise.

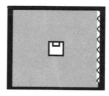

Typical history: The sizzling started right after the analog board was replaced.

Probable diagnosis: The problem is a bad ground.

Solution: Check for the presence of a grounding plate. Tighten the two grounding plate screws and verify that the ground wire is connected to the chassis. Also see the prior entry.

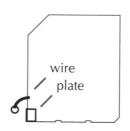

wire

plate

Approximate cost of repairing it yourself:		*15 min.*
Approximate third-party repair cost:		*$65.00*
1 hour labor	65.00	
Approximate dealer repair cost:		*$253.33*
1 new analog board	183.33	
1 hour labor	70.00	

Symptoms: The display is vertically compressed. It lacks height.

Typical history: The symptoms appeared out of the blue (not gradually, not immediately after the computer was board-swapped).

Probable diagnosis: The problem is on the analog board.

Solution: Replace the zener diode (IN5234B, ZD, 6.2V, ½-watt) at board reference CR15. Also see the next entry.

CR15

Approximate cost of repairing it yourself:		**$6.00**
1 IN5234B zener diode	6.00	*1 hour*
Approximate third-party repair cost:		**$77.00**
1 IN5234B zener diode	12.00	
1 hour labor	65.00	
Approximate dealer repair cost:		**$253.33**
1 new analog board	183.33	
1 hour labor	70.00	

Symptoms: The display is vertically compressed. It lacks height.

Typical history: The symptoms appeared immediately after the computer was board-swapped (not out of the blue).

Probable diagnosis: The new analog board is out of adjustment.

Solution: Adjust variable resistor R55 (labeled *Height)* until the display measures 4.75 inches high. If that doesn't do it, see the prior entry.

Height

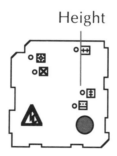

Approximate cost of repairing it yourself:		*30 min.*
Approximate third-party repair cost:		**$65.00**
1 hour labor	65.00	
Approximate dealer repair cost:		**$253.33**
1 new analog board	183.33	
1 hour labor	70.00	

Symptoms: The display is horizontally compressed. It lacks width.

Typical history: The symptoms appeared immediately after the computer was board-swapped (not out of the blue).

Probable diagnosis: The new analog board is out of adjustment.

Solution: Adjust tunable coil L2 (labeled *Width)* until the display measures 7.11 inches (approximately 7⅛ inches) wide.

Width

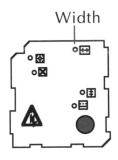

Approximate cost of repairing it yourself:		*30 min.*
Approximate third-party repair cost:		**$65.00**
1 hour labor	65.00	
Approximate dealer repair cost:		**$253.33**
1 new analog board	183.33	
1 hour labor	70.00	

Symptoms: The display is horizontally expanded. It's too wide.

Typical history: The symptoms appeared immediately after the computer was board-swapped (not out of the blue).

Probable diagnosis: The new analog board is out of adjustment.

Solution: Adjust tunable coil L2 (labeled *Width)* until the display measures 7.11 inches (approximately 7⅛ inches) wide.

Width

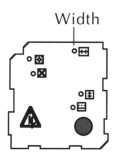

Approximate cost of repairing it yourself:		*30 min.*
Approximate third-party repair cost:		*$65.00*
1 hour labor	65.00	
Approximate dealer repair cost:		*$253.33*
1 new analog board	183.33	
1 hour labor	70.00	

Symptoms: The bottom of the display shakes (moves rapidly up and down) during a disk drive event or whenever a window is opened.

Probable diagnosis: The problem is on the analog board.

Solution: Replace the zener diode (IN5234B, ZD, 6.2V, ½-watt) at board reference CR15 on the analog board.

Approximate cost of repairing it yourself:		**$6.00**
1 IN5234B zener diode	6.00	**1 hour**
Approximate third-party repair cost:		**$77.00**
1 IN5234B zener diode	12.00	
1 hour labor	65.00	
Approximate dealer repair cost:		**$253.33**
1 new analog board	183.33	
1 hour labor	70.00	

Symptoms: The right side of the display moves in and out during a disk drive event or whenever a window is opened.

Probable diagnosis: The problem is on the analog board.

Solution: Replace the barrel rectifier (GI854, R-SI, 600V, 3A) at board reference CR5 on the analog board. Use a heavy-duty replacement part (MR824, R-SI, 400V, 5A) to avoid future repairs. If that doesn't do it, see the next entry.

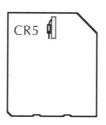

Approximate cost of repairing it yourself:		**$5.00**
1 MR824 rectifier	5.00	**1 hour**
Approximate third-party repair cost:		**$75.00**
1 MR824 rectifier	10.00	
1 hour labor	65.00	
Approximate dealer repair cost:		**$253.33**
1 new analog board	183.33	
1 hour labor	70.00	

Symptoms: Even after CR5 has been replaced, the right side of the display moves in and out during a disk drive event or whenever a window is opened.

Probable diagnosis: The problem is on the analog board.

Solution: Replace the horizontal output transistor (BU406) at board reference Q1. Also see the prior entry.

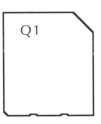

Approximate cost of repairing it yourself:		*$5.00*
1 BU406D transistor	5.00	*1 hour*
Approximate third-party repair cost:		*$75.00*
1 BU406D transistor	10.00	
1 hour labor	65.00	
Approximate dealer repair cost:		*$253.33*
1 new analog board	183.33	
1 hour labor	70.00	

Symptoms: There is no startup bong. The display is blank. The computer makes a high-pitched *chirp chirp chirp* noise.

Typical history: The right side of the display used to move in and out whenever a window was opened.

Probable diagnosis: The problem is on the analog board.

Solution: Replace the barrel rectifier (GI854, R-SI, 600V, 3A) at board reference CR5 on the analog board. Use a heavy-duty replacement part (MR824, R-SI, 400V, 5A) to avoid future repairs.

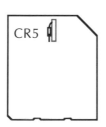

Approximate cost of repairing it yourself:		**$5.00**
1 MR824 rectifier	5.00	*1 hour*
Approximate third-party repair cost:		**$75.00**
1 MR824 rectifier	10.00	
1 hour labor	65.00	
Approximate dealer repair cost:		**$253.33**
1 new analog board	183.33	
1 hour labor	70.00	

Symptoms: There is no startup bong. The display is blank. The computer appears to be completely dead.

Typical history: Just before it died, the display went black and the computer made a high-pitched *chirp chirp chirp* noise. Prior to that, the right side of the display used to move in and out whenever a window was opened.

Probable diagnosis: The problem is on the analog board.

Solution: Replace the barrel rectifier (GI854, R-SI, 600V, 3A) at board reference CR5 on the analog board. Use a heavy-duty replacement part (MR824, R-SI, 400V, 5A) to avoid future repairs. Also replace the horizontal output transistor (BU406) at board reference Q1.

Approximate cost of repairing it yourself:		**$10.00**
1 MR824 rectifier	5.00	**1 hour**
1 BU406D transistor	5.00	
Approximate third-party repair cost:		**$85.00**
1 MR824 rectifier	10.00	
1 BU406D transistor	10.00	
1 hour labor	65.00	
Approximate dealer repair cost:		**$253.33**
1 new analog board	183.33	
1 hour labor	70.00	

Symptoms: The display intermittently blinks out (goes to solid black). White lines intermittently flash across the display. Tapping on the cabinet temporarily restores the display.

Probable diagnosis: The problem is a cracked solder joint on the analog board.

Solution: Check/resolder pin 1 (composite video) of the J4 connector.

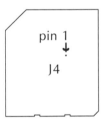

Approximate cost of repairing it yourself:		*30 min.*
Approximate third-party repair cost:		*$65.00*
1 hour labor	65.00	
Approximate dealer repair cost:		*$253.33*
1 new analog board	183.33	
1 hour labor	70.00	

Symptoms: The normal startup bong is present, but the display never comes up (remains solid black). Adjusting the front-panel brightness control does nothing. Tapping on the cabinet causes white lines to flash across the display.

Probable diagnosis: The problem is a cracked solder joint on the analog board.

Solution: Check/resolder pin 1 (composite video) of the J4 connector.

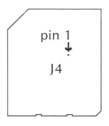

Approximate cost of repairing it yourself:		30 min.
Approximate third-party repair cost:		**$65.00**
1 hour labor	65.00	
Approximate dealer repair cost:		**$253.33**
1 new analog board	183.33	
1 hour labor	70.00	

Symptoms: There are two flashing, horizontal interference lines on the display. One is about one third of the way down. The other is about two thirds of the way down. Tapping on the cabinet causes the lines to jitter, but they never (or almost never) go away.

Probable diagnosis: The problem is a cracked solder joint on the analog board.

Solution: Check/resolder pin 1 (composite video) of the J4 connector.

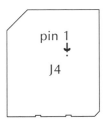

Approximate cost of repairing it yourself:		*30 min.*
Approximate third-party repair cost:		*$65.00*
1 hour labor	65.00	
Approximate dealer repair cost:		*$253.33*
1 new analog board	183.33	
1 hour labor	70.00	

Symptoms: The video display exhibits poor linearity. Items on the left are wider than items on the right.

Probable diagnosis: The problem is on the analog board.

Solution: Replace high-frequency capacitor C1 (3.9µ NP 25/35V HF) in the horizontal sweep circuit. Use a heavy-duty replacement part (3.9µ NP 100V HF) to avoid future repairs.

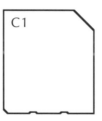

Approximate cost of repairing it yourself:		**$3.00**
1 3.9µ NP 100V HF capacitor	3.00	**1 hour**
Approximate third-party repair cost:		**$70.00**
1 3.9µ NP 100V HF capacitor	5.00	
1 hour labor	65.00	
Approximate dealer repair cost:		**$253.33**
1 new analog board	183.33	
1 hour labor	70.00	

Symptoms: A few minutes after startup, *relatively bright* diagonal lines appear on the display. If the power isn't switched off, the display gets darker and darker and the Mac begins to smoke.

Typical history: Prior to this, the display exhibited poor linearity.

Probable diagnosis: The problem is on the analog board.

Solution: Replace high-frequency capacitor C1 (3.9μ NP 25/35V HF). Use a heavy-duty replacement part (3.9μ NP 100V HF) to avoid future repairs. Also check/replace yoke plug J1 (may be burned).

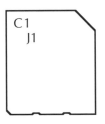

C1
J1

Approximate cost of repairing it yourself:		**$3.00**
1 3.9μ NP 100V HF capacitor	3.00	**1 hour**
Approximate third-party repair cost:		**$70.00**
1 3.9μ NP 100V HF capacitor	5.00	
1 hour labor	65.00	
Approximate dealer repair cost:		**$253.33**
1 new analog board	183.33	
1 hour labor	70.00	

Symptoms: On startup, the computer bongs, but the normal video display *does not* appear. Instead there is a *relatively bright* vertical line. If the power isn't switched off, the Mac begins to smoke.

Probable diagnosis: The problem is on the analog board.

Solution: Replace high-frequency capacitor C1 (3.9μ NP 25/35V HF). Use a heavy-duty replacement part (3.9μ NP 100V HF) to avoid future repairs. Also check/replace yoke plug J1 (may be burned).

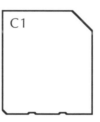

Approximate cost of repairing it yourself:		$3.00
1 3.9μ NP 100V HF capacitor	3.00	*1 hour*
Approximate third-party repair cost:		$70.00
1 3.9μ NP 100V HF capacitor	5.00	
1 hour labor	65.00	
Approximate dealer repair cost:		$253.33
1 new analog board	183.33	
1 hour labor	70.00	

Symptoms: On startup, the computer bongs, but the normal video display *does not* appear. Instead there is a *relatively dim* vertical line. If the power isn't switched off, the Mac begins to smoke.

Probable diagnosis: The problem is on the analog board.

Solution: Check/replace burned resistor R1 (220Ω, 1/ꟷwatt, 5%). To avoid immediate recurrence, vacuum-desolder linearity coil L1. Use 100% *fresh* solder (don't add solder; don't just reheat the joint).

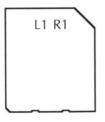

Approximate cost of repairing it yourself:		9¢
1 220Ω, 1/ꟷwatt, 5% resistor	.09	*1 hour*
Approximate third-party repair cost:		**$70.00**
1 220Ω, 1/ꟷwatt, 5% resistor	5.00	
1 hour labor	65.00	
Approximate dealer repair cost:		**$253.33**
1 new analog board	183.33	
1 hour labor	70.00	

Symptoms: After a short while, the video display collapses to a *relatively bright* vertical line. Tapping on the left side of the cabinet temporarily restores the full display or causes it to flash.

Probable diagnosis: The problem is a cracked solder joint on the analog board. The cracked joint may be covered by a foam pad.

Solution: Check/resolder pin 4 (top, horizontal yoke) of the J1 connector and check/resolder tunable coil L2 (marked width).

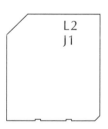

Approximate cost of repairing it yourself:		30 min.
Approximate third-party repair cost:		**$65.00**
1 hour labor	65.00	
Approximate dealer repair cost:		**$253.33**
1 new analog board	183.33	
1 hour labor	70.00	

Symptoms: After a short while, the video display collapses to a horizontal line. Tapping on the left side of the cabinet temporarily restores the full display or causes it to flash.

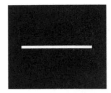

Probable diagnosis: The problem is a cracked solder joint on the analog board. The cracked joint may be covered by a foam pad.

Solution: Check/resolder pin 1 (bottom, vertical yoke) of the J1 connector and check/resolder C5 (47μ, 10V). Also see the next entry.

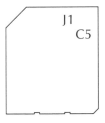

Approximate cost of repairing it yourself:	*30 min.*
Approximate third-party repair cost:	*$65.00*
1 hour labor 65.00	
Approximate dealer repair cost:	*$253.33*
1 new analog board 183.33	
1 hour labor 70.00	

Symptoms: On startup, the computer bongs, but the video display *does not* appear. Instead there is a *relatively bright* horizontal line. If the power isn't switched off, the Mac begins to smoke.

Probable diagnosis: The problem is on the analog board.

Solution: Check/replace burned transistor Q4 (2N4401), shorted transistor Q2 (MPSU51), open resistor R3 (1.5Ω, ¼-watt, 5%), zener diode CR15 (IN4735, ZD, 6.2V ½-watt) and other obviously burned parts in the vertical sweep circuit. Also see the prior entry.

Approximate cost of repairing it yourself:		$5.00
miscellaneous small parts	5.00	*1 hour*
Approximate third-party repair cost:		$75.00
miscellaneous small parts	10.00	
1 hour labor	65.00	
Approximate dealer repair cost:		$253.33
1 new analog board	183.33	
1 hour labor	70.00	

Symptoms: On startup, the computer bongs, but the normal video display *does not* appear. Instead, there is a tiny gray area, a *relatively bright* horizontal line and then three dotted horizontal lines. The bright horizontal line is flashing, and the cursor is just visible.

Probable diagnosis: The problem is on the analog board.

Solution: Check/replace field effect transistor Q5 (2N5485) in the vertical sweep circuit. Also see the prior entry.

Approximate cost of repairing it yourself:		79¢
1 2N5485 transistor	.79	*1 hour*
Approximate third-party repair cost:		*$70.00*
1 2N5485 transistor	5.00	
1 hour labor	65.00	
Approximate dealer repair cost:		*$253.33*
1 new analog board	183.33	
1 hour labor	70.00	

Symptoms: The video display is much too bright. Scan lines are visible even when the brightness control is turned down. Other than that, the computer is usable.

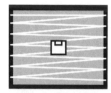

Typical history: The symptoms appeared out of the blue (not immediately after the computer was board-swapped).

Probable diagnosis: The problem is on the analog board.

Solution: Check/replace resistor R5 (470K, ¼-watt, 5%).

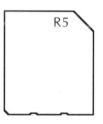

Approximate cost of repairing it yourself:		10¢
1 470K, ¼-watt, 5% resistor	.10	*1 hour*
Approximate third-party repair cost:		**$70.00**
1 470K, ¼-watt, 5% resistor	5.00	
1 hour labor	65.00	
Approximate dealer repair cost:		**$253.33**
1 new analog board	183.33	
1 hour labor	70.00	

Symptoms: The video display is much too bright. Scan lines are visible even when the brightness control is turned down. Otherwise, the computer is usable.

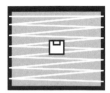

Typical history: The symptoms appeared immediately after the computer was board-swapped (not out of the blue).

Probable diagnosis: The new analog board is out of adjustment.

Solution: Adjust variable resistor R53 (labeled *Cut-off*) until the scan lines disappear.

Cut-off

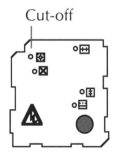

Approximate cost of repairing it yourself:		*30 min.*
Approximate third-party repair cost:		**$65.00**
1 hour labor	65.00	
Approximate dealer repair cost:		**$253.33**
1 new analog board	183.33	
1 hour labor	70.00	

Symptoms: There is raster but no video display (no desktop). The raster is very bright. Horizontal scan lines are visible. The computer isn't usable (because there's no desktop).

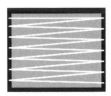

Probable diagnosis: The problem is on the analog board.

Solution: Replace the SN74LS38N chip (14-pin DIP, quad 2-input NAND) at board reference U2.

Approximate cost of repairing it yourself:		**35¢**
1 SN74LS38N chip	.35	*1 hour*
Approximate third-party repair cost:		**$70.00**
1 SN74LS38N chip	5.00	
1 hour labor	65.00	
Approximate dealer repair cost:		**$253.33**
1 new analog board	183.33	
1 hour labor	70.00	

Symptoms: The top half of the video display is somewhat squashed. There's a bright white line in the middle. The bottom half of the display is black.

Probable diagnosis: The problem is on the analog board.

Solution: Check/replace resistor R3 (1.5Ω, ¼-watt, 5%) and transistor Q1 (MPS U01) in the vertical sweep circuit.

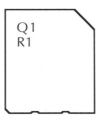

Approximate cost of repairing it yourself:		*$1.29*
1 1.5Ω, ¼-watt, 5% resistor	.10	*1 hour*
1 MPS U01 transistor	1.19	
Approximate third-party repair cost:		*$75.00*
2 miscellaneous parts	10.00	
1 hour labor	65.00	
Approximate dealer repair cost:		*$253.33*
1 new analog board	183.33	
1 hour labor	70.00	

Symptoms: The bottom half of the video display is somewhat squashed. There's a bright white line in the middle. The top half of the display is black.

Probable diagnosis: The problem is on the analog board.

Solution: Check/replace resistor R2 (1.5Ω, ¼-watt, 5%) and transistor Q2 (MPS U51) in the vertical sweep circuit.

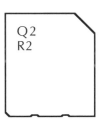

Approximate cost of repairing it yourself:		***$1.29***
1 1.5Ω, ¼-watt, 5% resistor	.10	***1 hour***
1 MPS U51 transistor	1.19	
Approximate third-party repair cost:		***$75.00***
2 miscellaneous parts	10.00	
1 hour labor	65.00	
Approximate dealer repair cost:		***$253.33***
1 new analog board	183.33	
1 hour labor	70.00	

Symptoms: The bottom half of the video display is so elongated that it disappears underneath the cabinet. Adjusting the Height control affects the top half of the display but doesn't affect the bottom.

Probable diagnosis: The problem is on the analog board.

Solution: Replace the LM324 chip (14-pin DIP, LP, quad op amp) at board reference U1.

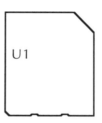

Approximate cost of repairing it yourself:		**39¢**
1 LM324 chip	.39	**1 hour**
Approximate third-party repair cost:		**$70.00**
1 LM324 chip	5.00	
1 hour labor	65.00	
Approximate dealer repair cost:		**$253.33**
1 new analog board	183.33	
1 hour labor	70.00	

Symptoms: The top half of the video display is so elongated that it disappears underneath the cabinet. Adjusting the Height control affects the bottom half of the display but doesn't affect the top.

Probable diagnosis: The problem is on the analog board.

Solution: Replace the LM324 chip (14-pin DIP, LP, quad op amp) at board reference U1.

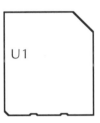

U1

Approximate cost of repairing it yourself:		39¢
1 LM324 chip	.39	*1 hour*
Approximate third-party repair cost:		**$70.00**
1 LM324 chip	5.00	
1 hour labor	65.00	
Approximate dealer repair cost:		**$253.33**
1 new analog board	183.33	
1 hour labor	70.00	

Symptoms: There is no startup bong. The raster shows tightly spaced horizontal lines. There is no desktop. The computer is unusable.

Typical history: The problem occurred out of the blue and spontaneously, not right after installing a programmer's switch.

Probable diagnosis: The problem is on the analog board.

Solution: Replace the SN74LS38N chip (14-pin DIP, quad 2-input NAND) at board reference U2.

U2

Approximate cost of repairing it yourself:		*35¢*
1 SN74LS38N chip	.35	*1 hour*
Approximate third-party repair cost:		**$70.00**
1 SN74LS38N chip	5.00	
1 hour labor	65.00	
Approximate dealer repair cost:		**$253.33**
1 new analog board	183.33	
1 hour labor	70.00	

Symptoms: On a Mac Plus there is no startup bong. The raster shows tightly spaced horizontal lines and is peppered with random dots. There is no desktop. The computer is unusable.

Typical history: The problem occurred when a programmer's switch was installed.

Probable diagnosis: The reset lever on the programmer's switch is making contact with the reset button on the logic board.

Solution: Check/reposition the programmer's switch. If necessary, trim and shorten the shafts.

Programmer's switch

Approximate cost of repairing it yourself:		*15 min.*
Approximate third-party repair cost:		**$65.00**
1 hour labor	65.00	
Approximate dealer repair cost:		**$445.00**
1 new logic board (Plus)	375.00	
1 hour labor	70.00	

Symptoms: On a Macintosh 128K, 512K or 512Ke, there is no startup bong. The display is laced with vertical lines and filled with a black-and-white checkerboard pattern.

Typical history: The problem occurred when a programmer's switch was installed.

Probable diagnosis: The reset lever on the programmer's switch is making contact with the reset button on the logic board.

Solution: Check/reposition the programmer's switch. If necessary, trim and shorten the shafts.

Programmer's switch

Approximate cost of repairing it yourself:		15 min.
Approximate third-party repair cost:		**$65.00**
1 hour labor	65.00	
Approximate dealer repair cost:		**$358.33**
1 new logic board (512K)	288.33	
1 hour labor	70.00	

Symptoms: On a Mac 512Ke, there is no startup bong. The display is filled with a black-and-white checkerboard pattern.

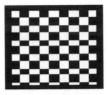

Typical history: The 512Ke has a SuperMac Enhance upgrade.

Probable diagnosis: The problem is in the processor clip.

Solution: For a temporary fix, detach and fold back the Enhance board, reseat the processor clip at location E5 to E8 on the 512Ke logic board *and* insulate the clip top with foam tape. For a permanent fix, replace the clip with a 64-pin (solder-type) header.

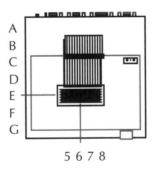

Approximate cost of repairing it yourself:		**$5.00**
1 64-pin solder-type header	5.00	**+ 8 hours**
Approximate third-party repair cost:		**$270.00**
1 64-pin header	10.00	
4 hours labor	260.00	
Approximate dealer repair cost:		**$1,210.00**
1 512Ke to Mac Plus upgrade	770.00	
1 2Mb RAM upgrade	440.00	

Symptoms: On a Mac 512Ke, there is no startup bong. The display is filled with a black-and-white checkerboard pattern.

Typical history: The 512Ke has a Levco MonsterMac upgrade.

Probable diagnosis: The problem is in the wiring harness.

Solution: For a temporary fix, reseat the wire between C24 and R32 at board location D2 to E2 on the Macintosh logic board. For a permanent fix, solder the wire in place. If that doesn't do it, see the next entry.

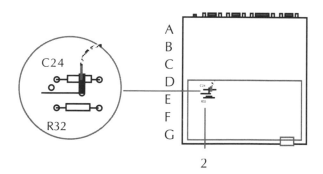

Approximate cost of repairing it yourself:		*1 hour*
Approximate third-party repair cost:		**$130.00**
2 hours labor	130.00	
Approximate dealer repair cost:		**$1,210.00**
1 512Ke to Mac Plus upgrade	770.00	
1 2Mb RAM upgrade	440.00	

Symptoms: On a Mac 512Ke, there is no startup bong. The display is filled with a black-and-white checkerboard pattern.

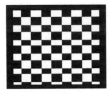

Typical history: The 512Ke has a Levco MonsterMac upgrade.

Probable diagnosis: One of the pin headers isn't making contact.

Solution: For a temporary fix, reseat the boards at location E5 to E8 on the 512Ke logic board. For a permanent fix, replace the OEM pin headers with two 64-pin IC sockets. Reconnect the two boards with a 64-pin socket header.

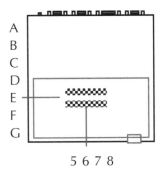

Approximate cost of repairing it yourself:		$9.00
miscellaneous parts	9.00	8 hours
Approximate third-party repair cost:		**$278.00**
miscellaneous parts	18.00	
4 hours labor	260.00	
Approximate dealer repair cost:		**$1,210.00**
1 512Ke to Mac Plus upgrade	770.00	
1 2Mb RAM upgrade	440.00	

Symptoms: There is no startup bong. The display is filled with alternating white-and-black vertical bars.

Typical history: The problem occurred right after a disk drive/ROM upgrade or a SCSI upgrade (right after you put everything back together).

Probable diagnosis: The problem is on the 512K logic board.

Solution: Verify that the ROM chips at board locations D6 and D8 are not reversed, backwards or otherwise incorrectly installed.

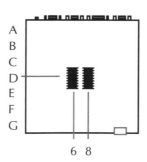

Approximate cost of repairing it yourself:		*30 min.*
Approximate third-party repair cost:		*$130.00*
2 hours labor	130.00	
Approximate dealer repair cost:		*$358.33*
1 new logic board (512K)	288.33	
1 hour labor	70.00	

Symptoms: On startup, you get a frozen floppy disk icon and a raster the size of a postage-stamp. The computer is unusable.

Typical history: The Macintosh is/was an upgraded 512K or 512Ke. The problem began immediately after a Dove/MacSnap 524 or 548 memory board was removed (pried up with a screwdriver).

Probable diagnosis: The problem is on the 512Ke logic board.

Solution: Check for and repair damaged circuit traces near the 74LS244 chips at board locations E12 and E13.

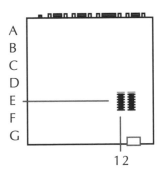

Approximate cost of repairing it yourself:		*2 hours*
Approximate third-party repair cost:		*$130.00*
2 hours labor	130.00	
Approximate dealer repair cost:		*$358.33*
1 new logic board (512K)	288.33	
1 hour labor	70.00	

Symptoms: There are consistent (repeatable) system errors that do not occur (cannot be repeated) on other Macs. The logic levels on the 74F253 chip (16-pin DIP, dual 4-input multiplexer, tri-state) at board location G13 are wrong.

Typical history: The Macintosh is/was an upgraded 512K or 512Ke. The problem began immediately after a Dove/MacSnap 524 or 548 memory board was removed (pried up with a screwdriver).

Probable diagnosis: The problem is on the 512K or 512Ke logic board. Most likely, circuit traces were cut by the screwdriver tip.

Solution: Check for and repair damaged circuit traces near the 41-256 DRAM chip at location G5.

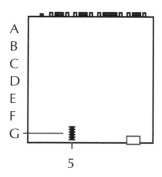

Approximate cost of repairing it yourself:		*2 hours*
Approximate third-party repair cost:		**$130.00**
2 hours labor	130.00	
Approximate dealer repair cost:		**$358.33**
1 new logic board (512K)	288.33	
1 hour labor	70.00	

Symptoms: There are consistent (repeatable) system errors that do not occur (cannot be repeated) on other Macs.

Typical history: The original 128K Macintosh has received an 800K DD/ROM upgrade and a Mac Plus or other logic board upgrade.

Probable diagnosis: The problem is on the original analog board (which has not been upgraded). The voltage is too low.

Solution: While measuring from pin 6 of the power/video cable to ground, adjust variable resistor R56 (labeled *Voltage)* for 5.0V DC. If the power supply won't go that high, see the next entry.

Voltage

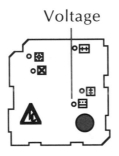

Approximate cost of repairing it yourself:		*30 min.*
Approximate third-party repair cost:		*$65.00*
1 hour labor	65.00	
Approximate dealer repair cost:		*$253.33*
1 new analog board	183.33	
1 hour labor	70.00	

Symptoms: There are consistent (repeatable) system errors that do not occur (cannot be repeated) on other Macs.

Typical history: The original 128K Macintosh has received an 800K DD/ROM upgrade and a Mac Plus or other logic board upgrade. The analog board can no longer produce 5.0V DC.

Probable diagnosis: The problem is on the original analog board (which has not been upgraded). The voltage is too low.

Solution: Check/replace the overvoltage reference diode (1N5349B, ZD, 12V, 5W) at board reference CR18 on the analog board. Also see the prior entry.

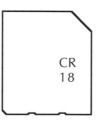

Approximate cost of repairing it yourself:		*$6.00*
1 1N5349B zener diode	6.00	+ *1 hour*
Approximate third-party repair cost:		*$71.00*
1 1N5349B zener diode	6.00	
1 hour labor	65.00	
Approximate dealer repair cost:		*$253.33*
1 new analog board	183.33	
1 hour labor	70.00	

Symptoms: A simple beep sound is OK, but right after a complex sound (boing, clank, monkey, etc.) the mouse pointer jumps, then it freezes and the Mac Plus locks up.

Probable diagnosis: The problem is on the Mac Plus logic board.

Solution: Replace the 6522-02PC chip (40-pin DIP, versatile interface adapter) at location D11.

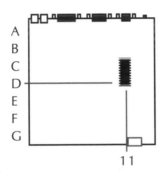

Approximate cost of repairing it yourself:		*$6.00*
1 6522-02PC VIA chip	6.00	*2 hours*
Approximate third-party repair cost:		*$142.00*
1 6522-02PC VIA chip	12.00	
2 hours labor	130.00	
Approximate dealer repair cost:		*$445.00*
1 new logic board (Plus)	375.00	
1 hour labor	70.00	

Symptoms: On startup, a Mac128K, 512K, 512Ke resets several times any ImageWriter II *directly connected* to the printer port. The first time you try to print you get a dialog box stating: *The printer is not responding,* but subsequent tries made during the same computer session work fine. If the same ImageWriter II is reconnected to the modem port, it appears to work normally. An ImageWriter I also appears to work normally, on either port.

Probable diagnosis: The problem is on the 512K or 512Ke logic board.

Solution: Check/replace the 26LS30 chip (16-pin DIP, dual differential RS422 party line/quad single-ended RS423 line driver) at board location B6.

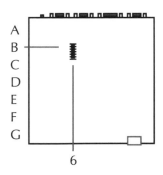

Approximate cost of repairing it yourself:		$2.49
1 · 26LS30 chip	2.49	*2 hours*
Approximate third-party repair cost:		$135.00
1 26LS30 chip	5.00	
2 hours labor	130.00	
Approximate dealer repair cost:		$358.33
1 new logic board (512K)	288.33	
1 hour labor	70.00	

Symptoms: A Mac 128K, 512K or 512Ke does not show up on an AppleTalk network. Otherwise, it appears to be normal.

Probable diagnosis: The problem is on the logic board.

Solution: Check/replace the 26LS30 chip (16-pin DIP, dual differential RS422 party line/quad single-ended RS423 line driver) at board location B6.

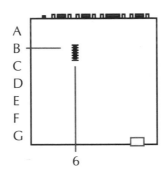

Approximate cost of repairing it yourself:		*$2.49*
1 26LS30 chip	2.49	*2 hours*
Approximate third-party repair cost:		*$135.00*
1 26LS30 chip	5.00	
2 hours labor	130.00	
Approximate dealer repair cost:		*$358.33*
1 new logic board (512K)	288.33	
1 hour labor	70.00	

Symptoms: On startup, a Mac Plus resets several times any ImageWriter II directly connected to the printer port. The first time you try to print you get a dialog box stating: *The printer is not responding*, but subsequent tries made during the same computer session work fine. If the same ImageWriter II is reconnected to the modem port, it appears to work normally. An ImageWriter I also appears to work normally, on either port.

Probable diagnosis: The problem is on the Mac Plus logic board.

Solution: Check/replace the 26LS30 chip (16-pin DIP, dual differential RS422 party line/quad single-ended RS423 line driver) at board location B3.

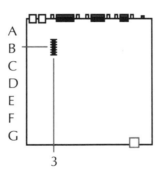

Approximate cost of repairing it yourself:		**$2.49**
1 26LS30 chip	2.49	**2 hours**
Approximate third-party repair cost:		**$135.00**
1 26LS30 chip	5.00	
2 hours labor	130.00	
Approximate dealer repair cost:		**$445.00**
1 new logic board (Mac Plus)	375.00	
1 hour labor	70.00	

Symptoms: The Mac Plus does not show up on an AppleTalk network. Otherwise, it appears to be normal.

Probable diagnosis: The problem is on the logic board.

Solution: Check/replace the 26LS30 chip (16-pin DIP, dual differential RS422 party line/quad single-ended RS423 line driver) at board location B3.

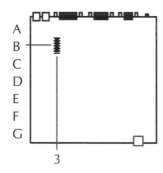

Approximate cost of repairing it yourself:		$2.49
1 26LS30 chip	2.49	2 hours
Approximate third-party repair cost:		$135.00
1 26LS30 chip	5.00	
2 hours labor	130.00	
Approximate dealer repair cost:		$445.00
1 new logic board (Mac Plus)	375.00	
1 hour labor	70.00	

Symptoms: On a Macintosh 512Ke the internal 800K disk drive works OK, but known-good external 800K disk drives do not work. Regardless of what disk you insert into the external DD, all you get is: *This disk is unreadable. Do you want to initialize it?*

Typical history: These very same disks work perfectly in other 800K disk drives. These very same external 800K disk drives work perfectly on other Macs (512Ke, Plus, SE).

Probable diagnosis: The problem is on the 512Ke logic board.

Solution: Check/replace the RC filter (20-pin, DIP, Apple part 115-0002) at location A13.

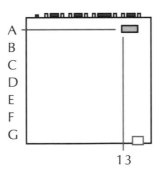

Approximate cost of repairing it yourself:		$12.00
1 Bourns filter	12.00	2 hours
Approximate third-party repair cost:		$154.00
1 Bourns filter	24.00	
2 hours labor	130.00	
Approximate dealer repair cost:		$358.33
1 new logic board (512K)	288.33	
1 hour labor	70.00	

Symptoms: On a Macintosh Plus the internal 800K disk drive works OK, but external 800K disk drives that are known to be good do not work. Regardless of what disk you insert into the external DD, all you get is: *This disk is unreadable. Do you want to initialize it?*

Typical history: These very same disks work perfectly in other 800K disk drives. These very same external 800K disk drives *work perfectly* on other Macs (512Ke, Plus, SE).

Probable diagnosis: The problem is on the Mac Plus logic board.

Solution: Check/replace the RC filter (20-pin, DIP, Apple part 115-0002) at location A11.

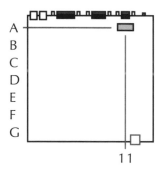

Approximate cost of repairing it yourself:		$12.00
1 Bourns filter	12.00	*2 hours*
Approximate third-party repair cost:		$154.00
1 Bourns filter	24.00	
2 hours labor	130.00	
Approximate dealer repair cost:		$445.00
1 new logic board (Plus)	375.00	
1 hour labor	70.00	

Symptoms: When floppy disks are inserted or ejected, they rub up against the cabinet opening.

Cabinet opening ——— [====] —— Disk

Typical history: The problem occurred right after an 800K DD/ROM upgrade or a disk-drive swap.

Probable diagnosis: The disk drive isn't centered on the cabinet opening.

Solution: Loosen/reposition the disk drive mounting screws.

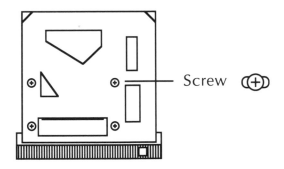

Screw

Approximate cost of repairing it yourself:	*15 min.*
Approximate third-party repair cost:	*$65.00*
1 hour labor 65.00	
Approximate dealer repair cost:	*$70.00*
1 hour labor 70.00	

Symptoms: On a Macintosh 512Ke with a SCSI upgrade, if there's an external hard drive connected to the SCSI port, it won't boot from a floppy disk unless the hard drive is also switched on.

Typical history: This same external hard drive works perfectly on other Macs. There's no need to power it up when all you want to do is play a game from a floppy disk.

Probable diagnosis: The problem is on the 512Ke logic board.

Solution: Replace the version-1 ROMs (marked 342-0341-A and 342-0342-A) at locations D6 and D8 with a set of version-3 ROMs (marked 342-0341-C and 342-0342-B).

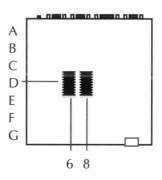

Approximate cost of repairing it yourself:		*$125.00*
1 set of version-3 ROMs	125.00	*1 hour*
Approximate third-party repair cost:		*$255.00*
1 set of version-3 ROMs	125.00	
2 hours labor	130.00	
Approximate dealer repair cost:		*$260.00*
1 set of version-3 ROMs	190.00	
1 hour labor	70.00	

Symptoms: On startup, a 512Ke (with SCSI upgrade) will not boot if the computer is switched on first, or if the external hard drive is switched on simultaneously. But, if you switch on the hard drive, wait 30 seconds and then switch on the computer, everything works OK.

Typical history: This same external hard drive works perfectly on other Macs. There's no need to wait 30 seconds before switching on the computer.

Probable diagnosis: The problem is on the 512Ke logic board.

Solution: Replace the version-2 ROMs (marked 342-0341-B and 342-0342-A) at locations D6 and D8 with a set of version-3 ROMs (marked 342-0341-C and 342-0342-B), or replace the hard drive.

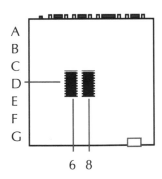

Approximate cost of repairing it yourself:		**$125.00**
1 set of version-3 ROMs	125.00	***1 hour***
Approximate third-party repair cost:		**$255.00**
1 set of version-3 ROMs	125.00	
2 hours labor	130.00	
Approximate dealer repair cost:		**$260.00**
1 set of version-3 ROMs	190.00	
1 hour labor	70.00	

Symptoms: If there's an external hard drive connected to the SCSI port, a Mac Plus won't boot from a floppy disk unless the hard drive is also switched on.

Typical history: This same external hard drive works perfectly on other Macs. There's no need to power it up when all you want to do is play a game from a floppy disk.

Probable diagnosis: The problem is on the Mac Plus logic board.

Solution: Replace the version-1 ROMs (marked 342-0341-A and 342-0342-A) at locations D6 and D8 with a set of version-3 ROMs (marked 342-0341-C and 342-0342-B).

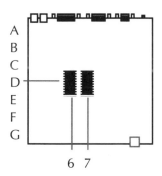

Approximate cost of repairing it yourself:		$125.00
1 set of version-3 ROMs	125.00	*1 hour*
Approximate third-party repair cost:		$255.00
1 set of version-3 ROMs	125.00	
2 hours labor	130.00	
Approximate dealer repair cost:		$260.00
1 set of version-3 ROMs	190.00	
1 hour labor	70.00	

Symptoms: A Mac Plus will not boot if the computer is switched on first, or if the external hard drive is switched on simultaneously. But if you switch on the hard drive, wait 30 seconds and then switch on the computer, everything works OK.

Typical history: This same external hard drive works perfectly on other Macs. There's no need to wait 30 seconds before switching on the computer.

Probable diagnosis: The problem is on the Mac Plus logic board.

Solution: Replace the version-2 ROMs (marked 342-0341-B and 342-0342-A) at locations D6 and D8 with a set of version-3 ROMs (marked 342-0341-C and 342-0342-B), or replace the hard drive.

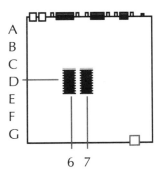

Approximate cost of repairing it yourself:		$125.00
1 set of version-3 ROMs	125.00	*1 hour*
Approximate third-party repair cost:		$255.00
1 set of version-3 ROMs	125.00	
2 hours labor	130.00	
Approximate dealer repair cost:		$260.00
1 set of version-3 ROMs	190.00	
1 hour labor	70.00	

Symptoms: On a Mac 128K, 512K or 512Ke everything the mouse pointer touches is automatically selected on this even when the mouse button is up.

Typical history: This very same mouse works perfectly on other Macs. Other mice malfunction exactly the same way on this Mac.

Probable diagnosis: The problem is on the *128K, 512K or 512Ke* logic board.

Solution: Check/replace the RC filter (20-pin, DIP, Apple part 115-0002) at location A13.

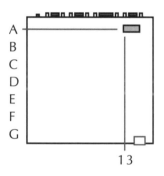

Approximate cost of repairing it yourself:		*$12.00*
1 Bourns filter	12.00	*2 hours*
Approximate third-party repair cost:		**$154.00**
1 Bourns filter	24.00	
2 hours labor	130.00	
Approximate dealer repair cost:		**$358.33**
1 new logic board (512K)	288.33	
1 hour labor	70.00	

Symptoms: On a Mac Plus, everything the mouse pointer touches is automatically selected, even when the mouse button is up.

Typical history: This very same mouse works perfectly on other Macs. Other mice malfunction exactly the same way on this Mac.

Probable diagnosis: The problem is on the Mac Plus logic board.

Solution: Check/replace the RC filter (20-pin, DIP, Apple part 115-0002) at location A11.

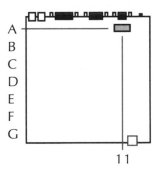

Approximate cost of repairing it yourself:		$12.00
1 Bourns filter	12.00	2 hours
Approximate third-party repair cost:		$154.00
1 Bourns filter	24.00	
2 hours labor	130.00	
Approximate dealer repair cost:		$445.00
1 new logic board (Plus)	375.00	
1 hour labor	70.00	

Symptoms: Everything the mouse pointer touches is automatically selected, even when the mouse button is up.

Typical history: Other mice work perfectly on this computer.

Probable diagnosis: The problem is inside the mouse.

Solution: Check/replace the micro switch under the mouse button.

Micro switch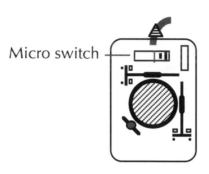

Approximate cost of repairing it yourself:		$2.00
1 micro switch	2.00	1 hour
Approximate third-party repair cost:		$69.00
1 micro switch	4.00	
1 hour labor	65.00	
Approximate dealer repair cost:		$93.33
1 new mouse	93.33	

Symptoms: The mouse pointer is jammed against the right side of the display. It goes up and down, but it doesn't go left.

Probable diagnosis: The problem is in the mouse cable.

Solution: Check/repair the brown wire, or replace the cable.

Mac End (DB9-P)	Mouse End (J1)
1 Ground	Black
2 +5V	Red
3 Ground	Black
4 Left	Brown
5 Right	Orange
6 Not connected	Not applicable
7 Button	Yellow
8 Down	Green
9 Up	Blue

Approximate cost of repairing it yourself:			***$15.00***
1 mouse cable		15.00	***30 min.***
Approximate third-party repair cost:			***$72.50***
1 mouse cable		40.00	
1 half hour labor		32.50	
Approximate dealer repair cost:			***$93.33***
1 new mouse		93.33	

Symptoms: The mouse pointer is jammed against the left side of the display. It goes up and down, but it doesn't go right.

Probable diagnosis: The problem is in the mouse cable.

Solution: Check/repair the orange wire, or replace the cable.

Mac End (DB9-P)	Mouse End (J1)
1 Ground	Black
2 +5V	Red
3 Ground	Black
4 Left	Brown
5 Right	Orange
6 Not connected	Not applicable
7 Button	Yellow
8 Down	Green
9 Up	Blue

Approximate cost of repairing it yourself:		***$15.00***
1 mouse cable	15.00	***30 min.***
Approximate third-party repair cost:		***$72.50***
1 mouse cable	40.00	
1 half hour labor	32.50	
Approximate dealer repair cost:		***$93.33***
1 new mouse	93.33	

Symptoms: The mouse pointer is jammed against the top of the display. It goes left and right, but it doesn't go down.

Probable diagnosis: The problem is in the mouse cable.

Solution: Check/repair the green wire, or replace the cable.

Mac End (DB9-P)	Mouse End (J1)
1 Ground	Black
2 +5V	Red
3 Ground	Black
4 Left	Brown
5 Right	Orange
6 Not connected	Not applicable
7 Button	Yellow
8 Down	Green
9 Up	Blue

Approximate cost of repairing it yourself:		***$15.00***
1 mouse cable	15.00	***30 min.***
Approximate third-party repair cost:		***$72.50***
1 mouse cable	40.00	
1 half hour labor	32.50	
Approximate dealer repair cost:		***$93.33***
1 new mouse	93.33	

Symptoms: The mouse pointer is jammed against the bottom of the display. It goes left and right, but it doesn't go up.

Probable diagnosis: The problem is in the mouse cable.

Solution: Check/repair the blue wire, or replace the cable.

Mac End (DB9-P)	Mouse End (J1)
1 Ground	Black
2 +5V	Red
3 Ground	Black
4 Left	Brown
5 Right	Orange
6 Not connected	Not applicable
7 Button	Yellow
8 Down	Green
9 Up	Blue

Approximate cost of repairing it yourself:		***$15.00***
1 mouse cable	15.00	***30 min.***
Approximate third-party repair cost:		***$72.50***
1 mouse cable	40.00	
1 half hour labor	32.50	
Approximate dealer repair cost:		***$93.33***
1 new mouse	93.33	

Symptoms: The mouse doesn't work at all. The pointer never appears. Clicking the button has no effect.

Typical history: Other mice work fine on this computer.

Probable diagnosis: The problem is in the mouse cable.

Solution: Check/repair the black and red wires, or replace the cable.

Mac End (DB9-P)	Mouse End (J1)
1 Ground	Black
2 +5V	Red
3 Ground	Black
4 Left	Brown
5 Right	Orange
6 Not connected	Not applicable
7 Button	Yellow
8 Down	Green
9 Up	Blue

Approximate cost of repairing it yourself:		**$15.00**
1 mouse cable	15.00	**30 min.**
Approximate third-party repair cost:		**$72.50**
1 mouse cable	40.00	
1 half hour labor	32.50	
Approximate dealer repair cost:		**$93.33**
1 new mouse	93.33	

Symptoms: The mouse jams when it's moved from side to side (left to right). The jam tends to lift the mouse right off the table.

Probable diagnosis: The problem is inside the mouse. The retainer at the top of the split plastic post (which bears the side-to-side interrupter axle) is broken. Instead of remaining horizontal, the side-to-side axle is riding up on the mouse ball.

Solution: Fashion a new bearing retainer from a wooden toothpick. Wedge the toothpick piece into the top of the broken bearing post. Test the mouse. When the side-to-side action is correct, cement the toothpick piece in place (but not the axle) with epoxy glue.

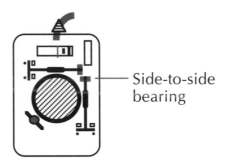

Side-to-side
bearing

Approximate cost of repairing it yourself:		*30 min.*
Approximate third-party repair cost:		*$65.00*
1 hour labor	65.00	
Approximate dealer repair cost:		*$93.33*
1 new mouse	93.33	

Symptoms: The mouse jams when it's moved from front to back (up and down). The jam tends to lift the mouse right off the table.

Probable diagnosis: The problem is inside the mouse. The retainer at the top of the split plastic post (which bears the up-and-down interrupter axle) is broken. Instead of remaining horizontal, the up-and-down axle is riding up on the mouse ball.

Solution: Fashion a new bearing retainer from a wooden toothpick. Wedge the toothpick piece into the top of the broken bearing post. Test the mouse. When the up-and-down action is correct, cement the toothpick piece in place (but not the axle) with epoxy glue.

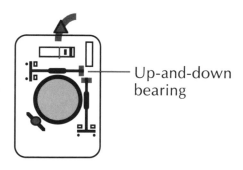

Up-and-down bearing

Approximate cost of repairing it yourself:		*30 min.*
Approximate third-party repair cost:		**$65.00**
1 hour labor	65.00	
Approximate dealer repair cost:		**$93.33**
1 new mouse	93.33	

Symptoms: The computer won't start. Startup disks are always ejected, but only when the keyboard (model M0110) is connected.

Typical history: The problem began shortly after a beverage was spilled on the keyboard.

Probable diagnosis: The problem is on the key-matrix PCB inside the keyboard.

Solution: Replace the 72LS123 chip (16-pin DIP, monostable multivibrator with clear) at board location U2.

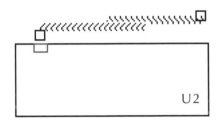

Approximate cost of repairing it yourself:		49¢
1 74LS123 chip	.49	*30 min.*
Approximate third-party repair cost:		**$70.00**
1 74LS123 chip	5.00	
1 hour labor	65.00	
Approximate dealer repair cost:		**$129.00**
1 new keyboard (Mac Plus)	129.00	

Symptoms: The keyboard is intermittent. Sometimes all of the keys work. Sometimes none of the keys work. Other keyboards work fine on this Mac.

Typical history: The problem began shortly after the keyboard was disconnected (and then reconnected).

Probable diagnosis: The problem is inside the keyboard. Most likely, the contacts on the RJ-11 jack are bent.

Solution: Straighten the contacts on the RJ-11 jack.

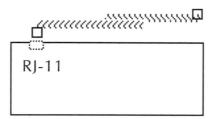

Approximate cost of repairing it yourself:		*5 min.*
Approximate third-party repair cost:		*$65.00*
1 hour labor	65.00	
Approximate dealer repair cost:		*$129.00*
1 new keyboard (Mac Plus)	129.00	

Symptoms: The keyboard is intermittent. Sometimes all of the keys work. Sometimes none of the keys work. Substituting other keyboards *does not* solve the problem.

Typical history: The problem began shortly after the keyboard was disconnected (and then reconnected).

Probable diagnosis: The problem is on the logic board. Most likely, the contacts on the RJ-11 jack are bent.

Solution: Straighten the contacts on the RJ-11 jack.

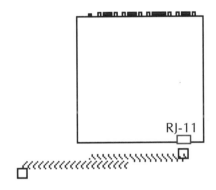

Approximate cost of repairing it yourself:		*30 min.*
Approximate third-party repair cost:		*$130.00*
2 hours labor	130.00	
Approximate dealer repair cost:		*$445.00*
1 new logic board (Mac Plus)	375.00	
1 hour labor	70.00	

Symptoms: The keyboard on a Mac 512Ke does not work. Substituting other keyboards *does not* solve the problem.

Typical history: The Macintosh is/was an upgraded 512K or 512Ke. The problem began immediately after a Dove MacSnap 524 or 548 memory board was removed (pried up with a screwdriver).

Probable diagnosis: The problem is on the 512Ke logic board. Most likely, circuit traces were cut by the screwdriver tip.

Solution: Check for and repair damaged circuit traces near the TSG PAL at board reference D3.

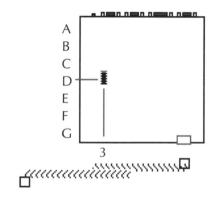

Approximate cost of repairing it yourself:		*2 hours*
Approximate third-party repair cost:		**$130.00**
2 hours labor	130.00	
Approximate dealer repair cost:		**$358.33**
1 new logic board (512K)	288.33	
1 hour labor	70.00	

Symptoms: A M0110 (128 or 512) keyboard does not work on any Mac.

Typical history: The problem occurred a telephone cable was used on the keyboard.

Probable diagnosis: The problem is in the keyboard.

Solution: Replace the 8021H (28-pin) chip at board reference U1.

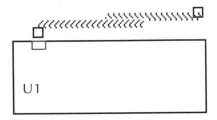

Approximate cost of repairing it yourself:		*$1.25*
1 8021H chip	1.25	*30 min.*
Approximate third-party repair cost:		*$90.00*
1 8021H chip	25.00	
1 hour labor	65.00	
Approximate dealer repair cost:		*$129.00*
1 new keyboard (Mac Plus)	129.00	

Symptoms: A M0110A (Mac Plus) keyboard does not work on any Mac.

Typical history: The problem occurred after a telephone cable was used on the keyboard.

Probable diagnosis: The problem is in the keyboard.

Solution: Replace the 8048 (40-pin DIP, MPU 8-bit) chip located under the spacebar.

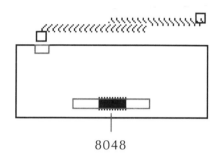

8048

Approximate cost of repairing it yourself:		*$1.25*
1 8048 chip	1.25	*30 min.*
Approximate third-party repair cost:		*$90.00*
1 8048 chip	25.00	
1 hour labor	65.00	
Approximate dealer repair cost:		*$129.00*
1 new keyboard (Mac Plus)	129.00	

Symptoms: The computer does not maintain the proper time and date.

Probable diagnosis: The problem is on the analog board.

Solution: Check/replace the clock battery (alkaline 4.5V, Eveready 523) at board location B1.

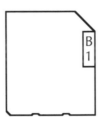

Approximate cost of repairing it yourself:		**$3.00**
1 alkaline battery	3.00	**1 min.**
Approximate third-party repair cost:		**$71.00**
1 alkaline battery	6.00	
1 hour labor	65.00	
Approximate dealer repair cost:		**$253.33**
1 new analog board	183.33	
1 hour labor	70.00	

Symptoms: The display is out of focus. Other than that, the computer is usable.

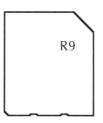

Typical history: The symptoms appeared out of the blue (not immediately after the computer was board-swapped).

Probable diagnosis: The problem is on the analog board.

Solution: Check/replace open resistor R9 (1MΩ, ½-watt, 5%). Also see the next entry.

Approximate cost of repairing it yourself:		15¢
1 1MΩ, 1/2W, 5% resistor	.15	*1 hour*
Approximate third-party repair cost:		*$70.00*
1 1MΩ, 1/2W, 5% resistor	5.00	
1 hour labor	65.00	
Approximate dealer repair cost:		*$253.33*
1 new analog board	183.33	
1 hour labor	70.00	

Symptoms: The display is out of focus. Other than that, the computer is usable.

Typical history: The symptoms appeared immediately after the computer was serviced or board-swapped (not out of the blue).

Probable diagnosis: The new analog board is out of adjustment.

Solution: Adjust variable resistor R54 (labeled *Focus*) for the best focus. If R54 makes no difference, see the prior entry.

Focus

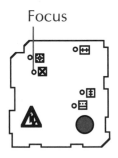

Approximate cost of repairing it yourself:		*30 min.*
Approximate third-party repair cost:		*$65.00*
1 hour labor	65.00	
Approximate dealer repair cost:		*$253.33*
1 new analog board	183.33	
1 hour labor	70.00	

Symptoms: The display is tilted. Other than that, the Mac is usable.

Typical history: The symptoms appeared immediately after the computer was board-swapped or serviced (not out of the blue).

Probable diagnosis: The yoke clamp (on the neck of the CRT) is loose.

Solution: Adjust/snug the yoke for a square picture.

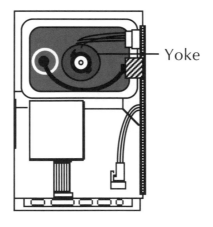

Yoke

Approximate cost of repairing it yourself:	***30 min.***
Approximate third-party repair cost:	***$65.00***
1 hour labor 65.00	
Approximate dealer repair cost:	***$70.00***
1 hour labor 70.00	

Symptoms: The display isn't rectangular. One or more of the edges is bowed. Other than that, the Mac is usable.

Typical history: The problem occurred right after completion of upgrade or service work.

Probable diagnosis: One of the yoke magnets is loose.

Solution: Identify/adjust the loose yoke magnet.

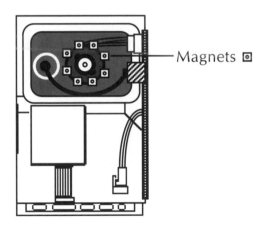

Approximate cost of repairing it yourself:		*30 min.*
Approximate third-party repair cost:		*$65.00*
1 hour labor	65.00	
Approximate dealer repair cost:		*$70.00*
1 hour labor	70.00	

Symptoms: The display is off center. Other than that, the Mac is usable.

Typical history: The problem occurred right after with the completion of upgrade or service work.

Probable diagnosis: The yoke rings are out of adjustment.

Solution: Adjust the yoke rings for a square picture.

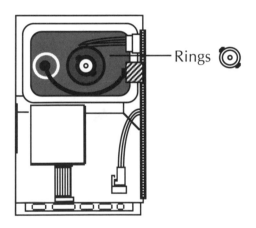

Approximate cost of repairing it yourself:		*15 min.*
Approximate third-party repair cost:		*$65.00*
1 hour labor	65.00	
Approximate dealer repair cost:		*$70.00*
1 hour labor	70.00	

Symptoms: The video display is shrunken. Other than that, the computer is usable.

Typical history: The problem occurred right after completion of upgrade or service work.

Probable diagnosis: The analog board is out of adjustment.

Solution: Adjust variable resistor R55 (labeled *Height)* and tunable coil L2 (labeled *Width)* for a 7.11 x 4.75-inch display.

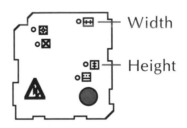

Approximate cost of repairing it yourself:	***30 min.***
Approximate third-party repair cost:	***$65.00***
1 hour labor 65.00	
Approximate dealer repair cost:	***$253.33***
1 new analog board 183.33	
1 hour labor 70.00	

Symptoms: On startup, the floppy disk icon appears, but the question mark does not blink. The internal 800K disk drive does not spin. Startup disks are neither read nor ejected.

Typical history: The problem occurred right after completion of upgrade or service work (right after you put everything back together).

Probable diagnosis: The disk drive cable is loose or disconnected.

Solution: Check/reconnect both ends of the disk drive cable.

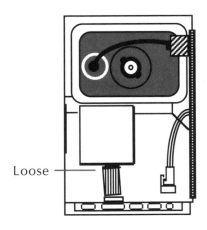

Loose

Approximate cost of repairing it yourself:		*15 min.*
Approximate third-party repair cost:		*$65.00*
1 hour labor	65.00	
Approximate dealer repair cost:		*$300.00*
1 800K mechanical assembly	230.00	
1 hour labor	70.00	

Symptoms: On startup, the Mac bongs, but then there is a *relatively bright* white dot in the center of the display.

Typical history: The problem occurred right after completion of upgrade or service work.

Probable diagnosis: The yoke cable is disconnected.

Solution: Reconnect the yoke cable to J1 on the analog board.

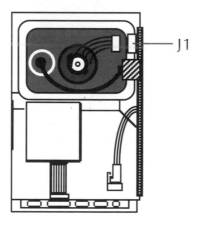

Approximate cost of repairing it yourself:		15 min.
Approximate third-party repair cost:		**$65.00**
1 hour labor	65.00	
Approximate dealer repair cost:		**$70.00**
1 hour labor	70.00	

Symptoms: On startup, there is a *relatively loud* sizzling noise. The display does not appear.

Typical history: The problem occurred right after completion of upgrade or service work (right after you put everything back together).

Probable diagnosis: The high voltage (HV) cable from the flyback transformer is disconnected.

Solution: Reconnect the HV cable from T1, the flyback transformer, to the anode well on the CRT.

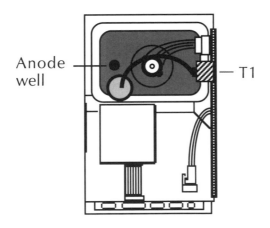

Approximate cost of repairing it yourself:		*15 min.*
Approximate third-party repair cost:		*$65.00*
1 hour labor	65.00	
Approximate dealer repair cost:		*$70.00*
1 hour labor	70.00	

Symptoms: There is no startup bong. There is no video. The display is dark, but bright flashes of light are coming from inside the computer. The whole inside of the Mac is arcing and sparking. It looks and sounds as if there's an arc welder in there!

Typical history: The Mac was dropped or was damaged in shipping.

Probable diagnosis: The neck of the cathode ray tube is broken. To prevent a fire, the neon bulb at board reference NE2 on the analog board is rapidly switching on and off.

Solution: Replace the CRT.

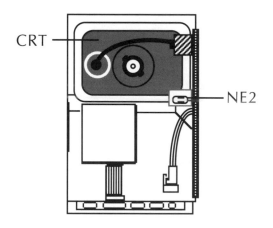

Approximate cost of repairing it yourself:		*$125.00*
1 9-inch CRT	125.00	*hour*
Approximate third-party repair cost:		*$315.00*
1 9-inch CRT	250.00	
1 hour labor	65.00	
Approximate dealer repair cost:		*$995.00*
1 new Mac Classic	995.00	

Symptoms: Occasionally, the display emits a bright flash of light. The effect is similar to a camera flash going off in your face.

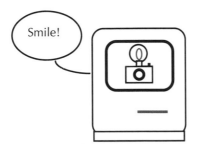

Probable diagnosis: The problem is a cracked solder joint on the analog board.

Solution: Check/resolder pin 1 (cut off) of the J2 connector.

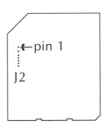

Approximate cost of repairing it yourself:		***30 min.***
Approximate third-party repair cost:		**$65.00**
1 hour labor	65.00	
Approximate dealer repair cost:		**$253.33**
1 new analog board	183.33	
1 hour labor	70.00	

Symptoms: There's no startup bong and no beep (or other) sound. Otherwise, the raster is normal, and the computer is usable.

Typical history: The problem occurred right after completion of upgrade or service work.

Probable diagnosis: The problem is on the analog board.

Solution: Check/reconnect the speaker input plug (if present) into the audio output jack at board reference J3. If that's not it, see the next entry.

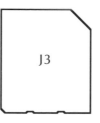

Approximate cost of repairing it yourself:		*15 min.*
Approximate third-party repair cost:		**$65.00**
1 hour labor	65.00	
Approximate dealer repair cost:		**$70.00**
1 hour labor	70.00	

Symptoms: There's no startup bong and no beep (or other) sound. Otherwise, the raster is normal, and the computer is usable.

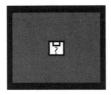

Typical history: The problem occurred right after completion of upgrade or service work.

Probable diagnosis: The RFI shield is shorting to the logic board.

Solution: Insulate the upper side of the RFI shield with two-inch packing tape. Also see the prior entry.

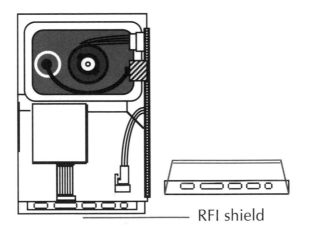

RFI shield

Approximate cost of repairing it yourself:		*15 min.*
Approximate third-party repair cost:		*$65.00*
1 hour labor	65.00	
Approximate dealer repair cost:		*$70.00*
1 hour labor	70.00	

Symptoms: On startup you get a sad Mac with error code 010601.

Typical history: The problem occurred right after completion of a 128K ROM upgrade on a 512K Mac.

Probable diagnosis: The ROMs are from different versions.

Solution: Replace the unmatched ROMs (marked 342-0341-B, 342-0342-B) at board locations D6 and D8 with a matched set of version-3 ROMs (marked 342-0341-C, 342-0342-B).

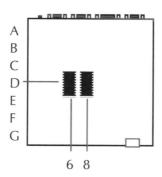

Approximate cost of repairing it yourself:		$125.00
1 set of version-3 ROMs	125.00	*1 hour*
Approximate third-party repair cost:		**$255.00**
1 set of version-3 ROMs	125.00	
2 hours labor	130.00	
Approximate dealer repair cost:		**$260.00**
1 set of version-3 ROMs	190.00	
1 hour labor	70.00	

Symptoms: On startup, a Mac 128K or 512K bongs, but then you get a sad Mac with error code 014120.

Typical history: The problem occurred right after completion of upgrade or service work on a Mac with 64K ROMs.

Probable diagnosis: The analog board is out of adjustment. The voltage is too low.

Solution: While measuring from pin 6 of the power/video cable to ground, adjust variable resistor R56 (labeled *Voltage)* for 5.0V DC.

Voltage

Approximate cost of repairing it yourself:	*30 min.*
Approximate third-party repair cost:	*$65.00*
1 hour labor 65.00	
Approximate dealer repair cost:	*$253.33*
1 new analog board 183.33	
1 hour labor 70.00	

Symptoms: On startup you get a sad Mac with error code 01FE01.

Typical history: The problem occurred right after completion of a 128K ROM upgrade on a 512K Mac.

Probable diagnosis: The ROMs are from different versions.

Solution: Replace the unmatched ROMs (marked 342-0341-C, 342-0342-A) at board locations D6 and D8 with a matched set of version-3 ROMs (marked 342-0341-C, 342-0342-B).

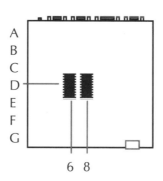

Approximate cost of repairing it yourself:		$125.00
1 set of version-3 ROMs	125.00	*1 hour*
Approximate third-party repair cost:		**$255.00**
1 set of version-3 ROMs	125.00	
2 hours labor	130.00	
Approximate dealer repair cost:		**$260.00**
1 set of version-3 ROMs	190.00	
1 hour labor	70.00	

Symptoms: On startup, you get a sad Mac with error code 030001, 030002, 030004, 030008, 030010, 030020, 030040 or 030080.

Typical history: The problem occurred out of the blue or right after installation of a SIMM upgrade.

Probable diagnosis: The problem is on the Mac Plus logic board.

Solution: Check/replace SIMMs 1 and 3 at locations F5-9 and G5-9.

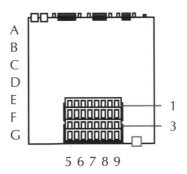

Approximate cost of repairing it yourself:		$10.00
1 41-256K SIMM	10.00	**1 hour**
Approximate third-party repair cost:		**$150.00**
1 41-256K SIMM	20.00	
2 hours labor	130.00	
Approximate dealer repair cost:		**$445.00**
1 new logic board (Plus)	375.00	
1 hour labor	70.00	

Symptoms: On startup, you get a sad Mac with error code 030100, 030200, 030400, 030800, 031000, 032000, 034000 or 038000.

Typical history: The problem occurred out of the blue or right after installation of a SIMM upgrade.

Probable diagnosis: The problem is on the Mac Plus logic board.

Solution: Check/replace SIMMs 2 and 4 at locations F5-9 and G5-9.

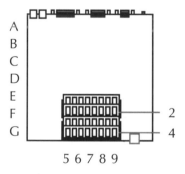

Approximate cost of repairing it yourself:		$10.00
1 41-256K SIMM	10.00	*1 hour*
Approximate third-party repair cost:		$150.00
1 41-256K SIMM	20.00	
2 hours labor	130.00	
Approximate dealer repair cost:		$445.00
1 new logic board (Plus)	375.00	
1 hour labor	70.00	

Symptoms: On startup, the computer bongs and you *almost* get to the desktop, but then you get a sad Mac with error code 0F000A.

Typical history: The Macintosh Plus (or 512Ke with SCSI upgrade) is connected to an external HD 20SC or other hard drive. If you disconnect the hard drive and boot from a floppy, it works OK.

Probable diagnosis: The hard drive has a bad partition map.

Solution: Boot the computer from a floppy disk, wait for the desktop to appear, and *then* turn on the drive. Use third-party SCSI formatting software (such as Silverlining version # 5.2/06, not Apple HD SC Setup) to repair the partition map (this won't always work).

Approximate cost of repairing it yourself:		**$135.00**
1 Silverlining (street price)	135.00	**30 min.**
Approximate third-party repair cost:		**$130.00**
2 hours labor	130.00	
Approximate dealer repair cost:		**$756.67**
1 HD20SC external mechanism	756.67	

Symptoms: On startup, there's no bong, and you get a sad Mac with error code 0F000D.

Typical history: The problem occurred right after installation of a programmer's switch.

Probable diagnosis: The interrupt lever on the programmer's switch is making contact with the interrupt button on the logic board.

Solution: Check/reposition the programmer's switch. If necessary, trim and shorten the shafts.

Approximate cost of repairing it yourself:		*15 min.*
Approximate third-party repair cost:		**$65.00**
1 hour labor	65.00	
Approximate dealer repair cost:		**$358.33**
1 new logic board (512K)	288.33	
1 hour labor	70.00	

Symptoms: On startup, the computer bongs and you *almost* get to the desktop, but then you get a sad Mac with error code 0F0002.

Typical history: The Macintosh is/was an upgraded 512K or 512Ke. The problem began immediately after a Dove/MacSnap 524 or 548 memory board was removed (pried up with a screwdriver).

Probable diagnosis: The problem is on the logic board.

Solution: Check for and repair damaged circuit traces near the AS253 chips at board locations G3, G4, F3 and F4.

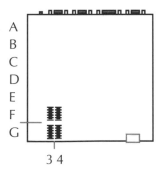

Approximate cost of repairing it yourself:		*2 hours*
Approximate third-party repair cost:		***$130.00***
2 hours labor	130.00	
Approximate dealer repair cost:		***$358.33***
1 new logic board (512K)	288.33	
1 hour labor	70.00	

Symptoms: On startup, the computer bongs and you *almost* get to the desktop, but then you get a sad Mac with error code 0F0002.

Typical history: The Macintosh Plus (or 512Ke with SCSI upgrade) is connected to an external HD 20SC or other hard drive. If you disconnect the hard drive and boot from a floppy, it works OK.

Probable diagnosis: The hard drive has a bad partition map.

Solution: Boot the computer from a floppy disk, wait for the desktop to appear, and *then* turn on the drive. Use third-party SCSI formatting software (such as Silverlining version # 5.2/06, not Apple HD SC Setup software) to repair the partition map (this doesn't always work).

Approximate cost of repairing it yourself:		***$135.00***
1 Silverlining (street price)	135.00	***30 min.***
Approximate third-party repair cost:		***$130.00***
2 hours labor	130.00	
Approximate dealer repair cost:		***$756.67***
1 HD20SC external mechanism	756.67	

Symptoms: On startup, the computer bongs and you *almost* get to the desktop, but then you get a sad Mac with error code 0F0003.

Typical history: The Macintosh Plus (or 512Ke with SCSI upgrade) is connected to an external HD 20SC or other hard drive. If you disconnect the hard drive and boot from a floppy, it works OK.

Probable diagnosis: The hard drive has a bad partition map.

Solution: Boot the computer from a floppy disk, wait for the desktop to appear, and *then* turn on the drive. Use third-party SCSI formatting software (such as Silverlining version # 5.2/06, not Apple HD SC Setup software) to repair the partition map (not always successful).

Approximate cost of repairing it yourself:		***$135.00***
1 Silverlining (street price)	135.00	***30 min.***
Approximate third-party repair cost:		***$130.00***
2 hours labor	130.00	
Approximate dealer repair cost:		***$756.67***
1 HD20SC external mechanism	756.67	

Symptoms: On startup, the computer bongs, but then you get a sad Mac with error code 0F0004.

Typical history: The problem occurred right after upgrade or service work on a 128K or 512K Mac with 64K ROMs.

Probable diagnosis: The analog board is out of adjustment.

Solution: Turn variable resistor R56 (labeled *Voltage*) fully counterclockwise. Restart and adjust R56 for 5.0V DC as measured from pin 6 of the power/video cable to chassis ground.

Voltage

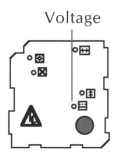

Approximate cost of repairing it yourself:		*15 min.*
Approximate third-party repair cost:		**$65.00**
1 hour labor	65.00	
Approximate dealer repair cost:		**$253.33**
1 new analog board	183.33	
1 hour labor	70.00	

Symptoms: On startup, a Mac 128K or 512K bongs, but then you get a sad Mac with error code 0F0064.

Probable diagnosis: The computer is incompatible with System software on the startup disk.

Solution: Replace the 64K ROM chips at board locations D6 and D8 with a set of 128K ROMs, or start up from a 400K disk formatted under the Macintosh File System (MFS).

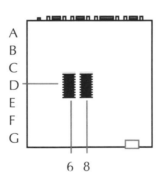

Approximate cost of repairing it yourself:		$125.00
1 set of 128K ROMs	125.00	*1 hour*
Approximate third-party repair cost:		$255.00
1 set of 128K ROMs	125.00	
2 hours labor	130.00	
Approximate dealer repair cost:		$260.00
1 set of version-3 ROMs	190.00	
1 hour labor	70.00	

Symptoms: On startup you get a sad Mac with error code nn0001 (where the value of nn is insignificant).

Typical history: The problem occurred out of the blue or right after installation of a 128K to 512K RAM upgrade.

Probable diagnosis: The problem is on the logic board.

Solution: Check/replace the RAM chip at board location F5.

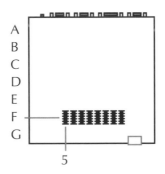

Approximate cost of repairing it yourself:		**$1.50**
1 41-256K 150NS RAM chip	1.50	**2 hours**
Approximate third-party repair cost:		**$135.00**
1 41-256K 150NS RAM chip	5.00	
2 hours labor	130.00	
Approximate dealer repair cost:		**$358.33**
1 new logic board (512K)	288.33	
1 hour labor	70.00	

Symptoms: On startup you get a sad Mac with error code nn0002 (where the value of nn is insignificant).

Typical history: The problem occurred out of the blue or right after installation of a 128K to 512K RAM upgrade.

Probable diagnosis: The problem is on the logic board.

Solution: Check/replace the RAM chip at board location F6.

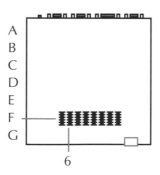

Approximate cost of repairing it yourself:		**$1.50**
1 41-256K 150NS RAM chip	1.50	**2 hours**
Approximate third-party repair cost:		**$135.00**
1 41-256K 150NS RAM chip	5.00	
2 hours labor	130.00	
Approximate dealer repair cost:		**$358.33**
1 new logic board (512K)	288.33	
1 hour labor	70.00	

Symptoms: On startup you get a sad Mac with error code nn0004 (where the value of nn is insignificant).

Typical history: The problem occurred out of the blue or right after installation of a 128K to 512K RAM upgrade.

Probable diagnosis: The problem is on the logic board.

Solution: Check/replace the RAM chip at board location F7.

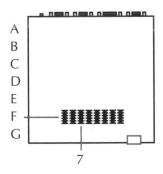

Approximate cost of repairing it yourself:		**$1.50**
1 41-256K 150NS RAM chip	1.50	**2 hours**
Approximate third-party repair cost:		**$135.00**
1 41-256K 150NS RAM chip	5.00	
2 hours labor	130.00	
Approximate dealer repair cost:		**$358.33**
1 new logic board (512K)	288.33	
1 hour labor	70.00	

Symptoms: On startup you get a sad Mac with error code nn0008 (where the value of nn is insignificant).

Typical history: The problem occurred out of the blue or right after the installation of a 128K to 512K RAM upgrade.

Probable diagnosis: The problem is on the logic board.

Solution: Check/replace the RAM chip at board location F8.

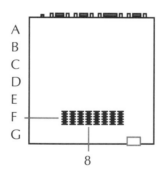

Approximate cost of repairing it yourself:		$1.50
1 41-256K 150NS RAM chip	1.50	2 hours
Approximate third-party repair cost:		$135.00
1 41-256K 150NS RAM chip	5.00	
2 hours labor	130.00	
Approximate dealer repair cost:		$358.33
1 new logic board (512K)	288.33	
1 hour labor	70.00	

Symptoms: On startup you get a sad Mac with error code nn0010 (where the value of nn is insignificant).

Typical history: The problem occurred out of the blue or right after the installation of a 128K to 512K RAM upgrade.

Probable diagnosis: The problem is on the logic board.

Solution: Check/replace the RAM chip at board location F9.

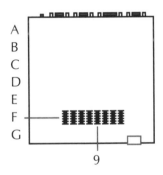

Approximate cost of repairing it yourself:		*$1.50*
1 41-256K 150NS RAM chip	1.50	*2 hours*
Approximate third-party repair cost:		*$135.00*
1 41-256K 150NS RAM chip	5.00	
2 hours labor	130.00	
Approximate dealer repair cost:		*$358.33*
1 new logic board (512K)	288.33	
1 hour labor	70.00	

Symptoms: On startup you get a sad Mac with error code nn0020 (where the value of nn is insignificant).

Typical history: The problem occurred out of the blue or right after the installation of a 128K to 512K RAM upgrade.

Probable diagnosis: The problem is on the logic board.

Solution: Check/replace the RAM chip at board location F10.

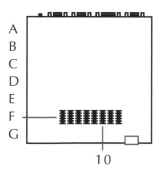

Approximate cost of repairing it yourself:		**$1.50**
1　41-256K 150NS RAM chip	1.50	**2 hours**
Approximate third-party repair cost:		**$135.00**
1　41-256K 150NS RAM chip	5.00	
2　hours labor	130.00	
Approximate dealer repair cost:		**$358.33**
1　new logic board (512K)	288.33	
1　hour labor	70.00	

Symptoms: On startup you get a sad Mac with error code nn0040 (where the value of nn is insignificant).

Typical history: The problem occurred out of the blue or right after installation of a 128K to 512K RAM upgrade.

Probable diagnosis: The problem is on the logic board.

Solution: Check/replace the RAM chip at board location F11.

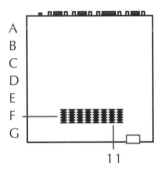

Approximate cost of repairing it yourself:		**$1.50**
1 41-256K 150NS RAM chip	1.50	**2 hours**
Approximate third-party repair cost:		**$135.00**
1 41-256K 150NS RAM chip	5.00	
2 hours labor	130.00	
Approximate dealer repair cost:		**$358.33**
1 new logic board (512K)	288.33	
1 hour labor	70.00	

Symptoms: On startup you get a sad Mac with error code nn0080 (where the value of nn is insignificant).

Typical history: The problem occurred out of the blue or right after installation of a 128K to 512K RAM upgrade.

Probable diagnosis: The problem is on the logic board.

Solution: Check/replace the RAM chip at board location F12.

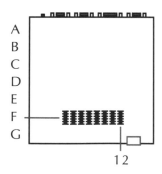

Approximate cost of repairing it yourself:		$1.50
1 41-256K 150NS RAM chip	1.50	2 hours
Approximate third-party repair cost:		**$135.00**
1 41-256K 150NS RAM chip	5.00	
2 hours labor	130.00	
Approximate dealer repair cost:		**$358.33**
1 new logic board (512K)	288.33	
1 hour labor	70.00	

Symptoms: On startup you get a sad Mac with error code nn0100 (where the value of nn is insignificant).

Typical history: The problem occurred out of the blue or right after installation of a 128K to 512K RAM upgrade.

Probable diagnosis: The problem is on the logic board.

Solution: Check/replace the RAM chip at board location G5.

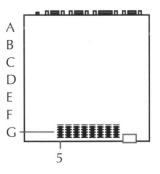

Approximate cost of repairing it yourself:		**$1.50**
1 41-256K 150NS RAM chip	1.50	**2 hours**
Approximate third-party repair cost:		**$135.00**
1 41-256K 150NS RAM chip	5.00	
2 hours labor	130.00	
Approximate dealer repair cost:		**$358.33**
1 new logic board (512K)	288.33	
1 hour labor	70.00	

Symptoms: On startup you get a sad Mac with error code nn0200 (where the value of nn is insignificant).

Typical history: The problem occurred out of the blue or right after the installation of a 128K to 512K RAM upgrade.

Probable diagnosis: The problem is on the logic board.

Solution: Check/replace the RAM chip at board location G6.

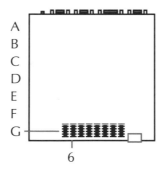

Approximate cost of repairing it yourself:		**$1.50**
1 41-256K 150NS RAM chip	1.50	**2 hours**
Approximate third-party repair cost:		**$135.00**
1 41-256K 150NS RAM chip	5.00	
2 hours labor	130.00	
Approximate dealer repair cost:		**$358.33**
1 new logic board (512K)	288.33	
1 hour labor	70.00	

Symptoms: On startup you get a sad Mac with error code nn0400 (where the value of nn is insignificant).

Typical history: The problem occurred out of the blue or right after installation of a 128K to 512K RAM upgrade.

Probable diagnosis: The problem is on the logic board.

Solution: Check/replace the RAM chip at board location G7.

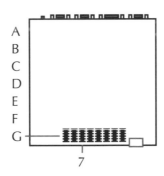

Approximate cost of repairing it yourself:		**$1.50**
1 41-256K 150NS RAM chip	1.50	**2 hours**
Approximate third-party repair cost:		**$135.00**
1 41-256K 150NS RAM chip	5.00	
2 hours labor	130.00	
Approximate dealer repair cost:		**$358.33**
1 new logic board (512K)	288.33	
1 hour labor	70.00	

Symptoms: On startup you get a sad Mac with error code nn800 (where the value of nn is insignificant).

Typical history: The problem occurred out of the blue or right after the installation of a 128K to 512K RAM upgrade.

Probable diagnosis: The problem is on the logic board.

Solution: Check/replace the RAM chip at board location G8.

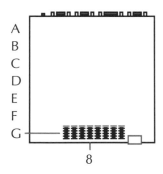

Approximate cost of repairing it yourself:		$1.50
1 41-256K 150NS RAM chip	1.50	*2 hours*
Approximate third-party repair cost:		***$135.00***
1 41-256K 150NS RAM chip	5.00	
2 hours labor	130.00	
Approximate dealer repair cost:		***$358.33***
1 new logic board (512K)	288.33	
1 hour labor	70.00	

Symptoms: On startup you get a sad Mac with error code nn1000 (where the value of nn is insignificant).

Typical history: The problem occurred out of the blue or right after installation of a 128K to 512K RAM upgrade.

Probable diagnosis: The problem is on the logic board.

Solution: Check/replace the RAM chip at board location G9.

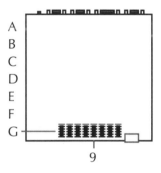

Approximate cost of repairing it yourself:		$1.50
1 41-256K 150NS RAM chip	1.50	2 hours
Approximate third-party repair cost:		$135.00
1 41-256K 150NS RAM chip	5.00	
2 hours labor	130.00	
Approximate dealer repair cost:		$358.33
1 new logic board (512K)	288.33	
1 hour labor	70.00	

Symptoms: On startup you get a sad Mac with error code nn2000 (where the value of nn is insignificant).

Typical history: The problem occurred out of the blue or right after installation of a 128K to 512K RAM upgrade.

Probable diagnosis: The problem is on the logic board.

Solution: Check/replace the RAM chip at board location G10.

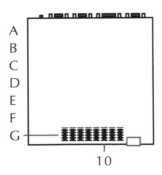

Approximate cost of repairing it yourself:		$1.50
1 41-256K 150NS RAM chip	1.50	2 hours
Approximate third-party repair cost:		$135.00
1 41-256K 150NS RAM chip	5.00	
2 hours labor	130.00	
Approximate dealer repair cost:		$358.33
1 new logic board (512K)	288.33	
1 hour labor	70.00	

Symptoms: On startup you get a sad Mac with error code nn4000 (where the value of nn is insignificant).

Typical history: The problem occurred out of the blue or right after installation of a 128K to 512K RAM upgrade.

Probable diagnosis: The problem is on the logic board.

Solution: Check/replace the RAM chip at board location G11.

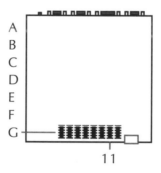

Approximate cost of repairing it yourself:		$1.50
1 41-256K 150NS RAM chip	1.50	2 hours
Approximate third-party repair cost:		$135.00
1 41-256K 150NS RAM chip	5.00	
2 hours labor	130.00	
Approximate dealer repair cost:		$358.33
1 new logic board (512K)	288.33	
1 hour labor	70.00	

Symptoms: On startup you get a sad Mac with error code nn8000 (where the value of nn is insignificant).

Typical history: The problem occurred out of the blue or right after installation of a 128K to 512K RAM upgrade.

Probable diagnosis: The problem is on the logic board.

Solution: Check/replace the RAM chip at board location G12.

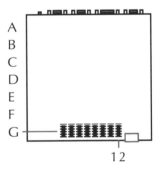

Approximate cost of repairing it yourself:		$1.50
1 41-256K 150NS RAM chip	1.50	2 hours
Approximate third-party repair cost:		$135.00
1 41-256K 150NS RAM chip	5.00	
2 hours labor	130.00	
Approximate dealer repair cost:		$358.33
1 new logic board (512K)	288.33	
1 hour labor	70.00	

Symptoms: On shutdown, the computer *momentarily* makes a loud burping noise. Otherwise, it seems OK.

Probable diagnosis: The problem is on the analog board.

Solution: Replace the 4N35 optoisolator IC (6-pin DIP, 3550V) at board reference U3.

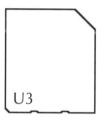

Approximate cost of repairing it yourself:		69¢
1 4N35 optoisolator	.69	*1 hour*
Approximate third-party repair cost:		**$70.00**
1 4N35 optoisolator	5.00	
1 hour labor	65.00	
Approximate dealer repair cost:		**$253.33**
1 new analog board	183.33	
1 hour labor	70.00	

Symptoms: On startup, the computer makes a soft ticking sound, as though there's a time bomb inside. Once you insert a disk, the ticking noise stops. After that, the computer seems OK.

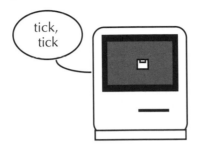

Probable diagnosis: The ticking noise is characteristic of certain 800K disk drives (part number MFD-51W-03). It's insignificant.

Solution: Ignore the ticking noise, or replace the disk drive.

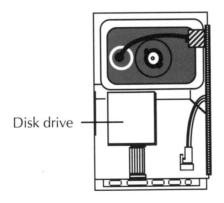

Disk drive

Approximate cost of repairing it yourself:		*zip*
Approximate third-party repair cost:		**$160.00**
1 800K DD swap	95.00	
1 hour labor	65.00	
Approximate dealer repair cost:		**$300.00**
1 new 800K drive assembly	230.00	
1 hour labor	70.00	

Symptoms: On a Mac 128K, 512K or 512Ke, there's no startup bong and no video display. You're sure that the problem isn't on the analog board, because the analog board works perfectly in another Mac.

Probable diagnosis: The problem is on the 128K or 512K logic board.

Solution: Check/replace the TSM PAL (Apple part 342-0254-A) at board location D1 and the LAG PAL (Apple part 342-0251-A) at E1.

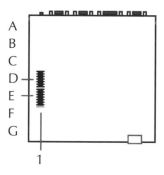

Approximate cost of repairing it yourself:		$20.00
1 PAL chip	20.00	*2 hours*
Approximate third-party repair cost:		***$170.00***
1 PAL chip	40.00	
2 hours labor	130.00	
Approximate dealer repair cost:		***$358.33***
1 new logic board (512K)	288.33	
1 hour labor	70.00	

Symptoms: On a Mac Plus there's no startup bong and no video display. You're sure that the problem isn't on the analog board, because the analog board works perfectly in another Mac.

Probable diagnosis: The problem is on the Mac Plus logic board.

Solution: Check/replace the LAG PAL (Apple part 342-0515-A) at board location E1, the BMU2 PAL (Apple part 342-0520-A) at E2 and the CAS PAL (Apple part 342-0519A) at E3.

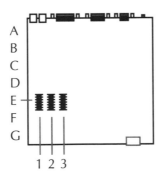

Approximate cost of repairing it yourself:		$20.00
1 PAL chip	20.00	2 hours
Approximate third-party repair cost:		$170.00
1 PAL chip	40.00	
2 hours labor	130.00	
Approximate dealer repair cost:		$445.00
1 new logic board (Plus)	375.00	
1 hour labor	70.00	

CHAPTER 2
MAC SE AND SE/30

Symptoms: There is a herringbone pattern throughout the display. Otherwise, the computer is usable.

Typical history: The computer is an original (early model) SE.

Probable diagnosis: The problem is on the analog board.

Solution: Replace the original flyback transformer (Apple part 157-0042A) at board reference T2 with a later type (157-0042C).

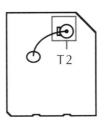

Approximate cost of repairing it yourself:		***$21.00***
1 flyback transformer	21.00	***1 hour***
Approximate third-party repair cost:		***$107.00***
1 flyback transformer	42.00	
1 hour labor	65.00	
Approximate dealer repair cost:		***$305.00***
1 new analog board	235.00	
1 hour labor	70.00	

Symptoms: The computer is excessively loud and/or the display intermittently jitters and shakes. Otherwise, the computer is usable.

Typical History: The computer is an original (early model) SE.

Probable diagnosis: The problem is on the analog board.

Solution: Replace the original crossflow fan at board reference B1 with a *brushless* 12VDC boxer fan.

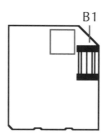

Approximate cost of repairing it yourself:		*$15.00*
1 brushless 12VDC boxer fan	15.00	*1 hour*
Approximate third-party repair cost:		*$105.00*
1 fan upgrade kit	40.00	
1 hour labor	65.00	
Approximate dealer repair cost:		*$305.00*
1 new analog board	235.00	
1 hour labor	70.00	

Symptoms: There is no startup bong. The computer makes a dreadful hissing/sizzling noise. The display is dark.

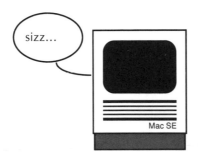

Probable diagnosis: The problem is on the analog board.

Solution: Check/replace the barrel rectifier (GI854, R-SI, 600V, 3A) at board reference CR2. If shorted (0.00 to 0.01Ω), substitute a heavy-duty replacement part (MR824, R-SI, 400V, 5A) to avoid future repairs.

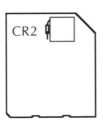

Approximate cost of repairing it yourself:		**$5.00**
1 MR824 rectifier	5.00	**1 hour**
Approximate third-party repair cost:		**$75.00**
1 MR824 rectifier	10.00	
1 hour labor	65.00	
Approximate dealer repair cost:		**$305.00**
1 new analog board	235.00	
1 hour labor	70.00	

Symptoms: There is no startup bong. The display is dark. The computer appears to be completely dead (no dreadful hissing/sizzling noise).

Probable diagnosis: The problem is on the analog board.

Solution: Check/replace the barrel rectifier (GI854, R-SI, 600V, 3A) at board reference CR3 (shorted). Use a heavy-duty replacement part (MR824, R-SI, 400V, 5A) to avoid future repairs. Also check/replace the BU406D transistor (horizontal output) at board reference Q2 (burned). If that doesn't do it, replace the flyback transformer at board reference T2. Also see the next entry.

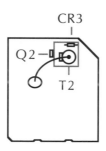

Approximate cost of repairing it yourself:		**$31.00**
1 MR824 rectifier	5.00	*1 hour*
1 BU406D transistor	5.00	
1 flyback transformer	21.00	
Approximate third-party repair cost:		**$127.00**
miscellaneous parts	62.00	
1 hour labor	65.00	
Approximate dealer repair cost:		**$305.00**
1 new analog board	235.00	
1 hour labor	70.00	

Symptoms: There is no startup bong. The display is black. The computer is completely dead (no fan or other noise).

Probable diagnosis: The problem may be in the Sony CR44 power supply.

Solution: Check/replace the on/off switch (Sony part 1-571-035-11) or substitute a generic switch made for panel cutouts measuring 1.125 inches x 1.072 inches. Also see the prior entry.

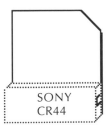

Approximate cost of repairing it yourself:		***$3.00***
1 on/off switch	3.00	***1 hour***
Approximate third-party repair cost:		***$71.00***
1 on/off switch	6.00	
1 hour labor	65.00	
Approximate dealer repair cost:		***$328.33***
1 new power supply	258.33	
1 hour labor	70.00	

Symptoms: On startup, the computer bongs, the fan turns and the internal hard drive spins (when present), but the blinking disk icon never appears. The display is dark. Turning up the front-panel brightness control has no effect.

Probable diagnosis: The problem is on the analog board.

Solution: Check/replace open resistor R22 (470K, ½-watt, 5%).

Approximate cost of repairing it yourself:		19¢
1 ½-watt resistor	.19	*1 hour*
Approximate third-party repair cost:		*$70.00*
1 ½-watt resistor	5.00	
1 hour labor	65.00	
Approximate dealer repair cost:		*$305.00*
1 new analog board	235.00	
1 hour labor	70.00	

Symptoms: The right side of the display wiggles (like a worm). There is a loud sizzling noise.

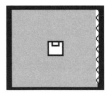

Typical history: The sizzling started right after the analog board was replaced.

Probable diagnosis: The problem is a bad ground.

Solution: Verify that the green ground wire (attached to the power supply) is connected to the chassis.

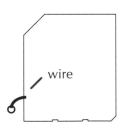

Approximate cost of repairing it yourself:		***30 min.***
Approximate third-party repair cost:		***$65.00***
1 hour labor	65.00	
Approximate dealer repair cost:		***$305.00***
1 new analog board	235.00	
1 hour labor	70.00	

Symptoms: The display is vertically compressed. It lacks height.

Typical history: The symptoms appeared immediately after the computer was board-swapped (not out of the blue).

Probable diagnosis: The new analog board is out of adjustment.

Solution: Adjust variable resistor R4 (labeled *Height)* until the display measures 4.75 inches high.

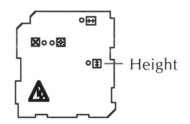

Approximate cost of repairing it yourself:		***30 min.***
Approximate third-party repair cost:		***$65.00***
1 hour labor	65.00	
Approximate dealer repair cost:		***$305.00***
1 new analog board	235.00	
1 hour labor	70.00	

Symptoms: The display is vertically expanded. It's too tall.

Typical history: The symptoms appeared immediately after the computer was board-swapped (not out of the blue).

Probable diagnosis: The new analog board is out of adjustment.

Solution: Adjust variable resistor R4 (labeled *Height)* until the display measures 4.75 inches high.

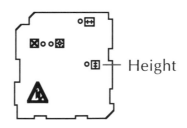

Approximate cost of repairing it yourself:		*30 min.*
Approximate third-party repair cost:		**$65.00**
1 hour labor	65.00	
Approximate dealer repair cost:		**$305.00**
1 new analog board	235.00	
1 hour labor	70.00	

Symptoms: The display is horizontally compressed. It lacks width.

Typical history: The symptoms appeared immediately after the computer was board-swapped (not out of the blue).

Probable diagnosis: The new analog board is out of adjustment.

Solution: Adjust tunable coil L2 (labeled *Width)* until the display measures 7.11 inches wide.

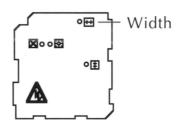 Width

Approximate cost of repairing it yourself:		*30 min.*
Approximate third-party repair cost:		**$65.00**
1 hour labor	65.00	
Approximate dealer repair cost:		**$305.00**
1 new analog board	235.00	
1 hour labor	70.00	

Symptoms: The display is horizontally expanded. It's too wide.

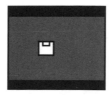

Typical history: The symptoms appeared immediately after the computer was board-swapped (not out of the blue).

Probable diagnosis: The new analog board is out of adjustment.

Solution: Adjust tunable coil L2 (labeled *Width)* until the display measures 7.11 inches wide.

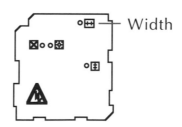

Approximate cost of repairing it yourself:		*30 min.*
Approximate third-party repair cost:		*$65.00*
1 hour labor	65.00	
Approximate dealer repair cost:		*$305.00*
1 new analog board	235.00	
1 hour labor	70.00	

Symptoms: The right side of the display shakes (moves in and out) during a disk drive event or whenever a window is opened.

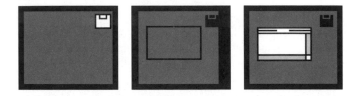

Probable diagnosis: The problem is on the analog board.

Solution: Replace the barrel rectifier (GI854, R-SI, 600V, 3A) at board reference CR2 on the analog board. Use a heavy-duty replacement part (MR824, R-SI, 400V, 5A) to avoid future repairs. If that doesn't do it, see the next entry.

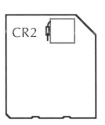

Approximate cost of repairing it yourself:		$5.00
1 MR824 rectifier	5.00	*1 hour*
Approximate third-party repair cost:		$75.00
1 MR824 rectifier	10.00	
1 hour labor	65.00	
Approximate dealer repair cost:		$305.00
1 new analog board	235.00	
1 hour labor	70.00	

Symptoms: Even after CR2 has been replaced, the right side of the display moves in and out during a disk drive event or whenever a window is opened.

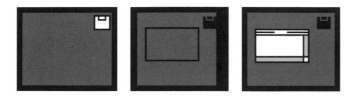

Probable diagnosis: The problem is on the analog board.

Solution: Replace the horizontal output transistor (BU406D) at board reference Q2. Also see the prior entry.

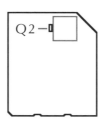

Approximate cost of repairing it yourself:		**$5.00**
1 BU406D transistor	5.00	***1 hour***
Approximate third-party repair cost:		**$75.00**
1 BU406D transistor	10.00	
1 hour labor	65.00	
Approximate dealer repair cost:		**$305.00**
1 new analog board	235.00	
1 hour labor	70.00	

Symptoms: On an SE/30, the display intermittently blinks out. White lines intermittently flash across the display. Tapping on the cabinet causes the problem to recur.

Probable diagnosis: The problem is a bad connection between the CRT socket board and the CRT.

Solution: Check the CRT socket board for a snug fit. Secure the CRT socket board to the neck of the CRT with a dab of hot glue.

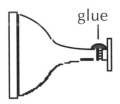

Approximate cost of repairing it yourself:		*1 hour*
Approximate third-party repair cost:		*$65.00*
1 hour labor	65.00	
Approximate dealer repair cost:		*$70.00*
1 hour labor	70.00	

Symptoms: The video display exhibits poor linearity. Items on the left are wider than items on the right.

Probable diagnosis: The problem is on the analog board.

Solution: Replace high-frequency capacitor C15 (3.9µ NP 25/35V HF). Use a heavy-duty replacement part (3.9µ NP 100V HF) to avoid future repairs.

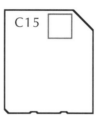

Approximate cost of repairing it yourself:		***$3.00***
1 3.9µ NP 100V HF capacitor	3.00	***1 hour***
Approximate third-party repair cost:		***$71.00***
1 3.9µ NP 100V HF capacitor	6.00	
1 hour labor	65.00	
Approximate dealer repair cost:		***$305.00***
1 new analog board	235.00	
1 hour labor	70.00	

Symptoms: A few minutes after startup, a vertical line appears on the right side of the video display, accompanied by diagonal lines. If the power isn't switched off, the display gets darker and darker and the Mac begins to smoke.

Typical history: Prior to this, the display exhibited poor linearity.

Probable diagnosis: The problem is on the analog board.

Solution: Replace high-frequency capacitor C15 (3.9μ NP 25/35V HF). Use a heavy-duty replacement part (3.9μ NP 100V HF) to avoid future repairs. Also, check/replace yoke plug P1 (may be burned).

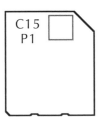

Approximate cost of repairing it yourself:		***$3.00***
1 3.9μ NP 100V HF capacitor	3.00	***1 hour***
Approximate third-party repair cost:		***$71.00***
1 3.9μ NP 100V HF capacitor	6.00	
1 hour labor	65.00	
Approximate dealer repair cost:		***$305.00***
1 new analog board	235.00	
1 hour labor	70.00	

Symptoms: On startup, the computer bongs but the normal video display *does not* appear. Instead there is a *very bright* vertical line. If the power isn't switched off, the Mac begins to smoke.

Probable diagnosis: The problem is on the analog board.

Solution: Replace high-frequency capacitor C15 (3.9μ NP 25/35V HF). Use a heavy-duty replacement part (3.9μ NP 100V HF) to avoid future repairs. Also, check/replace yoke plug P1 (may be burned).

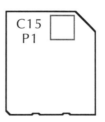

Approximate cost of repairing it yourself:		***$3.00***
1 3.9μ NP 100V HF capacitor	3.00	***1 hour***
Approximate third-party repair cost:		***$71.00***
1 3.9μ NP 100V HF capacitor	6.00	
1 hour labor	65.00	
Approximate dealer repair cost:		***$305.00***
1 new analog board	235.00	
1 hour labor	70.00	

Symptoms: On startup, the computer bongs but the normal video display *does not* appear. Instead there is a *relatively dim* vertical line. If the power isn't switched off, the Mac begins to smoke.

Probable diagnosis: The problem is on the analog board.

Solution: Check/replace burned resistor R19 (220Ω, ¼-watt 5%). To avoid immediate recurrence, vacuum-desolder linearity coil L3. Use 100% *fresh* solder (don't just reheat the joint).

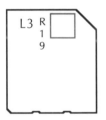

Approximate cost of repairing it yourself:		9¢
1 220Ω, ¼-watt 5% resistor	.09	*1 hour*
Approximate third-party repair cost:		**$70.00**
1 220Ω, ¼-watt 5% resistor	5.00	
1 hour labor	65.00	
Approximate dealer repair cost:		**$305.00**
1 new analog board	235.00	
1 hour labor	70.00	

Symptoms: After a short while, the video display collapses to a vertical line. Tapping on the left side of the cabinet temporarily restores the full display or causes it to flash.

Probable diagnosis: The problem is a cracked solder joint on the analog board.

Solution: Check/resolder pin 4 (top, horizontal yoke) of the P1 connector and check/resolder tunable coil L2 (marked *Width*).

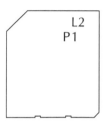

L2
P1

Approximate cost of repairing it yourself:		*30 min.*
Approximate third-party repair cost:		*$65.00*
1 hour labor	65.00	
Approximate dealer repair cost:		*$305.00*
1 new analog board	235.00	
1 hour labor	70.00	

Symptoms: After a short while, the video display collapses to a horizontal line. Tapping on the left side of the cabinet temporarily restores the full display or causes it to flash.

Probable diagnosis: The problem is a cracked solder joint on the analog board.

Solution: Check/resolder pin 1 (bottom, vertical yoke) of the P1 connector. Also see the next entry.

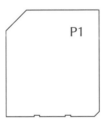

Approximate cost of repairing it yourself:		***30 min.***
Approximate third-party repair cost:		**$65.00**
1 hour labor	65.00	
Approximate dealer repair cost:		**$305.00**
1 new analog board	235.00	
1 hour labor	70.00	

Symptoms: On startup, the computer bongs but the normal video display *does not* appear. Instead there is a *very bright* horizontal line.

Typical history: The problem happened out of the blue. The display had not previously been intermittent.

Probable diagnosis: The problem is on the analog board.

Solution: Check/replace the TDA 1170 IC (12-pin TV, vertical deflection) at board reference U2. Also see the prior entry.

Approximate cost of repairing it yourself:		**$5.28**
1 TDA 1170 chip	5.28	**1 hour**
Approximate third-party repair cost:		**$75.56**
1 TDA 1170 chip	10.56	
1 hour labor	65.00	
Approximate dealer repair cost:		**$305.00**
1 new analog board	235.00	
1 hour labor	70.00	

Symptoms: On startup, the computer bongs and the blinking disk icon appears, but the video display is much too bright. Scan lines are visible even when the brightness control is turned down.

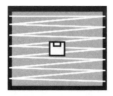

Typical history: The symptoms appeared out of the blue (not immediately after the computer was board-swapped).

Probable diagnosis: The problem is on the analog board.

Solution: Check/replace open resistors R20 (100K, ½-watt, 5%), and/or R21 (1M, ½-watt, 5%). Also see the next entry.

Approximate cost of repairing it yourself:		19¢
1 ½-watt resistor	.19	*1 hour*
Approximate third-party repair cost:		*$70.00*
1 ½-watt resistor	5.00	
1 hour labor	65.00	
Approximate dealer repair cost:		*$305.00*
1 new analog board	235.00	
1 hour labor	70.00	

Symptoms: On startup, the computer bongs and the blinking disk icon appears, but the video display is much too bright. Scan lines are visible even when the brightness control is turned down.

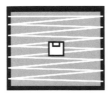

Typical history: The symptoms appeared immediately after the computer was board-swapped (not out of the blue).

Probable diagnosis: The new analog board is out of adjustment.

Solution: Adjust variable resistor R24 (labeled *Cut-off*) until the scan lines disappear. If that doesn't do it, see the prior entry.

Cut-off

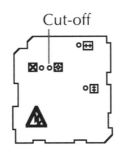

Approximate cost of repairing it yourself:		*30 min.*
Approximate third-party repair cost:		*$65.00*
1 hour labor	65.00	
Approximate dealer repair cost:		*$305.00*
1 new analog board	235.00	
1 hour labor	70.00	

Symptoms: There is raster but no video display. The raster is very bright. Horizontal scan lines are visible.

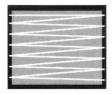

Probable diagnosis: The problem is on the analog board.

Solution: Replace the SN74LS38N chip (14-pin DIP, quad 2-input NAND) at board reference U1. If that's not it, see the next entry.

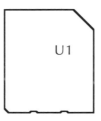

Approximate cost of repairing it yourself:		**35¢**
1 SN74LS38N chip	.35	**1 hour**
Approximate third-party repair cost:		**$70.00**
1 SN74LS38N chip	5.00	
1 hour labor	65.00	
Approximate dealer repair cost:		**$305.00**
1 new analog board	235.00	
1 hour labor	70.00	

Symptoms: There is raster but no video display. The raster is very bright. Horizontal scan lines are visible.

Probable diagnosis: The problem is on the CRT socket board.

Solution: Check/replace the 2N 3904 transistor (NPN, 0.6A, ½-watt, TO-92) at board reference Q1. Depending on the board revision Q1 could either be on the left or on the right. Also see the prior entry.

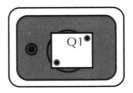

Approximate cost of repairing it yourself:		10¢
1 2N 3904 transistor	.10	*1 hour*
Approximate third-party repair cost:		$70.00
1 2N 3904 transistor	5.00	
1 hour labor	65.00	
Approximate dealer repair cost:		$87.00
1 new Apple CRT socket board	17.00	
1 hour labor	70.00	

Symptoms: The top half of the video display is somewhat squashed. There's a bright white line in the middle. The bottom half of the display is black.

Probable diagnosis: The problem is on the analog board.

Solution: Replace the TDA 1170 IC (12-pin TV, vertical deflection) at board reference U2.

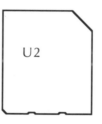

U2

Approximate cost of repairing it yourself:		*$5.28*
1 TDA 1170 chip	5.28	*1 hour*
Approximate third-party repair cost:		*$75.56*
1 TDA 1170 chip	10.56	
1 hour labor	65.00	
Approximate dealer repair cost:		*$305.00*
1 new analog board	235.00	
1 hour labor	70.00	

Symptoms: The bottom half of the video display is somewhat squashed. There's a bright white line in the middle. The top half of the display is black.

Probable diagnosis: The problem is on the analog board.

Solution: Replace the TDA 1170 IC (12-pin TV, vertical deflection) at board reference U2.

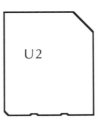

Approximate cost of repairing it yourself:		*$5.28*
1 TDA 1170 chip	5.28	*1 hour*
Approximate third-party repair cost:		*$75.56*
1 TDA 1170 chip	10.56	
1 hour labor	65.00	
Approximate dealer repair cost:		*$305.00*
1 new analog board	235.00	
1 hour labor	70.00	

Symptoms: The bottom half of the video display is so elongated that it disappears underneath the cabinet. Adjusting the Height control affects the top half of the display but does not affect the bottom.

Probable diagnosis: The problem is on the analog board.

Solution: Replace the TDA 1170 IC (12-pin TV, vertical deflection) at board reference U2.

Approximate cost of repairing it yourself:		**$5.28**
1 TDA 1170 chip	5.28	**1 hour**
Approximate third-party repair cost:		**$75.56**
1 TDA 1170 chip	10.56	
1 hour labor	65.00	
Approximate dealer repair cost:		**$305.00**
1 new analog board	235.00	
1 hour labor	70.00	

Symptoms: The top half of the video display is so elongated that it disappears underneath the cabinet. Adjusting the Height control affects the bottom half of the display but does not affect the top.

Probable diagnosis: The problem is on the analog board.

Solution: Replace the TDA 1170 IC (12-pin TV, vertical deflection) at board reference U2.

Approximate cost of repairing it yourself:		*$5.28*
1 TDA 1170 chip	5.28	*1 hour*
Approximate third-party repair cost:		*$75.56*
1 TDA 1170 chip	10.56	
1 hour labor	65.00	
Approximate dealer repair cost:		*$305.00*
1 new analog board	235.00	
1 hour labor	70.00	

Symptoms: A Mac SE has no startup bong. The display is filled with a black-and-white checkerboard pattern.

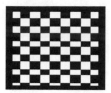

Typical history: The problem occurred after completion of an FDHD disk drive/ROM upgrade (right after you put everything back together).

Probable diagnosis: The problem is on the logic board.

Solution: Verify that the new ROMs and the new IWM at board locations D6, D7 and D8 are not reversed, backwards or otherwise incorrectly installed.

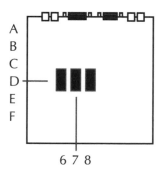

Approximate cost of repairing it yourself:		*15 min.*
Approximate third-party repair cost:		**$65.00**
1 hour labor	65.00	
Approximate dealer repair cost:		**$398.33**
1 new logic board (SE)	328.33	
1 hour labor	70.00	

Symptoms: A Mac SE/30 has no startup bong. The display is filled with a black-and-white checkerboard pattern.

Probable diagnosis: The problem on the SE/30 logic board.

Solution: Check/reseat the ROM SIMM.

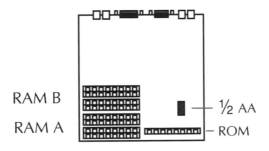

Approximate cost of repairing it yourself:		*1 hour*
Approximate third-party repair cost:		**$130.00**
2 hours labor	130.00	
Approximate dealer repair cost:		**$470.00**
1 new logic board (SE/30)	400.00	
1 hour labor	70.00	

Symptoms: A burning smell lingers about the computer. The internal hard drive spins, but doesn't mount. External SCSI devices don't mount either. Formatting software reports *broken bus* or *bus not terminated.*

Typical history: The problem occurred when you plugged a serial device or a parallel printer into the external SCSI port.

Probable diagnosis: The problem is on the Mac SE logic board.

Solution: Check/replace burned rectifier CR1 (1N4001) at board location B4. Also see the next entry.

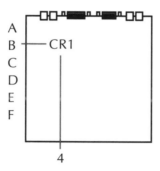

Approximate cost of repairing it yourself:		*10¢*
1 IN4001 rectifier	.10	*1 hour*
Approximate third-party repair cost:		*$135.00*
1 IN4001 rectifier	5.00	
2 hours labor	130.00	
Approximate dealer repair cost:		*$398.33*
1 new logic board (SE)	328.33	
1 hour labor	70.00	

Symptoms: The internal hard drive spins, but it doesn't mount. External SCSI devices (that work perfectly when connected to other Macs) don't mount either.

Typical history: The internal and external floppy drives work fine. Except for the SCSI problem, the computer appears to be normal.

Probable diagnosis: The problem is on the Mac SE logic board.

Solution: Check/replace the SCSI chip (NCR5380, 40-pin DIP) at board location B5–8. Also see the prior entry.

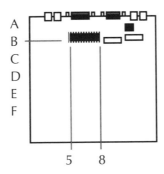

Approximate cost of repairing it yourself:		**18.00**
1 NCR5380	18.00	**2 hours**
Approximate third-party repair cost:		**$166.00**
1 NCR5380	36.00	
2 hours labor	130.00	
Approximate dealer repair cost:		**$398.33**
1 new logic board (SE)	328.33	
1 hour labor	70.00	

Symptoms: On startup, the desktop appears, but neither the keyboard nor the mouse work.

Typical history: The problem occurred when you connected or disconnected an ADB device while the computer was on.

Probable diagnosis: The problem is on the Mac SE logic board.

Solution: Check/replace the shorted filter (Apple part 155-0007-E) at board location A11.

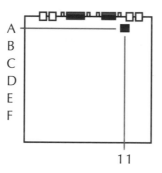

Approximate cost of repairing it yourself:		*$14.00*
1 Tokin filter	14.00	*2 hours*
Approximate third-party repair cost:		*$158.00*
1 Tokin filter	28.00	
2 hours labor	130.00	
Approximate dealer repair cost:		*$398.33*
1 new logic board (SE)	328.33	
1 hour labor	70.00	

Symptoms: A Mac SE does not maintain the proper time and date.

Probable diagnosis: The problem is on the Mac SE logic board.

Solution: Check/replace the clock battery (lithium, ½AA) at board location B4. Early models have 3V solder-in batteries with pigtail leads. Later models have 3.6V batteries that snap into battery boxes.

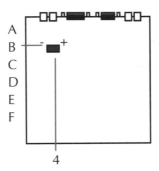

Approximate cost of repairing it yourself:		*$12.00*
1 lithium battery (½AA)	12.00	*1 hour*
Approximate third-party repair cost:		*$154.00*
1 lithium battery (½AA)	24.00	
2 hours labor	130.00	
Approximate dealer repair cost:		*$398.33*
1 new logic board (SE)	328.33	
1 hour labor	70.00	

Symptoms: A Mac SE/30 does not maintain the proper time and date.

Probable diagnosis: The problem is on the Mac SE/30 logic board.

Solution: Check/replace the clock battery (lithium 3.6V, ½AA, snap-in type).

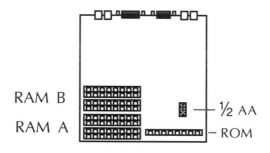

Approximate cost of repairing it yourself:		$12.00
1 lithium battery (3.6V, ½AA)	12.00	*1 hour*
Approximate third-party repair cost:		**$154.00**
1 lithium battery (3.6V, ½AA)	24.00	
2 hours labor	130.00	
Approximate dealer repair cost:		**$470.00**
1 new logic board (SE/30)	400.00	
1 hour labor	70.00	

Symptoms: On startup, you get a sad Mac with error code 00000001 over nnnnnnnn (where the values of n are insignificant).

Probable diagnosis: The problem is on the SE/30 logic board.

Solution: Check/reseat the ROM SIMM.

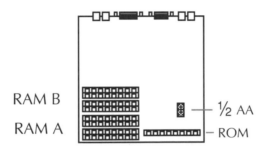

Approximate cost of repairing it yourself:		*1 hour*
Approximate third-party repair cost:		**$130.00**
2 hours labor	130.00	
Approximate dealer repair cost:		**$470.00**
1 new logic board (SE/30)	400.00	
1 hour labor	70.00	

Symptoms: On startup, you get a sad Mac with error code 00000002 over 000000nn (where the value of nn is insignificant).

Probable diagnosis: The problem is on the SE logic board.

Solution: Check/replace SIMM 1 on 820-0176 (original) logic boards. Check/replace SIMM 3 on 820-0250 (DIP SIMM) boards.

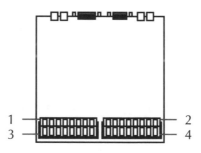

Approximate cost of repairing it yourself:		***$10.00***
1 SIMM (256K)	10.00	***1 hour***
Approximate third-party repair cost:		***$150.00***
1 SIMM (256K)	20.00	
2 hours labor	130.00	
Approximate dealer repair cost:		***$398.33***
1 new logic board (SE)	328.33	
1 hour labor	70.00	

Symptoms: On startup, you get a sad Mac with error code 00000002 over 00nn00nn (where the values of nn are insignificant).

Probable diagnosis: The problem is on the SE logic board.

Solution: Check/replace SIMM 1 on 820-0176 (original) logic boards. Check/replace SIMM 3 on 820-0250 (DIP SIMM) boards.

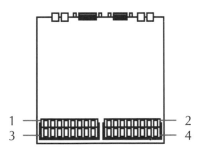

Approximate cost of repairing it yourself:		$10.00
1 SIMM (256K)	10.00	1 hour
Approximate third-party repair cost:		$150.00
1 SIMM (256K)	20.00	
2 hours labor	130.00	
Approximate dealer repair cost:		$398.33
1 new logic board (SE)	328.33	
1 hour labor	70.00	

Symptoms: On startup, you get a sad Mac with error code 00000002 over 0000nn00 (where the value of nn is insignificant).

Probable diagnosis: The problem is on the SE logic board.

Solution: Check/replace SIMM 2 on 820-0176 (original) logic boards. Check/replace SIMM 4 on 820-0250 (DIP SIMM) boards.

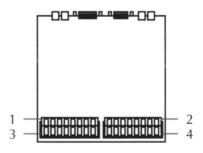

Approximate cost of repairing it yourself:		*$10.00*
1 SIMM (256K)	10.00	*1 hour*
Approximate third-party repair cost:		*$150.00*
1 SIMM (256K)	20.00	
2 hours labor	130.00	
Approximate dealer repair cost:		*$398.33*
1 new logic board (SE)	328.33	
1 hour labor	70.00	

Symptoms: On startup, you get a sad Mac with error code 00000002 over nn00nn00 (where the values of nn are insignificant).

Probable diagnosis: The problem is on the SE logic board.

Solution: Check/replace SIMM 2 on 820-0176 (original) logic boards. Check/replace SIMM 4 on 820-0250 (DIP SIMM) boards.

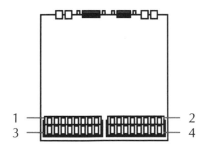

Approximate cost of repairing it yourself:		$10.00
1 SIMM (256K)	10.00	1 hour
Approximate third-party repair cost:		$150.00
1 SIMM (256K)	20.00	
2 hours labor	130.00	
Approximate dealer repair cost:		$398.33
1 new logic board (SE)	328.33	
1 hour labor	70.00	

Symptoms: On startup, you get a sad Mac with error code 00000003 over 000000nn (where the value of nn is insignificant).

Probable diagnosis: The problem is on the SE logic board.

Solution: Check/replace SIMM 1 on 820-0176 (original) logic boards. Check/replace SIMM 3 on 820-0250 (DIP SIMM) boards.

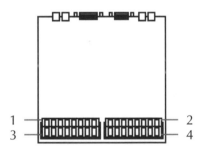

Approximate cost of repairing it yourself:		**$10.00**
1 SIMM (256K)	10.00	*1 hour*
Approximate third-party repair cost:		**$150.00**
1 SIMM (256K)	20.00	
2 hours labor	130.00	
Approximate dealer repair cost:		**$398.33**
1 new logic board (SE)	328.33	
1 hour labor	70.00	

Symptoms: On startup, you get a sad Mac with error code 00000003 over 00nn00nn (where the values of nn are insignificant).

Probable diagnosis: The problem is on the SE logic board.

Solution: Check/replace SIMM 1 on 820-0176 (original) logic boards. Check/replace SIMM 3 on 820-0250 (DIP SIMM) boards.

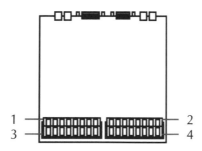

Approximate cost of repairing it yourself:		$10.00
1 SIMM (256K)	10.00	1 hour
Approximate third-party repair cost:		$150.00
1 SIMM (256K)	20.00	
2 hours labor	130.00	
Approximate dealer repair cost:		$398.33
1 new logic board (SE)	328.33	
1 hour labor	70.00	

Symptoms: On startup, you get a sad Mac with error code 00000003 over 0000nn00 (where the value of nn is insignificant).

Probable diagnosis: The problem is on the SE logic board.

Solution: Check/replace SIMM 2 on 820-0176 (original) logic boards. Check/replace SIMM 4 on 820-0250 (DIP SIMM) boards.

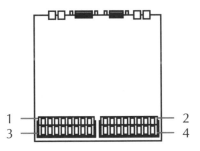

Approximate cost of repairing it yourself:		**$10.00**
1 SIMM (256K)	10.00	**1 hour**
Approximate third-party repair cost:		**$150.00**
1 SIMM (256K)	20.00	
2 hours labor	130.00	
Approximate dealer repair cost:		**$398.33**
1 new logic board (SE)	328.33	
1 hour labor	70.00	

Symptoms: On startup, you get a sad Mac with error code 00000003 over nn00nn00 (where the values of nn are insignificant).

Probable diagnosis: The problem is on the SE logic board.

Solution: Check/replace SIMM 2 on 820-0176 (original) logic boards. Check/replace SIMM 4 on 820-0250 (DIP SIMM) boards.

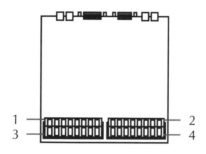

Approximate cost of repairing it yourself:		$10.00
1 SIMM (256K)	10.00	*1 hour*
Approximate third-party repair cost:		$150.00
1 SIMM (256K)	20.00	
2 hours labor	130.00	
Approximate dealer repair cost:		$398.33
1 new logic board (SE)	328.33	
1 hour labor	70.00	

Symptoms: On startup, you get a sad Mac with error code 00000004 over 000000nn (where the value of nn is insignificant).

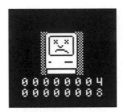

Probable diagnosis: The problem is on the Mac SE logic board.

Solution: Check/replace SIMM 3 on 820-0176 (original) logic boards. Check/replace SIMM 1 on 820-0250 (DIP SIMM) boards.

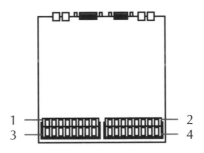

Approximate cost of repairing it yourself:		$10.00
1 SIMM (256K)	10.00	*1 hour*
Approximate third-party repair cost:		$150.00
1 SIMM (256K)	20.00	
2 hours labor	130.00	
Approximate dealer repair cost:		$398.33
1 new logic board (SE)	328.33	
1 hour labor	70.00	

Symptoms: On startup, you get a sad Mac with error code 00000004 over 00nn00nn (where the values of nn are insignificant).

Probable diagnosis: The problem is on the Mac SE logic board.

Solution: Check/replace SIMM 3 on 820-0176 (original) logic boards. Check/replace SIMM 1 on 820-0250 (DIP SIMM) boards.

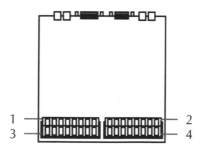

Approximate cost of repairing it yourself:		*$10.00*
1 SIMM (256K)	10.00	*1 hour*
Approximate third-party repair cost:		*$150.00*
1 SIMM (256K)	20.00	
2 hours labor	130.00	
Approximate dealer repair cost:		*$398.33*
1 new logic board (SE)	328.33	
1 hour labor	70.00	

Symptoms: On startup, you get a sad Mac with error code 00000004 over 0000nn00 (where the value of nn is insignificant).

Probable diagnosis: The problem is on the Mac SE logic board.

Solution: Check/replace SIMM 4 on 820-0176 (original) logic boards. Check/replace SIMM 2 on 820-0250 (DIP SIMM) boards.

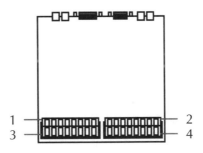

Approximate cost of repairing it yourself:		**$10.00**
1 SIMM (256K)	10.00	**1 hour**
Approximate third-party repair cost:		**$150.00**
1 SIMM (256K)	20.00	
2 hours labor	130.00	
Approximate dealer repair cost:		**$398.33**
1 new logic board (SE)	328.33	
1 hour labor	70.00	

Symptoms: On startup, you get a sad Mac with error code 00000004 over nn00nn00 (where the values of nn are insignificant).

Probable diagnosis: The problem is on the Mac SE logic board.

Solution: Check/replace SIMM 4 on 820-0176 (original) logic boards. Check/replace SIMM 2 on 820-0250 (DIP SIMM) boards.

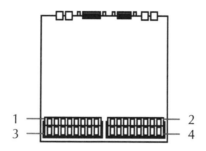

Approximate cost of repairing it yourself:		$10.00
1 SIMM (256K)	10.00	1 hour
Approximate third-party repair cost:		$150.00
1 SIMM (256K)	20.00	
2 hours labor	130.00	
Approximate dealer repair cost:		$398.33
1 new logic board (SE)	328.33	
1 hour labor	70.00	

Symptoms: On startup, you get a sad Mac with error code 00000005 over 000000nn (where the value of nn is insignificant).

Probable diagnosis: The problem is on the Mac SE logic board.

Solution: Check/replace SIMM 3 on 820-0176 (original) logic boards. Check/replace SIMM 1 on 820-0250 (DIP SIMM) boards.

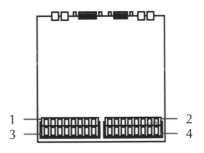

Approximate cost of repairing it yourself:		$10.00
1 SIMM (256K)	10.00	*1 hour*
Approximate third-party repair cost:		*$150.00*
1 SIMM (256K)	20.00	
2 hours labor	130.00	
Approximate dealer repair cost:		*$398.33*
1 new logic board (SE)	328.33	
1 hour labor	70.00	

Symptoms: On startup, you get a sad Mac with error code 00000005 over 00nn00nn (where the values of nn are insignificant).

Probable diagnosis: The problem is on the Mac SE logic board.

Solution: Check/replace SIMM 3 on 820-0176 (original) logic boards. Check/replace SIMM 1 on 820-0250 (DIP SIMM) boards.

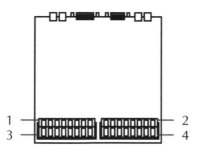

Approximate cost of repairing it yourself:		***$10.00***
1 SIMM (256K)	10.00	***1 hour***
Approximate third-party repair cost:		***$150.00***
1 SIMM (256K)	20.00	
2 hours labor	130.00	
Approximate dealer repair cost:		***$398.33***
1 new logic board (SE)	328.33	
1 hour labor	70.00	

Symptoms: On startup, you get a sad Mac with error code 00000005 over 0000nn00 (where the value of nn is insignificant).

Probable diagnosis: The problem is on the Mac SE logic board.

Solution: Check/replace SIMM 4 on 820-0176 (original) logic boards. Check/replace SIMM 2 on 820-0250 (DIP SIMM) boards.

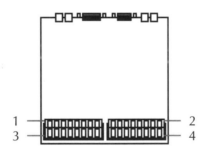

Approximate cost of repairing it yourself:		$10.00
1 SIMM (256K)	10.00	1 hour
Approximate third-party repair cost:		$150.00
1 SIMM (256K)	20.00	
2 hours labor	130.00	
Approximate dealer repair cost:		$398.33
1 new logic board (SE)	328.33	
1 hour labor	70.00	

Symptoms: On startup, you get a sad Mac with error code 00000005 over nn00nn00 (where the values of nn are insignificant).

Probable diagnosis: The problem is on the Mac SE logic board.

Solution: Check/replace SIMM 4 on 820-0176 (original) logic boards. Check/replace SIMM 2 on 820-0250 (DIP SIMM) boards.

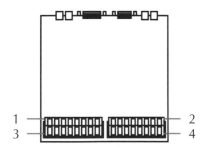

Approximate cost of repairing it yourself:		**$10.00**
1 SIMM (256K)	10.00	**1 hour**
Approximate third-party repair cost:		**$150.00**
1 SIMM (256K)	20.00	
2 hours labor	130.00	
Approximate dealer repair cost:		**$398.33**
1 new logic board (SE)	328.33	
1 hour labor	70.00	

Symptoms: On startup, you get a sad Mac with error code 0000000E over 000000nn (where the value of nn is insignificant).

Probable diagnosis: The problem is on the SE logic board.

Solution: Check/replace SIMM 1 on 820-0176 (original) logic boards. Check/replace SIMM 3 on 820-0250 (DIP SIMM) boards.

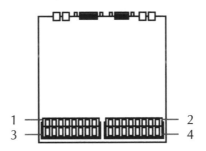

Approximate cost of repairing it yourself:		***$10.00***
1 SIMM (256K)	10.00	***1 hour***
Approximate third-party repair cost:		***$150.00***
1 SIMM (256K)	20.00	
2 hours labor	130.00	
Approximate dealer repair cost:		***$398.33***
1 new logic board (SE)	328.33	
1 hour labor	70.00	

Symptoms: On startup, you get a sad Mac with error code 0000000E over 00nn00nn (where the values of nn are insignificant).

Probable diagnosis: The problem is on the SE logic board.

Solution: Check/replace SIMM 1 on 820-0176 (original) logic boards. Check/replace SIMM 3 on 820-0250 (DIP SIMM) boards.

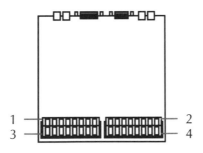

Approximate cost of repairing it yourself:		$10.00
1 SIMM (256K)	10.00	*1 hour*
Approximate third-party repair cost:		$150.00
1 SIMM (256K)	20.00	
2 hours labor	130.00	
Approximate dealer repair cost:		$398.33
1 new logic board (SE)	328.33	
1 hour labor	70.00	

Symptoms: On startup, you get a sad Mac with error code 0000000E over 0000nn00 (where the value of nn is insignificant).

Probable diagnosis: The problem is on the SE logic board.

Solution: Check/replace SIMM 2 on 820-0176 (original) logic boards. Check/replace SIMM 4 on 820-0250 (DIP SIMM) boards.

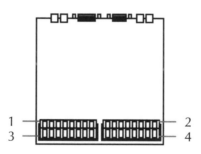

Approximate cost of repairing it yourself:		**$10.00**
1 SIMM (256K)	10.00	**1 hour**
Approximate third-party repair cost:		**$150.00**
1 SIMM (256K)	20.00	
2 hours labor	130.00	
Approximate dealer repair cost:		**$398.33**
1 new logic board (SE)	328.33	
1 hour labor	70.00	

Symptoms: On startup, you get a sad Mac with error code 0000000E over nn00nn00 (where the values of nn are insignificant).

Probable diagnosis: The problem is on the SE logic board.

Solution: Check/replace SIMM 2 on 820-0176 (original) logic boards. Check/replace SIMM 4 on 820-0250 (DIP SIMM) boards.

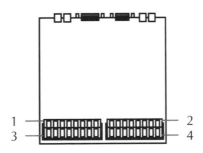

Approximate cost of repairing it yourself:		***$10.00***
1 SIMM (256K)	10.00	***1 hour***
Approximate third-party repair cost:		***$150.00***
1 SIMM (256K)	20.00	
2 hours labor	130.00	
Approximate dealer repair cost:		***$398.33***
1 new logic board (SE)	328.33	
1 hour labor	70.00	

Symptoms: On startup, the internal 20 MB hard drive peeps twice, then you get a sad Mac with error code 0000000F over 00000003.

Probable diagnosis: The internal hard drive (MiniScribe 8425S) has a bad driver map, bad partition signature or bad directory block.

Solution: Remove the internal hard drive from the Mac SE and install it in an external SCSI case. Boot the SE from a floppy disk, then after the desktop appears, switch on the external case.

To repair the malfunctioning MiniScribe drive (50/50 chance of success), launch DiskManager Mac version 2.24, and choose *Test Drive* from the Defect Management menu. If the test results indicate that bad blocks were found and rewritten, but the drive still won't mount, reformat the drive.

If the format operation fails, quit DMM and choose *Restart* from the Finder's Special menu. When the Finder's menu bar reappears, try holding down the mouse button. Holding down the mouse button will often mount a drive in these cases, even when the format operation failed.

If holding down the mouse button doesn't mount the drive, but the Finder indicates, *This is not a Macintosh disk. Do you want to initialize it?*, click *OK*. If any of these procedures mounts the drive, it'll be fine. It'll work as well as it ever did, for an indefinite period of time.

Approximate cost of repairing it yourself:		*$49.95*
1 DiskManager Mac (street price)	49.95	*1 hour*

Approximate third-party repair cost:		*$85.00*
20 MB @ 4.25 per MB	85.00	

Approximate dealer repair cost:		*$558.33*
1 new 3.5-inch 20 MB HDA	488.33	
1 hour labor	70.00	

Symptoms: On startup, you get part of a sad Mac with error code 0_0_0_0 over 0_F_0_F.

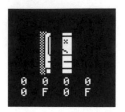

Probable diagnosis: The problem is on the Mac SE logic board.

Solution: Check/relatch SIMM 1 on 820-0176 (original) logic boards. Check/relatch SIMM 3 on 820-0250 (DIP SIMM) boards. If the latches are broken, replace the SIMM socket.

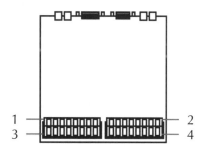

Approximate cost of repairing it yourself:		**$12.00**
1 SIMM socket	12.00	**2 hours**
Approximate third-party repair cost:		**$154.00**
1 SIMM socket	24.00	
2 hours labor	130.00	
Approximate dealer repair cost:		**$398.33**
1 new logic board (SE)	328.33	
1 hour labor	70.00	

Symptoms: On startup, you get part of a sad Mac with error code 0_0_0_5 over F_0_F_0.

Probable diagnosis: The problem is on the Mac SE logic board.

Solution: Check/relatch SIMM 4 on 820-0176 (original) logic boards. Check/relatch SIMM 2 on 820-0250 (DIP SIMM) boards. If the latches are broken, replace the SIMM socket.

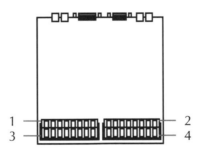

Approximate cost of repairing it yourself:		**$12.00**
1 SIMM socket	12.00	**2 hours**
Approximate third-party repair cost:		**$154.00**
1 SIMM socket	24.00	
2 hours labor	130.00	
Approximate dealer repair cost:		**$398.33**
1 new logic board (SE)	328.33	
1 hour labor	70.00	

Symptoms: On startup, the display fills with vertical bars and the smiling Mac never goes away. It looks like the little guy is in jail.

Typical history: The problem occurred right after memory upgrade from 1 MB to 2.5 MB.

Probable diagnosis: The problem is on the Mac SE logic board. The 1 MB SIMMs are in the wrong row.

Solution: Check/reinstall the SIMMs. On 820-0176 (original) logic boards, the 1 MB SIMMs go in sockets 1 and 2. On 820-0250 (DIP SIMM) logic boards, the 1 MB SIMMs go in sockets 3 and 4.

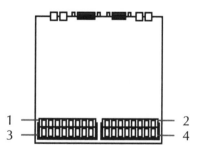

Approximate cost of repairing it yourself:		**30 min.**
Approximate third-party repair cost:		**$130.00**
2 hours labor	130.00	
Approximate dealer repair cost:		**$398.33**
1 new logic board (SE)	328.33	
1 hour labor	70.00	

Symptoms: On startup, the computer makes a tweeting noise.

Typical history: The problem occurred right after a memory upgrade.

Probable diagnosis: The problem is on the Mac SE logic board. One of the SIMMs is bad.

Solution: Check the SIMMs by substitution.

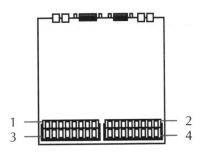

Approximate cost of repairing it yourself:		**30 min.**
Approximate third-party repair cost:		**$130.00**
2 hours labor	130.00	
Approximate dealer repair cost:		**$398.33**
1 new logic board (SE)	328.33	
1 hour labor	70.00	

Symptoms: On startup, the internal 20 MB drive spins but does not mount. If you boot from a floppy disk, third-party formatting software intermittently reports *broken bus* or *bus not terminated.*

Typical history: The drive was just serviced, or it was transferred to the Mac SE from an Apple HD20SC (where it worked fine).

Probable diagnosis: There are no terminators on the hard drive's embedded SCSI controller card.

Solution: Install/replace the dual in-line terminators (220/330Ω, 8-pin SIP) at board references RP1, RP2 and RP3. Be sure to observe polarity (the dot or the stripe)! Also see the next entry.

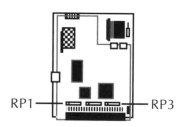

RP1 ——   —— RP3

Approximate cost of repairing it yourself:		*$1.00*
3 220/330 terminators	1.00	*30 min.*
Approximate third-party repair cost:		*$85.00*
20 MB @ 4.25 per MB	85.00	
Approximate dealer repair cost:		*$558.33*
1 new 3.5-inch 20 MB HDA	488.33	
1 hour labor	70.00	

Symptoms: On startup, the internal 20 MB drive spins but does not mount. Instead, you get the blinking floppy-disk icon. If you boot from a floppy disk, third-party formatting software intermittently reports *broken bus* or *bus not terminated.*

Typical history: This drive was just serviced, or it was transferred from an external Apple HD20SC (where it worked fine).

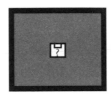

Probable diagnosis: A fuse is blown on the hard drive's embedded SCSI controller card.

Solution: Check/replace the pigtail fuse (Pico, 1A) at board reference F1. Also see the prior entry.

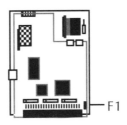

Approximate cost of repairing it yourself:		$2.00
1 1A Pico fuse	2.00	30 min.
Approximate third-party repair cost:		$85.00
20 MB @ 4.25 per MB	85.00	
Approximate dealer repair cost:		$558.33
1 new 3.5-inch 20 MB HDA	488.33	
1 hour labor	70.00	

Symptoms: On startup, the internal 20 MB drive spins but does not mount. Instead, you get the blinking floppy-disk icon. Third-party formatting software reports *error during inquiry command.*

Typical history: The problem occurred at the same time as unrelated upgrade work, right after you put everything back together.

Probable diagnosis: The SCSI data cable is loose, or one of the wires is internally broken.

Solution: Check/replace the SCSI data cable.

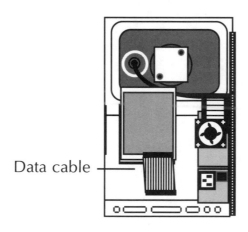

Data cable

Approximate cost of repairing it yourself:		$4.75
1 S50-18-S socket ribbon cable	4.75	30 min.
Approximate third-party repair cost:		$85.00
20 MB @ 4.25 per MB	85.00	
Approximate dealer repair cost:		$558.33
1 new 3.5-inch 20 MB HDA	488.33	
1 hour labor	70.00	

Symptoms: The display is tilted. Other than that, the Mac is usable.

Typical history: The symptoms appeared immediately after the computer was board-swapped or serviced (not out of the blue).

Probable diagnosis: The yoke clamp (on the neck of the CRT) is loose.

Solution: Adjust/rotate the yoke for a square picture.

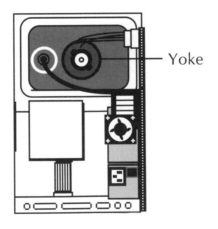

— Yoke

Approximate cost of repairing it yourself:		*30 min.*
Approximate third-party repair cost:		*$65.00*
1 hour labor	65.00	
Approximate dealer repair cost:		*$305.00*
1 new CRT	235.00	
1 hour labor	70.00	

Symptoms: The display isn't rectangular. One or more of the edges is bowed. Other than that, the Mac is usable.

Typical history: The problem occurred right after completion of upgrade or service work.

Probable diagnosis: One of the yoke magnets is loose.

Solution: Identify/adjust the loose yoke magnet.

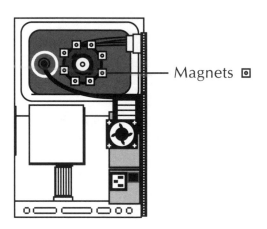

Magnets ▣

Approximate cost of repairing it yourself:		*30 min.*
Approximate third-party repair cost:		*$65.00*
1 hour labor	65.00	
Approximate dealer repair cost:		*$70.00*
1 hour labor	70.00	

Symptoms: There's no startup bong and no beep (or other) sound. Otherwise, the raster is normal, and the computer is usable.

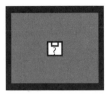

Typical history: The problem occurred shortly after installing a memory upgrade, an FDHD disk drive/ROM upgrade or an expansion card into the computer.

Probable diagnosis: The problem is on the logic board. The speaker cable is loose or disconnected.

Solution: Remove the logic board. Plug the speaker cable into J11.

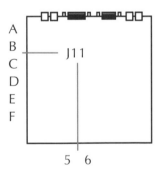

Approximate cost of repairing it yourself:		*15 min.*
Approximate third-party repair cost:		**$65.00**
1 hour labor	65.00	
Approximate dealer repair cost:		**$148.00**
1 front bezel/speaker assembly	78.00	
1 hour labor	70.00	

Symptoms: The upper disk drive doesn't work.

Typical history: The problem occurred right after completion of a memory upgrade or with the installation of an expansion card (right after you put everything back together).

Probable diagnosis: During installation, the upper disk drive data cable worked loose.

Solution: Check the disk drive end of the data cable for a snug fit.

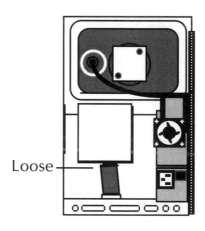

Loose

Approximate cost of repairing it yourself:		*15 min.*
Approximate third-party repair cost:		*$65.00*
1 hour labor	65.00	
Approximate dealer repair cost:		*$383.33*
1 new disk drive	313.33	
1 hour labor	70.00	

Symptoms: The video display is out of focus. Other than that, the computer is usable.

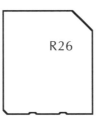

Typical history: The symptoms appeared out of the blue (not immediately after the computer was board-swapped).

Probable diagnosis: The problem is on the analog board.

Solution: Check/replace open resistor R26 (1MΩ, ½-watt, 5%). Also, see the next entry.

R26

Approximate cost of repairing it yourself:		*15¢*
1 1MΩ, ½-wattt, 5% resistor	.15	*1 hour*
Approximate third-party repair cost:		**$70.00**
1 1MΩ, ½-watt, 5% resistor	5.00	
1 hour labor	65.00	
Approximate dealer repair cost:		**$305.00**
1 new analog board	235.00	
1 hour labor	70.00	

Symptoms: The video display is out of focus. Other than that, the computer is usable.

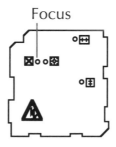

Typical history: The symptoms appeared immediately after the computer was serviced or board-swapped (not out of the blue).

Probable diagnosis: The new analog board is out of adjustment.

Solution: Adjust variable resistor R27 (labeled *Focus*) for the best all-around focus. If R27 makes no difference, see the prior entry.

Focus

Approximate cost of repairing it yourself:		*30 min.*
Approximate third-party repair cost:		*$65.00*
1 hour labor	65.00	
Approximate dealer repair cost:		*$305.00*
1 new analog board	235.00	
1 hour labor	70.00	

Symptoms: The video display is shrunken. Other than that, the computer is usable.

Typical history: The symptoms appeared right after installation of a memory upgrade or an expansion card.

Probable diagnosis: The analog board is out of adjustment.

Solution: Adjust variable resistor R4 (labeled *Height*) and tunable coil L2 (labeled *Width*) for a 7.11 x 4.75-inch display.

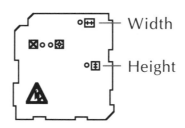

Approximate cost of repairing it yourself:		*30 min.*
Approximate third-party repair cost:		**$65.00**
1 hour labor	65.00	
Approximate dealer repair cost:		**$305.00**
1 new analog board	235.00	
1 hour labor	70.00	

Symptoms: On powerup, a heavily upgraded SE *intermittently* makes a *flup flup flup* noise and fails to start.

Typical history: When reverted to the stock configuration (1 MB, no expansion card), this same SE works perfectly.

Probable diagnosis: The problem is in the Astec power supply.

Solution: Check/replace the IRF 830 power MOSFET transistors at board references Q2 and Q3.

Approximate cost of repairing it yourself:		**$5.10**
1 IRF 830 MOSFET	5.10	***1 hour***
Approximate third-party repair cost:		**$75.20**
1 IRF 830 MOSFET	10.20	
1 hour labor	65.00	
Approximate dealer repair cost:		**$328.33**
1 new power supply	258.33	
1 hour labor	70.00	

Symptoms: On startup from the internal hard drive, you get a dialog box stating, *This disk is unreadable: Do you want to initialize it?* but the arrow points to the same hard drive that you just booted from!

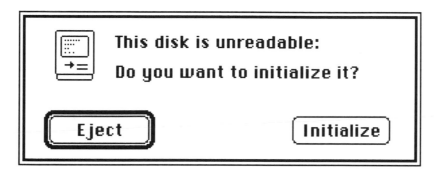

Probable diagnosis: The problem is on the SE logic board.

Solution: Check/replace the filter networks (20-pin DIP, Apple part 115-0002) at board references B9 and B11.

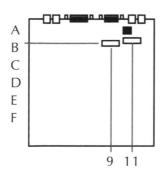

Approximate cost of repairing it yourself:		**$12.00**
1 Bourns filter	12.00	**2 hours**
Approximate third-party repair cost:		**$154.00**
1 Bourns filter	24.00	
2 hours labor	130.00	
Approximate dealer repair cost:		**$398.33**
1 new logic board (SE)	328.33	
1 hour labor	70.00	

Symptoms: On startup, you get a dialog box stating, *This disk is unreadable: Do you want to initialize it?* but the arrow points to a nonexistent external floppy drive!

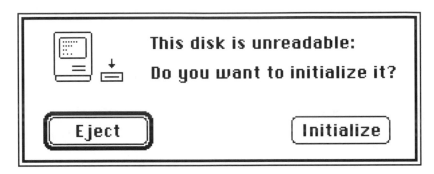

This disk is unreadable:

Do you want to initialize it?

Eject   Initialize

Probable diagnosis: The problem is on the SE logic board.

Solution: Check/replace the filter networks (20-pin DIP, Apple part 115-0002) at board references B9 and B11.

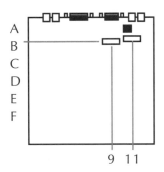

Approximate cost of repairing it yourself:		$12.00
1 Bourns filter	12.00	2 hours
Approximate third-party repair cost:		$154.00
1 Bourns filter	24.00	
2 hours labor	130.00	
Approximate dealer repair cost:		$398.33
1 new logic board (SE)	328.33	
1 hour labor	70.00	

CHAPTER 3
MAC II

Symptoms: The normal startup chime is present, but the internal hard drive doesn't make mounting noises, the disk drive doesn't pulse and *raster never comes up* on the monitor(s). If you unplug the internal hard drive and restart from a System disk, the internal disk drive doesn't spin and raster still doesn't come up on the monitor(s). Either way, there are no error sounds.

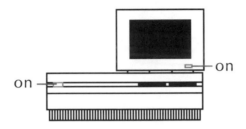

Probable diagnosis: The problem is on a NuBus card.

Solution: Shut down/remove the installed NuBus cards one at a time until normal operation is restored.

NuBus card

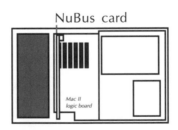

Approximate cost of repairing it yourself:		*30 min.* *+ card repairs*
Approximate third-party repair cost:		*$65.00*
1 hour labor	65.00	*+ card repairs*
Approximate dealer repair cost:		*$70.00*
1 hour labor	70.00	*+ cost of* *new card*

Symptoms: On startup, the normal startup chime is *quickly* followed by an error chord, then a *do-do-da-da* sound. The internal hard drive doesn't make its usual noises. The disk drive doesn't pulse. Raster never comes up on the monitor(s).

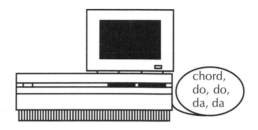

Typical history: The problem occurred out of the blue.

Probable diagnosis: There's a dust short on the logic board.

Solution: Remove the lid and the drive bay. Take the CPU cabinet outdoors and blow out the dust with an air compressor. Also see the next entry.

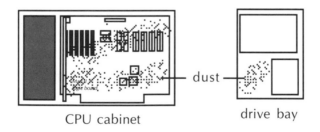

CPU cabinet   drive bay

Approximate cost of repairing it yourself:		*1 hour*
Approximate third-party repair cost:		**$195.00**
3 hours labor	195.00	
Approximate dealer repair cost:		**$210.00**
3 hours labor	210.00	

Symptoms: On startup, the normal startup chime is *quickly* followed by an error chord, then a *do-do-da-da* sound. The internal hard drive doesn't make its usual noises. The disk drive doesn't pulse. Raster never comes up on the monitor(s).

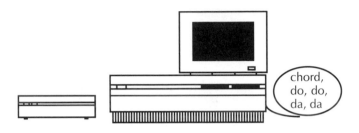

Typical history: The problem occurred right after you installed an external SCSI hard drive.

Probable diagnosis: The SCSI cable isn't plugged all the way into the 50-pin connector on the back of the external hard drive.

Solution: Check the SCSI cable. Make sure both ends are plugged all the way in. Make sure that the screws are tightened and make sure the bails are fastened. Also see the prior entry.

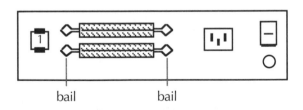

bail   bail

Approximate cost of repairing it yourself:	*2 min.*
Approximate third-party repair cost:	*$195.00*
3 hours labor 195.00	
Approximate dealer repair cost:	*$210.00*
3 hours labor 210.00	

Symptoms: On startup, you get the normal startup chime, the hard drive (if present) makes its usual noises, the raster starts to come up on the monitor, the disk drive pulses as usual and then (right about when the *Welcome to Macintosh* dialog box should appear) you get a *do-do-da-da* sound and the raster blacks out.

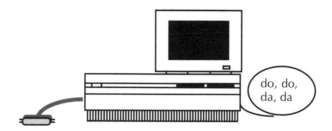

Typical history: The problem occurred right after you disconnected/removed the last SCSI device on the bus, but not the cable.

Probable diagnosis: There's a termination problem on the SCSI bus.

Solution: Install an external terminator on the open-ended SCSI cable that was left behind, or remove the cable and install a terminator (if necessary) on the SCSI device to which it *had been* connected. Also see the next entry.

Approximate cost of repairing it yourself:		$15.00
1 external terminator	15.00	2 min.
Approximate third-party repair cost:		$225.00
1 external terminator	30.00	
3 hours labor	195.00	
Approximate dealer repair cost:		$250.00
1 external terminator	40.00	
3 hours labor	210.00	

Symptoms: On startup, you get the normal startup chime, the hard drive (if present) makes its usual noises, the raster starts to come up on the monitor, the disk drive pulses as usual and then (right about when the *Welcome to Macintosh* dialog box should appear) you get a *do-do-da-da* sound and the raster blacks out.

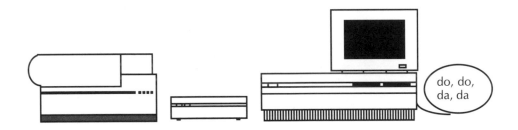

Typical history: The problem occurred when you installed a

second or third external SCSI device (generally a LaserWriter IISC or a Personal LaserWriter SC).

Probable diagnosis: The problem is on the SCSI bus. When the total cable length exceeds ten feet, an extra terminator may be required in the middle of the bus.

Solution: Substitute shorter SCSI cables, or install a *third* terminator in the middle of the bus. Also see the prior entry.

Approximate cost of repairing it yourself:			**$15.00**
1 external terminator		15.00	**2 min.**
Approximate third-party repair cost:			**$225.00**
1 external terminator		30.00	
3 hours labor		195.00	
Approximate dealer repair cost:			**$250.00**
1 external terminator		40.00	
3 hours labor		210.00	

Symptoms: On startup, you get the normal startup chime, then you get a single high note followed by a *do-do-da-da* sound and then the raster blacks out.

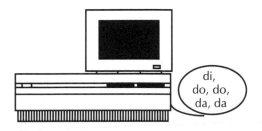

Typical history: The problem occurred when (or shortly after) you installed a RAM upgrade.

Probable diagnosis: The problem is on the logic board.

Solution: Check/replace the four SIMMs located in bank A.

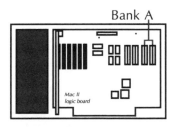

Approximate cost of repairing it yourself:		**$35.00**
1 SIMM (1 MB)	35.00	**1 hour**
Approximate third-party repair cost:		**$265.00**
1 SIMM (1 MB)	70.00	
3 hours labor	195.00	
Approximate dealer repair cost:		**$368.33**
1 SIMM (1 MB, 80 NS)	158.33	
3 hours labor	210.00	

Symptoms: On startup, you get the normal startup chime, then you get a high note, followed by an even higher note, followed by a *do-do-da-da* sound. Then the raster blacks out.

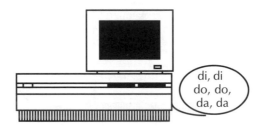

Typical history: The problem occurred when (or shortly after) you installed a RAM upgrade.

Probable diagnosis: The problem is on the logic board.

Solution: Check/replace the four SIMMs located in bank B.

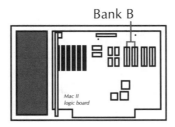

Approximate cost of repairing it yourself:		$35.00
1 SIMM (1 MB)	35.00	*1 hour*
Approximate third-party repair cost:		$265.00
1 SIMM (1 MB)	70.00	
3 hours labor	195.00	
Approximate dealer repair cost:		$368.33
1 SIMM (1 MB, 80 NS)	158.33	
3 hours labor	210.00	

Symptoms: On powerup, the green power supply light comes on, but the normal startup chime doesn't sound. Raster never comes up on the monitor.

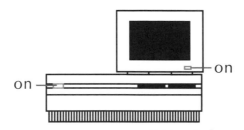

Probable diagnosis: The problem is on the Macintosh II logic board.

Solution: Check/replace the HMMU located at board reference U67 on the 820-0163-03 logic board and grid reference UG13 on the 820-0228-A logic board. If the black chip is spotted or shows signs of overheating, replace it with an MC68851RC16A PMMU (paged memory management unit). Also see the next entry.

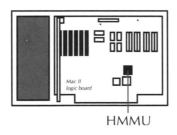

HMMU

Approximate cost of repairing it yourself:		$125.00
1 MC68851RC16A	125.00	30 min.
Approximate third-party repair cost:		$445.00
1 MC68851RC16A	250.00	
3 hours labor	195.00	
Approximate dealer repair cost:		$565.00
1 PMMU upgrade	495.00	
1 hour labor	70.00	

Symptoms: On powerup, the green power supply light comes on, but the normal startup chime doesn't sound. Raster never comes up on the monitor.

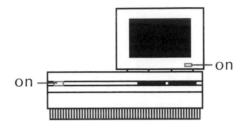

Typical history: The problem occurred when (or shortly after) you installed a PMMU upgrade.

Probable diagnosis: The problem is on the logic board. The PMMU is probably loose in the socket.

Solution: Check/replace the PMMU located at board reference U67 on the 820-0163-03 logic board and grid reference UG13 on the 820-0228-A logic board.

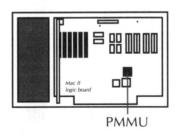

PMMU

Approximate cost of repairing it yourself:	***30 min.***
Approximate third-party repair cost:	***$195.00***
3 hours labor 195.00	
Approximate dealer repair cost:	***$210.00***
3 hours labor 210.00	

Symptoms: Mode32 won't install and/or virtual memory won't run even though there *is* a PMMU in the machine. Everything else seems to work OK.

Probable diagnosis: The problem is on the logic board. The PMMU is probably loose in the socket.

Solution: Check/replace the PMMU located at board reference U67 on the 820-0163-03 logic board and grid reference UG13 on the 820-0228-A logic board.

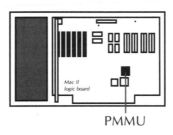

PMMU

Approximate cost of repairing it yourself:		*30 min.*
Approximate third-party repair cost:		**$195.00**
3 hours labor	195.00	
Approximate dealer repair cost:		**$210.00**
3 hours labor	210.00	

Symptoms: On startup, you get seven copies of the startup disk icon.

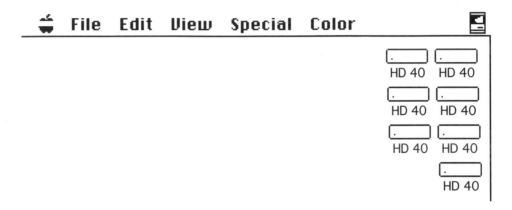

Typical history: The problem occurred when you installed an external SCSI drive.

Probable diagnosis: The problem is on the SCSI bus. Two devices have the same ID number.

Solution: Check/renumber the SCSI devices so that every device on the bus has a unique ID number between 0 and 6. By convention, internal hard drives are always to be 0. External devices can be any number between 1 and 6. The Mac itself is always 7.

Approximate cost of repairing it yourself:		***5 min.***
Approximate third-party repair cost:		***$65.00***
1 hour labor	65.00	
Approximate dealer repair cost:		***$70.00***
1 hour labor	70.00	

Symptoms: The internal hard drive works OK, but external hard drives (that work perfectly on other Macs) don't work on this machine.

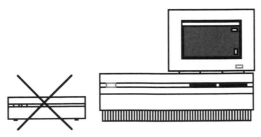

Typical history: The problem occurred when you plugged a parallel printer into the SCSI port.

Probable diagnosis: The problem is on the logic board.

Solution: Check/replace the fuse (1A, Pico) at board reference F1. Also see the next entry.

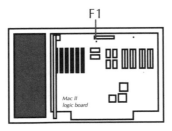

Approximate cost of repairing it yourself:		**$1.00**
1 Pico fuse (1A)	1.00	**1 hour**
Approximate third-party repair cost:		**$200.00**
1 Pico fuse (1A)	5.00	
3 hours labor	195.00	
Approximate dealer repair cost:		**$565.00**
1 new logic board (Mac II)	495.00	
1 hour labor	70.00	

Symptoms: Internal and external hard drives (that work perfectly on other Macs) don't work on this machine.

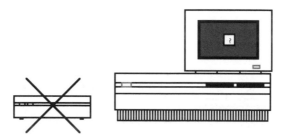

Typical history: The problem occurred after you connected or disconnected a SCSI cable while the power was on.

Probable diagnosis: The problem is on the Mac II logic board.

Solution: Check/replace the SCSI chip (53C80-P44, SMD) at board reference U45 on the 820-0163-03 logic board and grid reference B8 on the 820-0228-A logic board. Also see the prior entry.

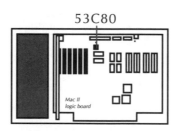

Approximate cost of repairing it yourself:		**$18.00**
1 53C80-P44 (surface mount)	18.00	**1 hour**
Approximate third-party repair cost:		**$231.00**
1 53C80-P44 (surface mount)	36.00	
3 hours labor	195.00	
Approximate dealer repair cost:		**$565.00**
1 new logic board (Mac II)	495.00	
1 hour labor	70.00	

Symptoms: On startup, the desktop appears, but neither the keyboard nor the mouse works.

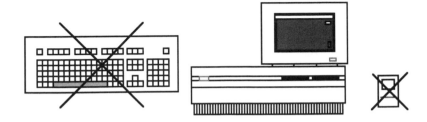

Typical history: The problem occurred after you connected or disconnected an ADB device while the computer was on.

Probable diagnosis: The problem is on the Mac II logic board.

Solution: Check/replace the fuse (1A, Pico) at board reference F2. Also see the next entry.

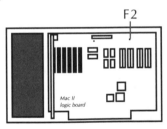

Approximate cost of repairing it yourself:		**$1.00**
1 Pico fuse (1A)	1.00	**1 hour**
Approximate third-party repair cost:		**$200.00**
1 Pico fuse (1A)	5.00	
3 hours labor	195.00	
Approximate dealer repair cost:		**$565.00**
1 new logic board (Mac II)	495.00	
1 hour labor	70.00	

Symptoms: On startup, the desktop appears, but neither the keyboard nor the mouse works.

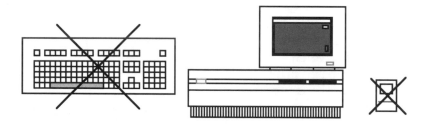

Typical history: The problem occurred after you connected or disconnected an ADB device while the computer was on.

Probable diagnosis: The problem is on the Mac II logic board.

Solution: Check/replace the shorted filter (Apple part 155-0007-E) at location L7 on the 820-0163-03 logic board and grid reference A14 on the 820-0228-A logic board. Also see the prior entry.

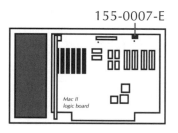

155-0007-E

Mac II
logic board

Approximate cost of repairing it yourself:		**$14.00**
1 ADB filter, Tokin D-16C	14.00	**2 hours**
Approximate third-party repair cost:		**$223.00**
1 ADB filter, Tokin D-16C	28.00	
3 hours labor	195.00	
Approximate dealer repair cost:		**$565.00**
1 new logic board (Mac II)	495.00	
1 hour labor	70.00	

Symptoms: On startup, the desktop appears, but neither the modem nor the printer works.

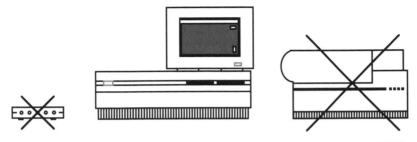

Probable diagnosis: The problem is on the Mac II logic board.

Solution: Check/replace the AM26LS30 chips at board references U70 and U71 on the 820-0163-03 logic board and grid references A14 and B14 on the 820-0228-A logic board.

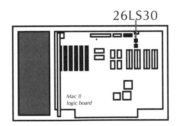

Approximate cost of repairing it yourself:		***$5.00***
1 26LS30	5.00	***2 hours***
Approximate third-party repair cost:		***$205.00***
1 26LS30	10.00	
3 hours labor	195.00	
Approximate dealer repair cost:		***$565.00***
1 new logic board (Mac II)	495.00	
1 hour labor	70.00	

Symptoms: When an HP DeskWriter that works perfectly on other Macs is directly connected to the printer port and properly selected in the Chooser, it prints *Error trap 10864* and then cancels the print job.

Error trap 10864

Typical history: Other printers directly connected to the printer port seem to work fine.

Probable diagnosis: The problem is on the Mac II logic board (not in the DeskWriter).

Solution: Check/replace the R/C network (20-pin DIP, Apple part 115-0002) at board reference RP14.

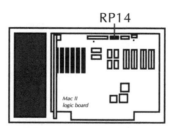

Approximate cost of repairing it yourself:		$12.00
1 Bourns filter	12.00	2 hours
Approximate third-party repair cost:		$154.00
1 Bourns filter	24.00	
2 hours labor	130.00	
Approximate dealer repair cost:		$565.00
1 new logic board (Mac II)	495.00	(average cost)
1 hour labor	70.00	

Symptoms: When an HP DeskWriter that works perfectly on other Macs is directly connected to the modem port and properly selected in the Chooser, it prints *Error trap 10864* and then cancels the print job.

Error trap 10864

Typical history: Other printers connected to the modem port seem to work fine.

Probable diagnosis: The problem is on the Mac II logic board (not in the DeskWriter).

Solution: Check/replace the R/C network (20-pin DIP, Apple part 115-0002) at board reference RP15.

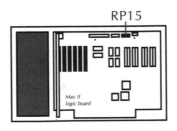

Approximate cost of repairing it yourself:		***$12.00***
1 Bourns filter	12.00	***2 hours***
Approximate third-party repair cost:		***$154.00***
1 Bourns filter	24.00	
2 hours labor	130.00	
Approximate dealer repair cost:		***$565.00***
1 new logic board (Mac II)	495.00	***(average cost)***
1 hour labor	70.00	

Symptoms: The Mac II does not maintain the time and date. Whenever the power cord is disconnected, the date goes back to 1904.

Probable diagnosis: The problem is on the Mac II logic board.

Solution: Check/replace the clock battery (lithium, ½ AA) at board location B1 (820-0163-03 logic board). Early models have 3V solder-in batteries with pigtail leads. Later models have 3.6V batteries that snap into battery boxes.

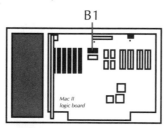

Approximate cost of repairing it yourself:		$12.00
1 lithium battery (½AA)	12.00	2 hours
Approximate third-party repair cost:		$219.00
1 lithium battery (½AA)	24.00	
3 hours labor	195.00	
Approximate dealer repair cost:		$565.00
1 new logic board (Mac II)	495.00	
1 hour labor	70.00	

Symptoms: The Mac II is hard starting. When the Power On key is pressed it doesn't always start!

Power On key

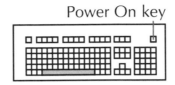

Probable diagnosis: The problem is on the Mac II logic board.

Solution: Check/replace the battery (lithium, ½ AA) at board location B2 (820-0163-03 logic board). Early models have 3V solder-in batteries with pig tail leads. Later models have 3.6V batteries that snap into battery boxes.

B2

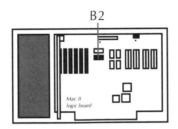

Approximate cost of repairing it yourself:		***$12.00***
1 lithium battery (½AA)	12.00	***2 hours***
Approximate third-party repair cost:		***$219.00***
1 lithium battery (½AA)	24.00	
3 hours labor	195.00	
Approximate dealer repair cost:		***$565.00***
1 new logic board (Mac II)	495.00	
1 hour labor	70.00	

Hardware affected: Mac IIci with 3.5-inch Toshiba 106 hard drive.

Symptoms: On startup, the normal startup chime is followed by a do-do-da-da sound, then you get a sad Mac with error code 0000000F over 00000001.

Probable diagnosis: The problem is on the internal hard drive.

Solution: To restore normal operation, shut down and disconnect the internal hard drive.

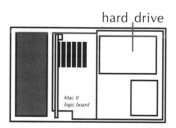

Approximate cost of repairing it yourself:		***30 min.***
drive repairs		
Approximate third-party repair cost:		***$65.00***
1 hour labor	65.00	*+ drive repairs*
Approximate dealer repair cost:		***$70.00***
1 hour labor	70.00	*+ cost of*

new drive

CHAPTER 4

FLOPPY DISK DRIVES

Hardware affected: Apple/Sony OA-D34V 400K disk drive (internal or external).

Symptoms: The eject mechanism sticks or no longer works at all.

Typical history: The problem developed gradually, over a period of time.

Probable diagnosis: The grease used on the eject levers (located on the right side of the drive) has dried out and turned to glue.

Solution: Remove the sticky dried-out grease with paper towels and cotton swabs. Relubricate the eject levers with WD-40.

Eject levers

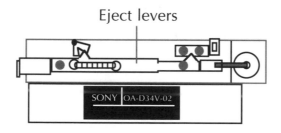

SONY OA-D34V-02

Approximate cost of repairing it yourself:		*1 hour*
Approximate third-party repair cost:		*$65.00*
1 hour labor	65.00	
Approximate dealer repair cost:		*$315.00*
1 new 400K disk mechanism	245.00	
1 hour labor	70.00	

Hardware affected: Apple/Sony OA-D34V 400K disk drive (internal or external).

Symptoms: Regardless of which disk you insert, the computer says, *This disk is unreadable: Do you want to initialize it?*

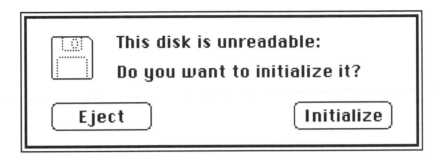

Typical history: The problem started right after a stuck disk was forcibly ejected from the drive (yanked out with pliers).

Probable diagnosis: The forcible eject dislocated the pressure pad, which is now loose (somewhere inside the drive).

Solution: Pop the loose pad into its mounting bracket (located directly above the read/write head). Also see the prior entry.

 —— Pressure pad

Approximate cost of repairing it yourself:		*1 hour*
Approximate third-party repair cost:		**$65.00**
1 hour labor	65.00	
Approximate dealer repair cost:		**$315.00**
1 new 400K disk mechanism	245.00	
1 hour labor	70.00	

Hardware affected: Apple/Sony OA-D34V 400K disk drive (internal or external).

Symptoms: Regardless of which disk you insert, the computer says, *This disk is unreadable: Do you want to initialize it?*

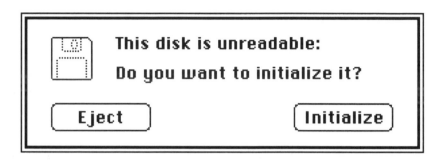

Typical history: The problem started out of the blue (not right after a stuck disk was yanked out with pliers).

Probable diagnosis: The 400K read/write head is dirty.

Solution: Clean the read/write head with a *single-sided* cleaning diskette, preferably moistened with isopropyl alcohol. If that doesn't do it, see the prior entry.

 — Read/write head

Approximate cost of repairing it yourself:		*5 min.*
Approximate third-party repair cost:		**$65.00**
1 hour labor	65.00	
Approximate dealer repair cost:		**$315.00**
1 new 400K disk mechanism	245.00	
1 hour labor	70.00	

Hardware affected: Apple/Sony OA-D34V 400K disk drive (internal or external).

Symptoms: When copying disks or files, you get a dialog box that says, *The file "File Name" could not be read and was skipped.*

Typical history: The problem may have developed gradually, or it may have started right after the drive was serviced.

Probable diagnosis: The pressure pad spring is weak or improperly adjusted. There's not enough tension on the head.

Solution: Move the pressure pad spring to the next notch (on the mounting bracket) so that it places more tension on the head.

Approximate cost of repairing it yourself:		*1 hour*
Approximate third-party repair cost:		*$65.00*
1 hour labor	65.00	
Approximate dealer repair cost:		*$315.00*
1 new 400K disk mechanism	245.00	
1 hour labor	70.00	

Hardware affected: Apple/Sony OA-D34V 400K disk drive (internal or external).

Symptoms: Regardless of which disk you insert, the computer says *This is not a Macintosh disk: Do you want to initialize it?*

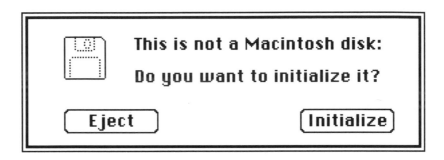

Typical history: The same 400K disks work fine in other drives.

Probable diagnosis: The stepper motor is out of alignment.

Solution: Perform the track zero alignment procedure described starting on page 274.

Approximate cost of repairing it yourself:		*1 hour*
Approximate third-party repair cost:		**$65.00**
1 hour labor	65.00	
Approximate dealer repair cost:		**$315.00**
1 new 400K disk mechanism	245.00	
1 hour labor	70.00	

Hardware affected: Apple/Sony MFD-51W 800K internal disk drive.

Symptoms: Even when there is no disk in the drive, it spins and makes continuous eject noises.

Typical history: The problem occurred after swapping the drive, but not the cable.

Probable diagnosis: The problem is in the disk drive data cable.

Solution: Replace the red-striped data cable with a yellow-striped data cable. Alternatively, disconnect the existing wires leading to pins 9 and 20 at the socket header (on one end of the red-striped cable).

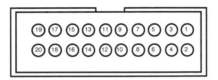

Approximate cost of repairing it yourself:		*1 hour*
Approximate third-party repair cost:		**$65.00**
1 hour labor	65.00	
Approximate dealer repair cost:		**$300.00**
1 new 800K disk mechanism	230.00	
1 hour labor	70.00	

Hardware affected: Apple/Sony MFD-51W 800K disk drive (internal or external).

Symptoms: The eject mechanism sticks or no longer works at all.

Typical history: The problem developed gradually, over a period of time.

Probable diagnosis: The OEM grease used on the eject levers (located at the top of the drive) has dried out and turned to glue.

Solution: Remove the sticky dried-out grease with paper towels and cotton swabs. Relubricate the eject levers with WD-40. To remove a stuck disk from the drive (without damaging the read/write heads), see the disassembly instructions at the end of this chapter.

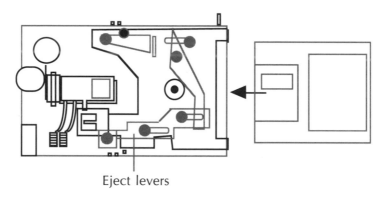

Eject levers

Approximate cost of repairing it yourself:		*1 hour*
Approximate third-party repair cost:		**$65.00**
1 hour labor	65.00	
Approximate dealer repair cost:		**$300.00**
1 new 800K disk mechanism	230.00	
1 hour labor	70.00	

Hardware affected: Apple/Sony MFD-51W 800K disk drive (internal or external).

Symptoms: Regardless of which disk you insert, the computer says, *This disk is unreadable: Do you want to initialize it?*

Typical history: The problem started right after a stuck disk was forcibly ejected from the drive (yanked out with pliers).

Probable diagnosis: During the forcible eject, the open disk shutter dislocated the upper read/write head.

Solution: Replace the 800K read/write head assembly (Sony part A-8010-223-A). If necessary, perform the track zero alignment procedure described starting on page 274.

Approximate cost of repairing it yourself:		***$75.00***
1 800K head assembly	75.00	***1 hour***
Approximate third-party repair cost:		***$140.00***
1 800K head assembly	75.00	
1 hour labor	65.00	
Approximate dealer repair cost:		***$300.00***
1 new 800K disk mechanism	230.00	
1 hour labor	70.00	

Hardware affected: Apple/Sony MFD-51W 800K disk drive (internal or external).

Symptoms: Regardless of which disk you insert, the computer says, *This disk is unreadable: Do you want to initialize it?*

Typical history: The problem started out of the blue (not right after a stuck disk was yanked out with pliers).

Probable diagnosis: The read/write head is dirty.

Solution: Clean the read/write head with a *double-sided* cleaning diskette, preferably moistened with isopropyl alcohol. Also see the next entry.

Approximate cost of repairing it yourself:		***5 min.***
Approximate third-party repair cost:		**$65.00**
1 hour labor	65.00	
Approximate dealer repair cost:		**$300.00**
1 new 800K disk mechanism	230.00	
1 hour labor	70.00	

Hardware affected: Apple/Sony MFD-51W 800K disk drive (internal or external).

Symptoms: Regardless of which disk you insert, the computer says, *This disk is unreadable: Do you want to initialize it?*

Typical history: The problem started during a heat wave (90° to 100°) after the drive had been in use for several hours.

Probable diagnosis: The drive got too hot to continue working.

Solution: Shut down and allow the drive to cool. To prevent recurrence, aim a small table fan at the computer equipment.

Approximate cost of repairing it yourself:		*zip*
Approximate third-party repair cost:		**$65.00**
1 hour labor	65.00	
Approximate dealer repair cost:		**$300.00**
1 new 800K disk mechanism	230.00	
1 hour labor	70.00	

Hardware affected: Apple/Sony MFD-51W 800K disk drive (internal or external).

Symptoms: Regardless of what program you happen to be running, you intermittently get a dialog stating, *Sorry, a system error occurred. ID=10.*

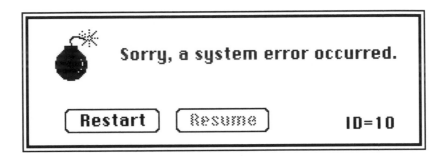

Typical history: The problem generally occurs in warm weather, or after the drive has been in use for several hours, when you choose *Open, Save, Quit* or some other menu item.

Probable diagnosis: The drive got too hot to continue working.

Solution: Shut down and allow the drive to cool. To prevent recurrence, aim a small table fan at the computer equipment.

Approximate cost of repairing it yourself:		*zip*
Approximate third-party repair cost:		*$65.00*
1 hour labor	65.00	
Approximate dealer repair cost:		*$300.00*
1 new 800K disk mechanism	230.00	
1 hour labor	70.00	

Hardware affected: Apple/Sony MFD-51W 800K disk drive (internal or external).

Symptoms: Regardless of what program you happen to be running, you intermittently get a dialog stating, *Sorry, a system error occurred. ID=15*

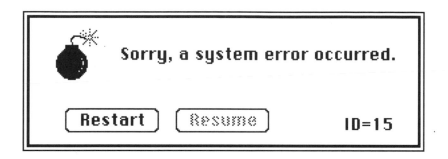

Typical history: The problem generally occurs in warm weather, or after the drive has been in use for several hours, when you choose *Open, Save, Quit* or some other menu item.

Probable diagnosis: The drive got too hot to continue working.

Solution: Shut down and allow the drive to cool. To prevent recurrence, aim a small table fan at the computer equipment.

Approximate cost of repairing it yourself:		*zip*
Approximate third-party repair cost:		*$65.00*
1 hour labor	65.00	
Approximate dealer repair cost:		*$300.00*
1 new 800K disk mechanism	230.00	
1 hour labor	70.00	

Hardware affected: Apple/Sony MFD-51W 800K disk drive (internal or external).

Symptoms: When copying files from 800K disks, you get a dialog box stating, *The file "File Name" could not be read and was skipped;* but when copying files from 400K disks, everything works perfectly.

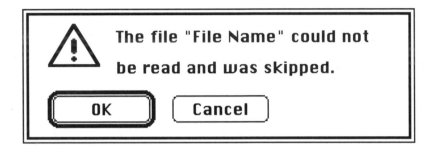

> **⚠ The file "File Name" could not be read and was skipped.**
>
> [**OK**]   [**Cancel**]

Typical history: The problem developed gradually, in combination with an eject problem.

Probable diagnosis: The upper head assembly is bent. There's not enough pressure on the top side of the disk.

Solution: Replace the 800K read/write head assembly (Sony part A-8010223-A). If necessary, perform the track zero alignment procedure (see page 274).

Approximate cost of repairing it yourself:		**$75.00**
1 800K head assembly	75.00	*1 hour*
Approximate third-party repair cost:		**$140.00**
1 800K head assembly	75.00	
1 hour labor	65.00	
Approximate dealer repair cost:		**$300.00**
1 new 800K disk mechanism	230.00	
1 hour labor	70.00	

Hardware affected: Apple/Sony MFD-51W 800K disk drive (internal or external).

Symptoms: Regardless of which 800K disk you insert, the computer says, *This is not a Macintosh disk: Do you want to initialize it?;* but 400K disks read/write perfectly.

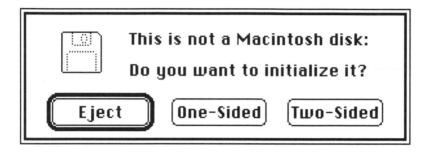

This is not a Macintosh disk:

Do you want to initialize it?

[Eject] [One-Sided] [Two-Sided]

Typical history: The problem developed together with an eject problem. The same 800K disks work fine in other drives.

Probable diagnosis: The upper read/write head is bent. It's no longer in contact with the top side of the disk.

Solution: Replace the 800K read/write head assembly (Sony part A-8010223-A). If necessary, perform the track zero alignment procedure (see page 274).

Approximate cost of repairing it yourself:		**$75.00**
1 800K head assembly	75.00	**1 hour**
Approximate third-party repair cost:		**$140.00**
1 800K head assembly	75.00	
1 hour labor	65.00	
Approximate dealer repair cost:		**$300.00**
1 new 800K disk mechanism	230.00	
1 hour labor	70.00	

Hardware affected: Apple/Sony MFD-75W 1.4MB disk drive (internal or external).

Symptoms: Occasionally, when you insert a disk, nothing happens.

Probable diagnosis: One of the microswitches is sticky.

Solution: Lubricate the sticky microswitch with WD-40.

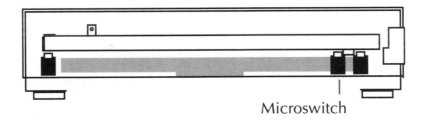

Microswitch

Approximate cost of repairing it yourself:		*30 min.*
Approximate third-party repair cost:		*$65.00*
1 hour labor	65.00	
Approximate dealer repair cost:		*$383.33*
1 1.4MB disk mechanism assembly	313.33	
1 hour labor	70.00	

Hardware affected: Apple/Sony MFD-75W 1.4MB disk drive (internal or external).

Symptoms: Sometimes, even when there is no disk in the drive, it spins and makes continuous eject noises.

Probable diagnosis: One of the microswitches is sticky.

Solution: Lubricate the sticky microswitch with WD-40.

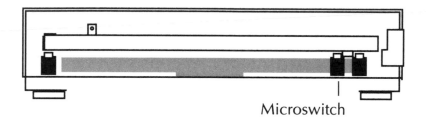

Microswitch

Approximate cost of repairing it yourself:		*30 min.*
Approximate third-party repair cost:		*$65.00*
1 hour labor	65.00	
Approximate dealer repair cost:		*$383.33*
1 1.4MB disk mechanism assembly	313.33	
1 hour labor	70.00	

Hardware affected: Apple/Sony MFD-75W 1.4MB disk drive (internal or external).

Symptoms: The eject mechanism sticks or no longer works at all.

Typical history: The problem developed gradually, over a period of time.

Probable diagnosis: The OEM grease used on the eject levers has dried out and turned to glue.

Solution: Remove the sticky dried-out grease with paper towels and cotton swabs. Relubricate the eject levers with WD-40. To remove a stuck disk from the drive (without damaging the heads), see the disassembly instructions at the end of this chapter.

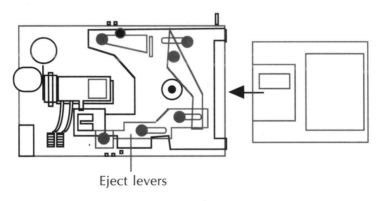

Eject levers

Approximate cost of repairing it yourself:		*1 hour*
Approximate third-party repair cost:		**$65.00**
1 hour labor	65.00	
Approximate dealer repair cost:		**$383.33**
1 1.4MB disk mechanism assembly	313.33	
1 hour labor	70.00	

Hardware affected: Apple/Sony MFD-75W 1.4MB disk drive (internal or external).

Symptoms: Regardless of which disk you insert, the computer says, *This disk is unreadable: Do you want to initialize it?*

Typical history: The problem started right after a stuck disk was forcibly ejected from the drive (yanked out with pliers).

Probable diagnosis: During the forcible eject, the open disk shutter dislocated the upper read/write head.

Solution: Replace the 1.4MB read/write head assembly (Sony part A-8010-251-A). If necessary, perform the track zero alignment procedure (see page 274).

Approximate cost of repairing it yourself:		***$125.00***
1 1.4MB head assembly	125.00	***1 hour***
Approximate third-party repair cost:		***$190.00***
1 1.4MB head assembly	125.00	
1 hour labor	65.00	
Approximate dealer repair cost:		***$383.33***
1 1.4MB disk mechanism assembly	313.33	
1 hour labor	70.00	

Hardware affected: Apple/Sony MFD-75W 1.4MB disk drive (internal or external).

Symptoms: Regardless of which disk you insert, the computer says, *This disk is unreadable: Do you want to initialize it?*

Typical history: The problem started out of the blue (not right after a stuck disk was yanked out with pliers).

Probable diagnosis: The read/write head is dirty.

Solution: Clean the read/write head with a *double-sided* cleaning diskette, preferably moistened with isopropyl alcohol.

Approximate cost of repairing it yourself:		***5 min.***
Approximate third-party repair cost:		***$65.00***
1 hour labor	65.00	
Approximate dealer repair cost:		***$383.33***
1 1.4MB disk mechanism assembly	313.33	
1 hour labor	70.00	

Hardware affected: Apple/Sony MFD-75W 1.4MB disk drive (internal or external).

Symptoms: When copying files from 1.4MB and/or 800K disks, you invariably get a dialog box stating,*The file "File Name" could not be read and was skipped;* but when copying files from 400K disks, everything works perfectly.

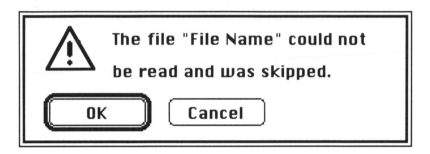

> ⚠ **The file "File Name" could not**
>
> **be read and was skipped.**
>
> **OK**   **Cancel**

Typical history: The problem developed gradually, in combination with an eject problem.

Probable diagnosis: The upper head assembly is bent. There's not enough pressure on the top side of the disk.

Solution: Replace the 1.4MB read/write head assembly (Sony part A-8010-251-A). If necessary, perform the track zero alignment procedure described starting on page 274.

Approximate cost of repairing it yourself:		***$125.00***
1 1.4MB head assembly	125.00	***1 hour***
Approximate third-party repair cost:		***$190.00***
1 1.4MB head assembly	125.00	
1 hour labor	65.00	
Approximate dealer repair cost:		***$383.33***
1 1.4MB disk mechanism assembly	313.33	
1 hour labor	70.00	

Hardware affected: Apple/Sony MFD-75W 1.4MB disk drive (internal or external).

Symptoms: Regardless of which 1.4MB or 800K disk you insert, the computer says, *This is not a Macintosh disk: Do you want to initialize it?;* but 400K disks work perfectly.

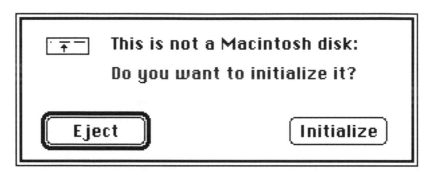

Typical history: The problem developed suddenly, in combination with an eject problem.

Probable diagnosis: The upper head assembly is bent. It's no longer in contact with the top side of the disk.

Solution: Replace the 1.4MB read/write head assembly (Sony part A-8010-251-A). If necessary, perform the track zero alignment procedure.

Approximate cost of repairing it yourself:		**$125.00**
1 1.4MB head assembly	125.00	*1 hour*
Approximate third-party repair cost:		**$190.00**
1 1.4MB head assembly	125.00	
1 hour labor	65.00	
Approximate dealer repair cost:		**$383.33**
1 1.4MB disk mechanism assembly	313.33	
1 hour labor	70.00	

Replacing disk drive heads without test instruments

The head-replacement procedure given in the official *Sony Micro Floppydisk Drive Service Manual* requires an oscilloscope, an MFD function checker, an IF board, a special test jig and a Sony SMC-70 computer. This setup allows factory service centers to do precision work in the shortest possible time, but it is also possible for *mechanically inclined* people to do a reasonably good job at home, with ordinary hand tools and the Mac you already own.

Bear in mind, though, that mastering this procedure is like learning to ride a bike: There's a knack to it. Written instructions are not enough. The only way to learn it is to practice, practice and practice some more, until you finally get it.

Materials required

- a new head carriage assembly, Sony part A-8010-223-A (800K) or A-8010-251-A (1.4MB)

- a #0 Phillips-head screwdriver with a two-inch shaft

- a 5⁄64-inch Allen driver with a two-inch insulated shaft

- two initialized, unlocked 800K disks

- five to ten initialized, locked 800K disks (Miscellaneous public domain disks are excellent for this purpose.)

- a two-foot data cable with 20-pin insulation displacement connectors (IDCs) on either end (make sure pins 9 and 20 are disconnected) or a DB19-P to 20-pin IDC cable taken from an external 800K or 1.4MB disk drive (DD) cabinet

- any Macintosh equipped with a working 800K or 1.4MB drive and a second (internal or external) DD connector

Disassembly and replacement instructions

All part names used in this section are consistent with the part names given in the Sony service manuals. Diagrams come after (not before) the written instructions. Look at the next diagram (not the previous one) for an illustration of what you're reading.

1. Remove the disk drive from the computer or external cabinet.

2. Disconnect the data cable.

3. Remove the disk drive from its metal mounting bracket. Brackets vary, but generally there are two screws along each side. Remove the screws and slide the drive forward.

4. If necessary, eject the stuck disk by simultaneously disengaging the disk-notch pawl located on the left side of the cassette holder assembly and pushing on the eject button. Disengage the disk-notch pawl by pulling (slightly) in the direction indicated by the arrow.

Eject button

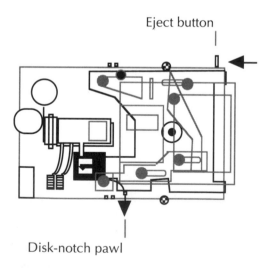

Disk-notch pawl

5. Lower the cassette holder assembly (to put it in "disk-in" mode) by engaging the trigger arm located on the right side of the cassette holder. Push gently in the direction indicated by the arrow.

Trigger arm

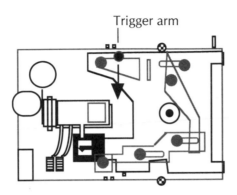

6. Using an ordinary pin, carefully release the cassette holder springs from the DD frame. There are two springs, one per side, located about halfway down each loading rail. Stretch/release only the bottom of the springs (not the tops).

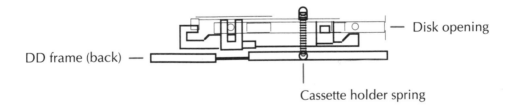

Disk opening

DD frame (back)

Cassette holder spring

7. Remove the black plastic head stop. Note that the center arm is barbed. The barb fits into a notch on the cassette holder assembly. Lift up on the center arm to disengage it from the notch, and slide the head stop toward the back of the drive.

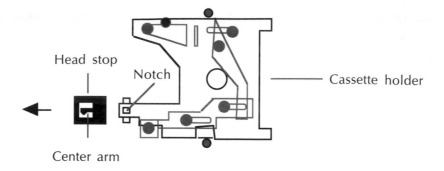

Head stop

Notch

Cassette holder

Center arm

8. Remove the cassette holder from the disk drive frame. Lift up on the front of the assembly, then push the eject button about halfway in (if necessary), then lift up on the back of the assembly.

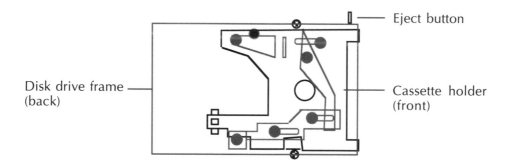

Eject button

Disk drive frame (back)

Cassette holder (front)

9. Carefully remove any dust, dried-up grease, etc. from the cassette holder assembly. Relubricate with WD-40 as necessary.

10. Carefully remove any dust, dried-up grease, etc. from the slide plate. Relubricate with WD-40 as necessary.

Slide plate

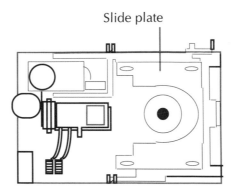

11. Examine the disk-notch pawl at the left-rear corner of the cassette holder assembly. Push the lever in the direction indicated by the arrow. Upon pushing the lever, the disk notch pawl will appear in the opening as shown. If necessary (because a disk was forcibly ejected with pliers and the pawl arm is horribly mangled), bend the pawl arm back into shape, then reinstall the cassette holder assembly and verify that the eject function works reliably.

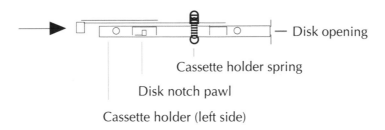

Disk opening

Cassette holder spring

Disk notch pawl

Cassette holder (left side)

12. When you're satisfied that the eject problem (if any) has been fixed, remove the head carriage assembly. Unplug the two ribbon cables; remove the two Phillips head screws on the slide-guide shaft (do not loosen the third brass-color screw!); lift up on the left side of the head carriage assembly, and disengage it from the rotor shaft.

When lifting, be careful not to lose the rubber cap at the front end of the slide-guide shaft. Sometimes it's glued to the disk drive frame; sometimes it isn't.

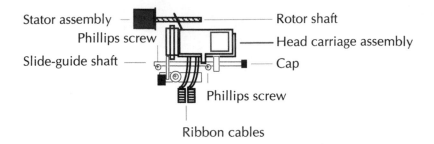

13. Slip the slide-guide shaft out of the old head carriage assembly. Slip the slide-guide shaft into the new head carriage assembly. Cap the slide-guide shaft, if necessary.

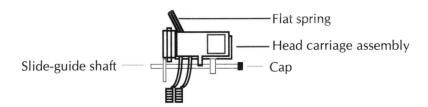

14. Hold the new head carriage assembly at an angle. Sandwich the rotor shaft between the head wire and the flat spring. Butt the head carriage assembly up against the track 00 sensor, then position the slide-guide shaft so that rubber cap is against the disk drive frame.

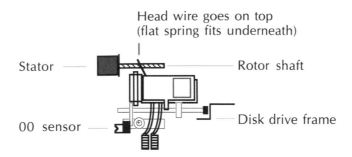

Head wire goes on top
(flat spring fits underneath)

Stator — Rotor shaft

00 sensor — Disk drive frame

15. Reinstall the two black Phillips head screws over the slide-guide shaft and reconnect the two ribbon cables. The rearmost cable plugs into connector CN6, the frontmost cable plugs into CN5.

16. Make sure that the head wire is in a groove, not riding on top of the rotor shaft.

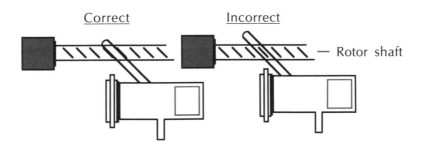

Correct   Incorrect

Rotor shaft

17. Reinstall the cassette holder assembly. While observing the roller bearings on the sides of the cassette holder, lower it gently over the slide plate (attached to the disk drive frame), then work the eject button until the cassette holder assembly falls into place.

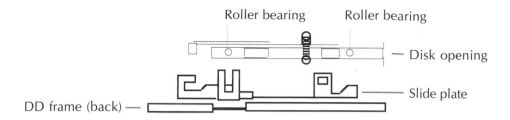

18. Reattach the cassette holder springs. Using a pin, carefully reconnect the bottoms of the cassette holder springs to the disk drive frame. Don't stretch the springs one millimeter more than necessary!

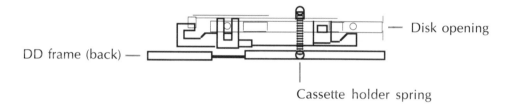

19. Reattach the black plastic head stop. Hold it at angle, so that you can easily slip it under the head lifter without having to pry the heads apart, then slide the head stop toward the front of the drive so that the barb falls into the notch. Be very careful not to pry the heads apart!

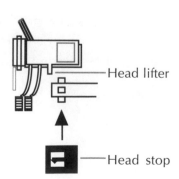

20. Push the eject button all the way in (to set the carriage to "disk-out" mode).

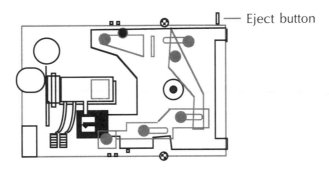

Eject button

21. Carefully withdraw the rubber protector from between the upper and lower heads. Be very careful not to pry the heads apart!

22. Make sure the Mac is turned off, then reconnect the data cable (otherwise you may damage the disk drive electronics). When the cable is securely connected, hold the drive by the edges so that the flywheel underneath spins freely and then turn on the Mac.

Insert a reliable System disk in the working disk drive, then try reading some locked, initialized disks in the drive you just fixed. If they all mount, you're all done. Reinstall the drive in its metal mounting bracket, then reinstall the assembly in the computer or external case.

If you get a dialog box saying: 1) *The disk "Disk Name" needs minor repairs. Do you want to repair it?* or 2) *This disk is unreadable: Do you want to initialize it?* or 3) *This disk is damaged: Do you want to initialize it?* click the *Eject* button, and proceed to the next step.

Track zero alignment procedure

23. Verify the disk drive's general operating condition by inserting a disk you know is good (but that you don't care about) and clicking *Initialize* or *Two-Sided* in the alert box that appears. If the disk formats and mounts, it won't be readable in other drives, but at least you'll know that except for alignment, the disk drive is OK.

If the disk doesn't format, loosen the brass screw on the track 00 sensor and move the sensor assembly just a little. Start by lining up the V on the back of the sensor base with the line etched into the disk drive frame. Tighten the screw, and then try initializing another disk. Until you can initialize a disk, you can't go any further. If you're not able to initialize any disk, then the drive may have an electrical problem (someone may have yanked the data cable while the Mac was on), or the new head assembly may be damaged (someone may have spread the heads apart during the installation).

If you can initialize a disk, try mounting some locked, initialized disks. If they all mount, you're all done. Reinstall the drive in its metal mounting bracket, then reinstall the assembly into the computer or external drive case. If they don't all mount, proceed to the next step.

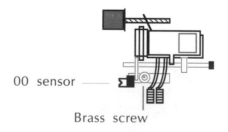

00 sensor

Brass screw

24. When the drive can initialize a disk, but can't read disks that you know are good, it means that the stepping motor assembly (consisting of the stator and the rotor) is out of alignment. Mark the original position of the stator assembly on the disk drive frame (draw

a line with a pencil or a felt marker), then loosen the mounting bracket screws (just a little) with a $\frac{5}{64}$-inch hex driver.

Note that the stator assembly mounting bracket is made of spring steel. When the hex screws are tight, or when the stator assembly is pushed in, turning the stator housing does not turn the rotor shaft. But when the screws are just loose enough so that the stator assembly is sprung out, turning the stator housing *does* turn the rotor shaft. It's important to loosen the hex screws just enough to spring the mounting bracket. If the hex screws are too loose or too tight, there won't be any spring action, the rotor shaft won't turn as you turn the stator housing, and you won't accomplish anything in the next step.

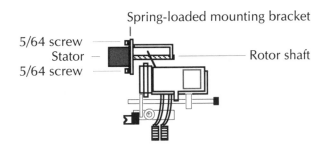

25. If you haven't done so already, mark the original position of the stator housing on the disk drive frame, then turn the housing just a hair one way or the other so that the rotor shaft turns, then snug the screws and try reading a known-good disk again. If you get a dialog box stating, *The disk "Disk Name" needs minor repairs. Do you want to repair it?*, click the *Cancel* button, loosen the screws, turn the stator housing a little more in the same direction, snug the screws tighter and try again. Continue until either the disk mounts or you get a dialog box stating, *This disk is damaged: Do you want to initialize it?* or *This disk is unreadable: Do you want to initialize it?*

If the disk mounts, proceed to the next step. If you get either dialog box *(This disk is damaged* or *This disk is unreadable),* then either you went too far, or you've been turning the stator housing the wrong way. Loosen the screws and turn the housing the other way until the disk mounts.

26. When the disk mounts, try mounting some other disks that you know are good. If problems persist—if disk contents appear, but not disk icons, or some disks mount but some don't, or it takes too long to build the desktop—continue fine-tuning the stator alignment until each and every one of the disks mounts normally.

   When making final adjustments, pay attention to the way the drive sounds. Without instruments, you have to rely on your hearing to tell whether the alignment is correct, just like a seasoned mechanic tuning an engine by ear.

27. Remount the drive in its metal mounting bracket.

28. Reinstall the drive in the computer or external cabinet.

CHAPTER 5
HARD DRIVES AND OTHER PERIPHERALS

Hardware affected: Any external hard drive.

Symptoms: The disk-access LED doesn't work.

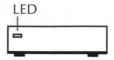

Probable diagnosis: The LED cable is backwards, loose or disconnected.

Solution: Check/tighten/reverse the LED connections.

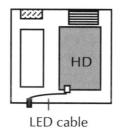

LED cable

Approximate cost of repairing it yourself:		*30 min.*
Approximate third-party repair cost:		*$65.00*
1 hour labor	65.00	
Approximate dealer repair cost:		*$558.33*
1 new 3.5-inch 20 MB HDA (min)	488.33	
1 hour labor	70.00	

Hardware affected: Any external hard drive.

Symptoms: On startup, the drive spins but does not mount. Instead, you get the blinking floppy-disk icon. Third-party formatting software reports *error during inquiry command.*

Typical history: The problem occurred after power supply repair work, right after you put everything back together.

Probable diagnosis: The SCSI data cable is loose, or one of its 50 internal wires is broken.

Solution: Check/replace the SCSI data cable.

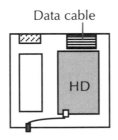

Data cable

Approximate cost of repairing it yourself:		***$1.00***
1 foot of 50 conductor ribbon cable	1.00	***1 hour***
Approximate third-party repair cost:		***$85.00***
20 MB @ 4.25 per MB	85.00	
Approximate dealer repair cost:		***$558.33***
1 new 3.5-inch 20 MB HDA	488.33	
1 hour labor	70.00	

Hardware affected: Any Apple HD 20 SC, Mac SE or Mac XL with an internal Miniscribe 8425SA SCSI drive.

Symptoms: On startup, the 20 MB hard drive peeps twice, then you get a sad Mac and the desktop never appears.

Probable diagnosis: The internal 3.5-inch 20 MB drive mechanism (Miniscribe 8425SA) has a bad master directory block.

Solution: Boot the computer from a floppy disk. Use third-party SCSI formatting software (like DiskManager Mac version 2.24, not Apple HD SC Setup) to test the drive. If testing reports that bad blocks were found and rewritten, but the drive still won't mount, reformat the drive.

If the format operation fails, reboot from the floppy disk, and once the menu bar appears, hold down the mouse button. Holding down the mouse button will often mount a drive in these cases, even when the format operation failed. If holding down the mouse button doesn't mount the drive, but the Finder indicates *This is not a Macintosh disk. Do you want to initialize it?*, click *OK*.

If any of these procedures mounts the drive, it'll be fine. It'll work as well as it ever did, for an indefinite period of time.

Approximate cost of repairing it yourself:		**$49.95**
1 DiskManager Mac (street price)	49.95	**1 hour**
Approximate third-party repair cost:		**$85.00**
20 MB @ 4.25 per MB	85.00	
Approximate dealer repair cost:		**$558.33**
1 new 3.5-inch 20 MB HDA	488.33	
1 hour labor	70.00	

Hardware affected: Any Apple HD 20 SC, Mac SE or Mac XL with an internal Miniscribe 8425SA SCSI drive.

Symptoms: On startup, the disk access light comes on and stays on, but the hard drive doesn't make the usual beep noises and it never spins. Eventually, you get a floppy disk icon with a blinking question mark.

Probable diagnosis: The problem may be mechanical (related to the spinner motor) or it may be electrical (related to the ROM chip).

Solution: Verify the drive mechanism by substituting a controller card that's known to be good. If the mechanism spins, installing a controller card with the same ROM and PCB revisions as the failed card may restore full operation. If the drive mechanism fails to spin, the original controller card may still be good, and under opposite circumstances, it might be used to repair another drive. Bear in mind that new parts for the Miniscribe 8425 are very tough to come by. Success generally requires a *large* stock of junk drives to take parts from.

Approximate cost of repairing it yourself:		*not practical*
Approximate third-party repair cost:		**$85.00**
20 MB @ 4.25 per MB	85.00	
Approximate dealer repair cost:		**$558.33**
1 new 3.5-inch 20 MB HDA	488.33	
1 hour labor	70.00	

Hardware affected: Any Apple HD 20 SC, Mac SE or Mac XL with an internal Miniscribe 8425SA SCSI drive.

Symptoms: On startup, the drive makes its usual beep noises but it doesn't mount. Instead, it makes a continuous *clunk-clunk* noise.

Probable diagnosis: The problem is in the ROM chip (revisions vary) located on the embedded controller card.

Solution: Replace the ROM chip with a used chip bearing *identical* revision information. Bear in mind that new parts for the Miniscribe 8425 are very tough to come by. Success generally requires a *large* stock of junk drives to take parts from.

Approximate cost of repairing it yourself:		*not practical*
Approximate third-party repair cost:		*$85.00*
20 MB @ 4.25 per MB	85.00	
Approximate dealer repair cost:		*$558.33*
1 new 3.5-inch 20 MB HDA	488.33	
1 hour labor	70.00	

Hardware affected: Any Apple HD 40 SC or Macintosh II with an internal Quantum QA250 SCSI drive.

Symptoms: On startup, the drive spins but does not mount. If you boot from a floppy disk and run Apple HD SC Setup version 2.0 or later, you get a dialog box that says, *Drive selection failed. Unable to locate a suitable drive connected to the SCSI port.*

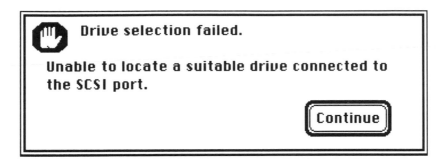

Probable diagnosis: The SCSI driver has been damaged or replaced by optimizer software, protection software or a generic SCSI utility.

Solution: Reinstall a suitable SCSI driver by updating the drive with Apple HD SC Setup version 1.5 (not Apple HD SC Setup version 2.0 or later). If this diagnosis is correct, the drive will mount with all data intact, and it should work fine for an indefinite period of time.

Approximate cost of repairing it yourself:		***10 min.***
Approximate third-party repair cost:		***$170.00***
40 MB @ 4.25 per MB	170.00	
Approximate dealer repair cost:		***$670.00***
1 new 3.5-inch 40 MB HDA	600.00	
1 hour labor	70.00	

Hardware affected: Any Apple HD 40 SC, Mac SE or Mac II with an internal Sony SRD 2040A 40 MB SCSI drive.

Symptoms: On startup, the disk access light (not visible on a Mac II) comes on and stays on, but the drive does not spin. If the computer isn't shut off immediately, the drive gets very hot and you smell burning grease.

Probable diagnosis: The hard disks are stuck. Either there's too much resistance on the drive bearing, or one of the heads is stuck to the media.

Solution: Fold back the embedded controller card and spin the motor (to get it started) by hand. Nine times out of ten, once you put the controller card back on, the drive will work fine, for an indefinite period of time.

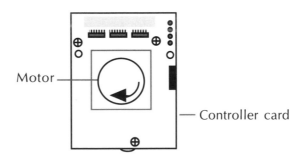

Motor

Controller card

Approximate cost of repairing it yourself:		*1 hour*
Approximate third-party repair cost:		**$170.00**
40 MB @ 4.25 per MB	170.00	
Approximate dealer repair cost:		**$670.00**
1 new 3.5-inch 40 MB HDA	600.00	
1 hour labor	70.00	

Hardware affected: CMS PRO60 or any other external hard drive with Lien Engineering power supply, board number 10-8707A.

Symptoms: The power switch is on and the power cord is connected, but the unit is dead. The drive does not spin. The cooling fan does not turn. The power supply LED does not light. The unit makes no sound whatsoever.

Probable diagnosis: The problem is in the power supply.

Solution: Check/replace transistor Q1 (2SC 3150, T-NPN, SI, high-speed switch) and pigtail fuse F1 (1A) .

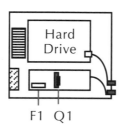

F1   Q1

Approximate cost of repairing it yourself:		*$4.50*
1 2SC 3150 transistor	4.00	*1 hour*
1 pigtail fuse (1A)	.50	
Approximate third-party repair cost:		*$255.00*
60 MB @ 4.25 per MB	255.00	
Approximate dealer repair cost:		*$795.00*
1 new 80M HDA	725.00	
1 hour labor	70.00	

Hardware affected: CMS PRO80-II/i, Jasmine 80 or any other external hard drive with a Quantum Q280 (80 MB) mechanism.

Symptoms: The drive spins but occasionally doesn't mount. Formatting software intermittently reports *broken bus* or *bus not terminated.*

Typical history: The unit had been working fine, but it failed *immediately* after its SCSI cable was disconnected/reconnected while the power was on.

Probable diagnosis: A fuse is blown on the embedded controller card.

Solution: Check/replace the pigtail fuse (Pico, 1A) at board reference F1.

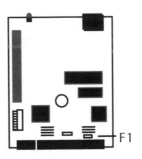

Approximate cost of repairing it yourself:		$2.00
1 1A Pico fuse	2.00	*1 hour*
Approximate third-party repair cost:		$340.00
80 MB @ 4.25 per MB	340.00	
Approximate dealer repair cost:		$795.00
1 new 80M HDA	725.00	
1 hour labor	70.00	

Hardware affected: CMS PRO80-II/i, Jasmine 80 or any other external hard drive with a Quantum Q280 (80 MB) mechanism.

Symptoms: When copying files you get a dialog box stating, *The file "File Name" could not be read and was skipped.*

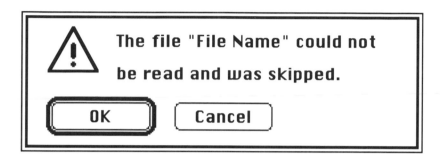

Typical history: The problem started right after the drive was optimized or updated using a generic SCSI utility.

Probable diagnosis: The updated SCSI driver (using blind reads and writes) is incompatible with this drive (which requires handshaking).

Solution: Reinstall compatible SCSI drivers using the OEM SCSI utility or use Silverlining version 5.2/06 to install compatible drivers by choosing *SCSI Read/Write Loops...* from the Drive menu and selecting *Standard Mac Handshake* from the dialog box.

Approximate cost of repairing it yourself:		***$135.00***
1 Silverlining (street price)	135.00	***30 min.***
Approximate third-party repair cost:		***$340.00***
80 MB @ 4.25 per MB	340.00	
Approximate dealer repair cost:		***$795.00***
1 new 80M HDA	725.00	
1 hour labor	70.00	

Hardware affected: CMS P1 100-SE/r or any other external hard drive with Conner CP3100 (100 MB) mechanism.

Symptoms: The drive spins but does not mount. Formatting software intermittently reports *broken bus* or *bus not terminated*.

Typical history: The CP3100 worked fine before as an internal drive, but failed *immediately* after it was mounted in an external enclosure.

Probable diagnosis: One of the mounting screws has disconnected CR15 on the embedded controller card.

Solution: Remove the screw. Inspect/resolder/replace CR15.

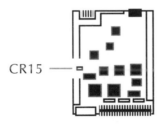

CR15

Approximate cost of repairing it yourself:	*1 hour*
Approximate third-party repair cost:	*$425.00*
100 MB @ 4.25 per MB 425.00	
Approximate dealer repair cost:	*$795.00*
1 new 80M HDA 725.00	
1 hour labor 70.00	

Hardware affected: Hisper 20 or any other external hard drive with a Seagate ST225N (20 MB) mechanism.

Symptoms: The drive mounts, but it's *painfully* slow and prone to system errors. Reformatting/reinstalling drivers isn't possible because the OEM SCSI software no longer recognizes this drive.

Typical history: The problem started right after a disk-tools editor was used to update, optimize or write new sectors to the drive.

Probable diagnosis: The OEM SCSI driver has been corrupted.

Solution: Reformat the drive with DiskManager Mac version 2.24 by choosing *Format options...* from the Defect Management menu and selecting *Use manufacturer's default format* from the dialog box.

Approximate cost of repairing it yourself:		**$49.95**
1 DiskManager Mac (street price)	49.95	**1 hour**
Approximate third-party repair cost:		**$85.00**
20 MB @ 4.25 per MB	85.00	
Approximate dealer repair cost:		**$756.67**
1 HD20SC external mechanism	756.67	

Hardware affected: Jasmine 20 or any other external hard drive with a Miniscribe 8425SA (20 MB) mechanism.

Symptoms: The drive spins but occasionally does not mount. Formatting software intermittently reports *broken bus* or *bus not terminated.*

Typical history: The unit had been working fine, but it failed *immediately* after its SCSI cable was disconnected/reconnected while the power was on.

Probable diagnosis: A fuse is blown on the embedded SCSI controller card.

Solution: Check/replace the pigtail fuse (Pico, 1A) at board reference F1.

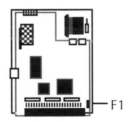

Approximate cost of repairing it yourself:		*$2.00*
1 1A Pico fuse	2.00	*1 hour*
Approximate third-party repair cost:		*$85.00*
20 MB @ 4.25 per MB	85.00	
Approximate dealer repair cost:		*$558.33*
1 new 3.5-inch 20 MB HDA	488.33	
1 hour labor	70.00	

Hardware affected: Jasmine Direct Drive 40 external hard drive with 3.5-inch Quantum 40 Prodrive (40 MB) mechanism.

Symptoms: The power switch is on and the fan spins, but the hard drive does not start. Tapping on, picking up or moving the enclosure may start the drive.

Probable diagnosis: One of the insulation displacement connectors (IDCs) on the power supply cable is intermittent.

Solution: Strip and solder *both* ends of *each* wire to the insulation displacement connectors.

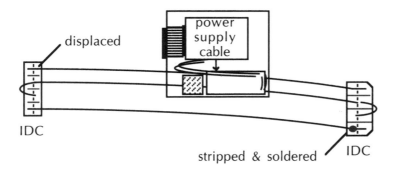

Approximate cost of repairing it yourself:		*1 hour*
Approximate third-party repair cost:		**$170.00**
40 MB @ 4.25 per MB	170.00	
Approximate dealer repair cost:		**$670.00**
1 new 3.5-inch 40 MB HDA	600.00	
1 hour labor	70.00	

Hardware affected: Jasmine Direct Drive 80 external hard drive with 5.25-inch Quantum Q280 (80 MB) mechanism.

Symptoms: The power switch is on and the fan spins, but the hard drive does not start. Tapping on, picking up or moving the enclosure may start the drive.

Probable diagnosis: One of the insulation displacement connectors (IDCs) on the power supply cable is intermittent.

Solution: Strip and solder *both* ends of *each* wire to the insulation displacement connectors.

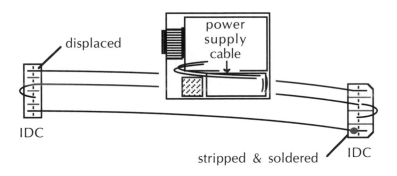

Approximate cost of repairing it yourself:		*1 hour*
Approximate third-party repair cost:		**$340.00**
80 MB @ 4.25 per MB	340.00	
Approximate dealer repair cost:		**$795.00**
1 new 5.25-inch 80 MB HDA	725.00	
1 hour labor	70.00	

Hardware affected: Jasmine 100, MicroTech Nova 50 or other external hard drive with Power General Series 3045 power supply.

Symptoms: The power switch is on and the power cord is connected, but the unit is dead. The power supply LED doesn't light. The drive doesn't spin. The fan doesn't turn. The unit makes no sound whatsoever.

Probable diagnosis: The problem is in the power supply.

Solution: Desolder/check/replace resistor R3 (200K, 2W, 5%). If exact replacement resistor is unavailable, substitute 220K, 2W, 2%.

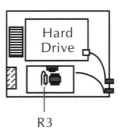

R3

Approximate cost of repairing it yourself:		*$2.00*
1 220K, 2W, 2% resistor	2.00	*1 hour*
Approximate third-party repair cost:		*$425.00*
100 MB @ 4.25 per MB	425.00	
Approximate dealer repair cost:		*$795.00*
1 new 5.25-inch 80 MB HDA	725.00	
1 hour labor	70.00	

Hardware affected: LaCie Cirrus 80 external hard drive with Computer Products model ML40-3101 power supply (35W 115/230 VAC).

Symptoms: The power switch is on and the cord is connected, but the drive doesn't spin. The cooling fan doesn't turn. The unit makes no sound whatsoever.

Typical history: The problem occurred out of the blue, while the drive was on during a *momentary* power failure.

Probable diagnosis: The problem is in the power supply.

Solution: Check/replace fuse F2 (3A), transistor Q3 (SGS 12015-D/2SC 3039), resistor R1 (56K, ¼-watt, 5%) and resistor R4 (470K, ½-watt, 5%).

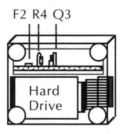

Approximate cost of repairing it yourself:		$6.18
1 Pico fuse (3A)	2.00	*1 hour*
1 2SC 3039 transistor	4.00	
1 56K, ¼-watt resistor	.09	
1 470K, ½-watt 5% resistor	.09	
Approximate third-party repair cost:		**$340.00**
80 MB @ 4.25 per MB	340.00	
Approximate dealer repair cost:		**$795.00**
1 new 5.25-inch 80 MB HDA	725.00	
1 hour labor	70.00	

Hardware affected: Mirror/MagNet 40/40 external hard drive with integral tape backup.

Symptoms: When connected to a Mac II along with other external SCSI devices, the drive spins but does not mount.

Typical history: This very same drive worked fine on a Mac Plus where it was the *only* drive.

Probable diagnosis: There's an ID conflict on the SCSI bus. Two ID numbers are occupied by the Mirror/MagNet 40/40. The tape drive is at ID 1. The hard drive is at ID 5. If any other devices on the SCSI bus share these numbers, the Mirror/MagNet 40/40 won't mount.

Solution: Verify that the Mirror/MagNet drive is the only device occupying IDs 1 and 5. Renumber the other devices as necessary. Verify that the ID selector switch on the back of the Mirror/MagNet 40/40 is set to 5 (not 1 or any other number).

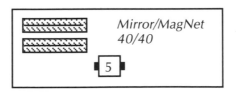

Approximate cost of repairing it yourself:		*10 min.*
Approximate third-party repair cost:		**$170.00**
40 MB @ 4.25 per MB	170.00	
Approximate dealer repair cost:		**$670.00**
1 new 3.5-inch 40 MB HDA	600.00	
1 hour labor	70.00	

Hardware affected: Peak 20 external hard drive with 5.25-inch Miniscribe (20 MB) mechanism.

Symptoms: The power switch is on and the fan spins, but the hard drive does not start. Tapping on, picking up or moving the enclosure may start the drive.

Probable diagnosis: One of the insulation displacement connectors (IDCs) on one of the *two* power supply cables is intermittent.

Solution: Strip and solder *both* ends of *each* wire to the insulation displacement connectors on *both* power supply cables. (Only one of the two cables is shown in the diagram.)

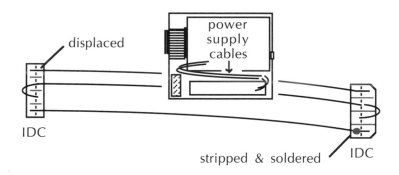

Approximate cost of repairing it yourself:		*1 hour*
Approximate third-party repair cost:		**$85.00**
20 MB @ 4.25 per MB	85.00	
Approximate dealer repair cost:		**$558.33**
1 new 3.5-inch 20 MB HDA	488.33	
1 hour labor	70.00	

Hardware affected: Rodime Systems 20 Plus external hard drive with 5.25-inch Seagate ST225N (20 MB) mechanism.

Symptoms: If this drive is powered up when you turn on your Mac Plus, the red drive light blinks, and then you get a sad Mac with error code 0F000A. If you try to mount the drive using SCSI Probe 2.01, you get a system error, ID=02. Other utilities report Mac Error #5.

Typical history: This drive was tested using Apple HD SC Setup software (version 1.5). The *Update* button was clicked, and then a dialog box appeared saying, *This is not a Macintosh disk, do you want to initialize it?* At that point, the *Cancel* button was clicked.

Probable diagnosis: The partition map is invalid.

Solution: Boot the computer from a floppy disk, wait for the desktop to appear and *then* turn on the drive. Use third-party SCSI formatting software (like Silverlining version 5.2/06) not Apple HD SC Setup software, to repair the partition map.

Approximate cost of repairing it yourself:		**$135.00**
1 Silverlining (street price)	135.00	***30 min.***
Approximate third-party repair cost:		**$85.00**
20 MB @ 4.25 per MB	85.00	
Approximate dealer repair cost:		**$558.33**
1 new 3.5-inch 20 MB HDA	488.33	
1 hour labor	70.00	

Hardware affected: SuperMac DataFrame 40XP external hard drive with Computer Products model ML40-3101 power supply (35W 115/230 VAC).

Symptoms: The power switch is on and the power cord is connected, but the enclosure is dead. The green LED doesn't light. The drive doesn't spin. The unit makes no sound whatsoever.

Typical history: The problem occurred out of the blue, while the drive was on during a *momentary* power failure.

Probable diagnosis: The problem is in the power supply.

Solution: Check/replace fuse F2 (3A), transistor Q3 (SGS 12015-D/2SC 3039), resistor R1 (56K, ¼-watt, 5%) and resistor R4 (470K, ½-watt, 5%).

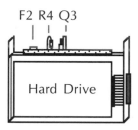

Approximate cost of repairing it yourself:		$6.18
1 Pico fuse (3A)	2.00	*1 hour*
1 2SC 3039 transistor	4.00	
1 56K, ¼-watt resistor	.09	
1 470K, ½-watt resistor	.09	
Approximate third-party repair cost:		**$170.00**
40 MB @ 4.25 per MB	170.00	
Approximate dealer repair cost:		**$670.00**
1 new 3.5-inch 40 MB HDA	600.00	
1 hour labor	70.00	

Hardware affected: SuperMac DataFrame 40XP external hard drive with 5.25-inch NEC mechanism.

Symptoms: The power switch is on, the green LED *does* light, but the hard drive doesn't spin. Tapping on, picking up or moving the enclosure may start the drive.

Probable diagnosis: One of the insulation displacement connectors (IDCs) on the power supply cable is intermittent.

Solution: Strip and solder *both* ends of *each* wire to the insulation displacement connectors.

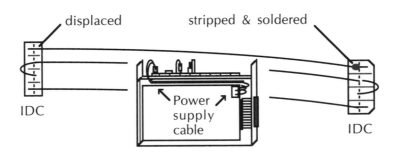

Approximate cost of repairing it yourself:		*1 hour*
Approximate third-party repair cost:		***$170.00***
40 MB @ 4.25 per MB	170.00	
Approximate dealer repair cost:		***$670.00***
1 new 3.5-inch 40 MB HDA	600.00	
1 hour labor	70.00	

Hardware affected: Warp 9/Photon external hard drive with 3.5-inch Lapine mechanism.

Symptoms: The drive spins, but the red LED in the front panel doesn't work, and the drive doesn't mount.

Typical history: This very same drive worked fine on a Mac Plus where it was the *only* drive, but it failed as soon as it was connected to a Mac with an internal hard drive. The LED problem began right after the enclosure was taken apart and then reassembled.

Probable diagnosis: Originally, there was a SCSI ID conflict. The Photon drive is jumpered for ID 0. When connected to a SCSI bus where an internal drive is also jumpered for ID 0, the Photon drive won't mount. Now, the LED cable is severed and short-circuiting.

Solution: Check/replace the front panel LED. Check/rejumper the SCSI IDs, or move the Photon unit back to the Mac Plus.

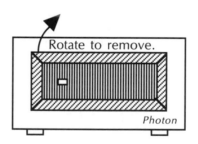

Approximate cost of repairing it yourself:		**20¢**
1 rectangular LED	.20	**1 hour**
Approximate third-party repair cost:		**$85.00**
20 MB @ 4.25 per MB	85.00	
Approximate dealer repair cost:		**$558.33**
1 new 3.5-inch 20 MB HDA	488.33	
1 hour labor	70.00	

Hardware affected: Apple CD S

Symptoms: An Apple CD SC is unable to read a disk.

Probable diagnosis: Accumulated dust is affecting the head mechanism.

Solution: Blow out the accumulated dust with compressed air. To prevent recurrence of this problem, disconnect the intake fan.

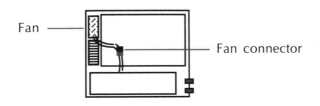

Fan ——————

—— Fan connector

Approximate cost of repairing it yourself:		*1 hour*
Approximate third-party repair cost:		**$65.00**
1 hour labor	65.00	
Approximate dealer repair cost:		**$500.00**
1 new CD ROM drive	500.00	

Hardware affected: Apple Scanner (original 300 dpi model).

Symptoms: The scanner works fine when it's the only external device on the SCSI bus, but it intermittently locks the system and/or prevents the Mac from booting when other external devices (hard drive, LaserWriter II SC, et) are added to the bus.

Probable diagnosis: The problem is on the Apple Scanner logic board.

Solution: Break off the filter networks at board locations CA4, CA5 and CA6. No replacements are necessary.

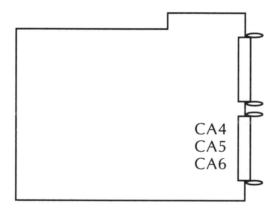

CA4
CA5
CA6

Approximate cost of repairing it yourself:		*30 min.*
Approximate third-party repair cost:		*$65.00*
1 hour labor	65.00	
Approximate dealer repair cost:		*$253.33*
1 new main logic board	183.33	
1 hour labor	70.00	

Hardware affected: Hayes Smartmodem 2400 model number 231AA.

Symptoms: The modem turns on and the power light comes on, but there is no transmit or receive.

Typical history: The modem had been connected to the printer port, not the modem port, of a Mac 512Ke. The problem occurred when you turned on AppleTalk (via the Control Panel or the Chooser DA) while the modem was on.

Probable diagnosis: The problem is on the modem PCB.

Solution: Check/replace the MC1489 chip (14-pin DIP, quad line receiver, same as 75189) at board reference U22.

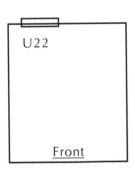

Approximate cost of repairing it yourself:		**$1.25**
1 75189 chip	1.25	**1 hour**
Approximate third-party repair cost:		**$70.00**
1 75189 chip	5.00	
1 hour labor	65.00	
Approximate dealer repair cost:		**$379.00**
1 Apple modem, 2400 baud	379.00	

Hardware affected: Hewlett Packard DeskJet/Plus/500.

Symptoms: After printing one page the printer stops, and the *on line* light blinks (green) even though the printer isn't out of paper.

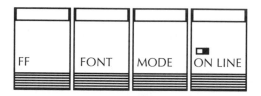

Probable diagnosis: The problem is in the printer mechanism.

Solution: Check/resynchronize the transmission levers (located under the top cover assembly).

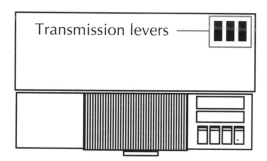

Approximate cost of repairing it yourself:		*15 min.*
Approximate third-party repair cost:		*$65.00*
1 hour labor	65.00	
Approximate dealer repair cost:		*$599.00*
1 new StyleWriter printer	599.00	

Hardware affected: Hewlett Packard DeskWriter.

Symptoms: After a few lines, the DeskWriter prints *Datacomm buffer overrun—no DTR handshaking* and ejects the page. Only the smallest (one paragraph long) files can be printed.

Datacomm buffer overrun - no DTR handshaking

Typical History: The DeskWriter is connected to a Mac II running virtual memory. The installed printer driver is version 2.1 or earlier.

Probable diagnosis: Virtual memory does not support DTR handshaking.
Solution: Open the Memory control panel. Turn off virtual memory.

 Virtual Memory
○ On
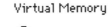 ◉ Off

Approximate cost of repairing it yourself:		*2 min.*
Approximate third-party repair cost:		**$65.00**
1 hour labor	65.00	
Approximate dealer repair cost:		**$599.00**
1 new StyleWriter printer	599.00	

Hardware affected: Hewlett Packard DeskWriter.

Symptoms: In response to the *Macintosh Print...* command, the DeskWriter invariably prints *Datacomm Error—please check baud rate* and ejects the page. No part of the file is printed.

Datacomm Error - please check baud rate

Typical History: The DeskWriter is connected to a Mac II equipped with a CSI-Hurdler serial card.

Probable diagnosis: The DeskWriter is communicating at 57,600 baud. Hurdler cards manufactured before Fall of 1991 don't support 57,600 baud.

Solution: Disconnect the DeskWriter from the Hurdler card. Reconnect it to one of the Mac's built-in serial ports.

Approximate cost of repairing it yourself:		*2 min.*
Approximate third-party repair cost:		*$65.00*
1 hour labor	65.00	
Approximate dealer repair cost:		*$599.00*
1 new StyleWriter printer	599.00	

Hardware affected: Hewlett Packard DeskWriter.

Symptoms: If the computer is on when you switch on the DeskWriter, it starts to print garbage characters in reverse video. The garbage keeps coming out page after page. There's no way to have the Mac and the DeskWriter powered up at the same time.

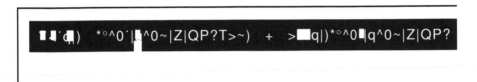

Probable diagnosis: The DeskWriter is connected to the printer port and AppleTalk is turned on, but the DeskWriter is connected via a serial cable (not connected via a LocalTalk cable).

Solution: Open the Chooser DA and deactivate AppleTalk.

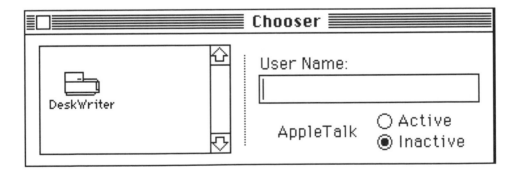

Approximate cost of repairing it yourself:		*2 min.*
Approximate third-party repair cost:		**$114.95**
1 LocalTalk cable	49.95	
1 hour labor	65.00	
Approximate dealer repair cost:		**$599.00**
1 new StyleWriter printer	599.00	

Hardware affected: Hewlett Packard DeskWriter.

Symptoms: In response to the Macintosh *Print...* command, the DeskWriter prints *Error trap 10864* and ejects the page. No part of the file is printed.

Error trap 10864

Probable diagnosis: The problem is on the Macintosh logic board (not in the DeskWriter).

Solution: Check/replace the R/C network (20-pin DIP, Apple part 115-0002 or SMD, Apple part 115-50002) wired to the printer port. Styles and board references vary from CPU to CPU.

115-0002

Approximate cost of repairing it yourself:		*$12.00*
1 Bourns filter	12.00	*2 hours*
Approximate third-party repair cost:		*$154.00*
1 Bourns filter	24.00	
2 hours labor	130.00	
Approximate dealer repair cost:		*$570.00*
1 new logic board	500.00	*(average cost)*
1 hour labor	70.00	

CHAPTER 6
EXTERNAL MONITORS

Hardware affected: AppleColor High-Resolution RGB monitor.

Symptoms: There's a thin horizontal line located about 2¼ inches up from the bottom of the screen. The thin line is stationary. It never goes away. It's visible in all programs.

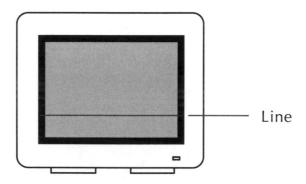 — Line

Probable diagnosis: The thin line is a characteristic of the particular Trinitron CRT (Sony part M34JNQ10X) used in this monitor. There's nothing to be done about it.

Solution: Ignore the line or switch to a different brand of monitor.

Approximate cost of repairing it yourself:	*zip*
Approximate third-party repair cost:	*zip*
Approximate dealer repair cost:	*zip*

Hardware affected: AppleColor High-Resolution RGB monitor.

Symptoms: The display is fine at 640 x 480, but when expanded to 672 x 512 or 704 x 512 using MaxAppleZoom (MAZ), it rolls from top to bottom (no vertical hold).

Probable diagnosis: The problem is on the D board.

Solution: Carefully adjust variable resistor RV507, labeled *V.HOLD*, counterclockwise for a stable picture. A *very slight* turn is generally all that's required.

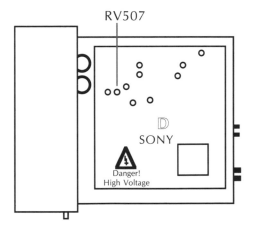

Approximate cost of repairing it yourself:	*1 hour*
Approximate third-party repair cost:	**$65.00**
1 hour labor	65.00
Approximate dealer repair cost:	**$70.00**
1 hour labor	70.00

Hardware affected: AppleColor High-Resolution RGB monitor.

Symptoms: The display is fine at 640 x 480, but when it's expanded to 672 x 512 or 704 x 512 using MAZ, the left side folds over.

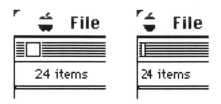

Probable diagnosis: The problem is on the D board.

Solution: Carefully turn variable resistor RV501, labeled *H.HOLD*, counterclockwise until the left side of the display unfolds.

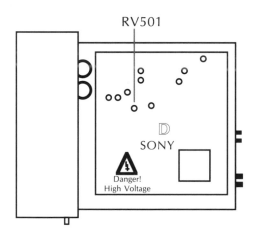

Approximate cost of repairing it yourself:	*1 hour*
Approximate third-party repair cost:	*$65.00*
1 hour labor 65.00	
Approximate dealer repair cost:	*$70.00*
1 hour labor 70.00	

Hardware affected: AppleColor High-Resolution RGB monitor.

Symptoms: For the first ten to fifteen minutes of operation, the display intermittently jitters in and out of focus. Once it warms up, it's OK.

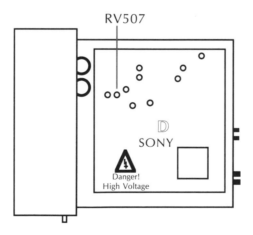

Probable diagnosis: The problem is on the D board.

Solution: Carefully turn variable resistor RV507, labeled *V.HOLD*, counterclockwise for a stable picture. A *very slight* turn is generally all that's required. Also see the next entry.

Approximate cost of repairing it yourself:		*1 hour*
Approximate third-party repair cost:		**$65.00**
1 hour labor	65.00	
Approximate dealer repair cost:		**$70.00**
1 hour labor	70.00	

Hardware affected: AppleColor High-Resolution RGB monitor.

Symptoms: The display is always out of focus.

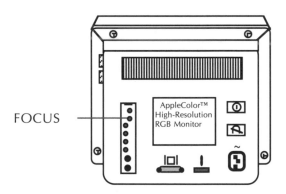

Probable diagnosis: The problem is on the H board, located under the control cover plate at the back of the monitor.

Solution: Carefully adjust the variable resistor RV 701, labeled *FOCUS*, for a sharp, clear picture. Also see the next entry.

FOCUS

Approximate cost of repairing it yourself:	*5 min.*
Approximate third-party repair cost:	*$65.00*
1 hour labor	65.00
Approximate dealer repair cost:	*$70.00*
1 hour labor	70.00

Hardware affected: AppleColor High-Resolution RGB monitor.

Symptoms: The display is covered with red, green or blue shadows. In extreme cases, it may resemble a 3-D comic book as seen without the special eyeglasses.

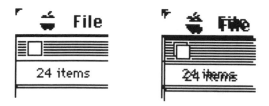

Probable diagnosis: The problem is on the H board, located under the control cover plate at the back of the monitor.

Solution: Carefully adjust the variable resistors labeled *V-TWIST* and *H-STAT*, until the colored shadows disappear.

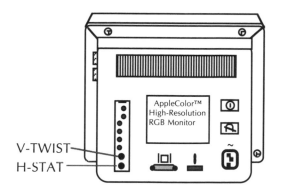

Approximate cost of repairing it yourself:		*5 min.*
Approximate third-party repair cost:		**$65.00**
1 hour labor	65.00	
Approximate dealer repair cost:		**$70.00**
1 hour labor	70.00	

Hardware affected: AppleColor High-Resolution RGB monitor.

Symptoms: There is a very noticeable red shadow in the upper right corner of the display.

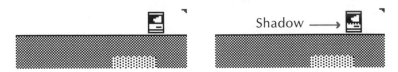

Typical history: No matter how you adjust the *H-STAT* and *V-TWIST* controls (located on the H board), you can't solve the problem.

Probable diagnosis: An unmarked coil, mounted horizontally on top of the CRT yoke, is out of adjustment.

Solution: Carefully adjust the unmarked coil until the red shadow disappears.

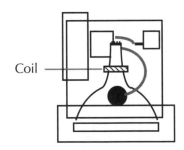

Approximate cost of repairing it yourself:		*1 hour*
Approximate third-party repair cost:		*$65.00*
1 hour labor	65.00	
Approximate dealer repair cost:		*$70.00*
1 hour labor	70.00	

Hardware affected: AppleColor High-Resolution RGB monitor.

Symptoms: There is a *very noticeable* blue shadow on the left side of the display. Other areas have thinner blue shadows.

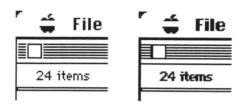

Typical history: No matter how you adjust the *H-STAT* and *V-TWIST* controls (on the H board), you can't solve the problem.

Probable diagnosis: The problem is on the C board.

Solution: Carefully adjust variable resistor RV703, labeled *H.STAT*, until the blue shadows disappear.

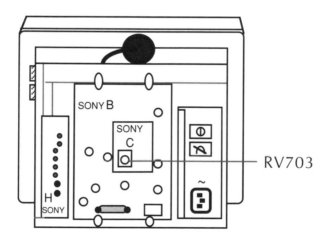

Approximate cost of repairing it yourself:	*1 hour*
Approximate third-party repair cost:	*$65.00*
1 hour labor 65.00	
Approximate dealer repair cost:	*$70.00*
1 hour labor 70.00	

Hardware affected: AppleColor High-Resolution RGB monitor.

Symptoms: All of a sudden, there seem to be colored blotches on the display.

Typical history: The problem occurred right after you lifted the monitor (to clean underneath it?) while the power was on.

Probable diagnosis: Moving the monitor without turning off the power magnetized the CRT.

Solution: Demagnetize the CRT by pressing the degauss switch.

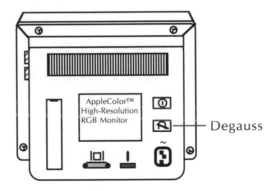

Approximate cost of repairing it yourself:		*1 min.*
Approximate third-party repair cost:		**$65.00**
1 hour labor	65.00	
Approximate dealer repair cost:		**$70.00**
1 hour labor	70.00	

Hardware affected: AppleColor High-Resolution RGB monitor.

Symptoms: The entire display is tinted red. Everything looks pink!

Probable diagnosis: The problem is on the B board.

Solution: Carefully adjust variable resistor RV711, labeled *R.BKG*, clockwise until the red tint just disappears. A *very slight* clockwise turn is generally all that's required.

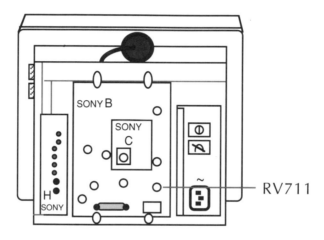

Approximate cost of repairing it yourself:		*1 hour*
Approximate third-party repair cost:		**$65.00**
1 hour labor	65.00	
Approximate dealer repair cost:		**$70.00**
1 hour labor	70.00	

Hardware affected: AppleColor High-Resolution RGB monitor.

Symptoms: The entire display is tinted green. Everything looks sick!

Probable diagnosis: The problem is on the B board.

Solution: Carefully adjust variable resistor RV721, labeled *G.BKG*, clockwise until the green tint just disappears. A *very slight* clockwise turn is generally all that's required.

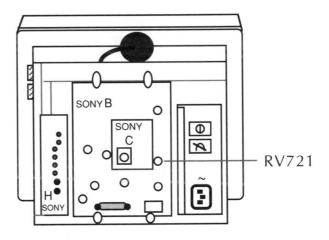

Approximate cost of repairing it yourself:		*1 hour*
Approximate third-party repair cost:		**$65.00**
1 hour labor	65.00	
Approximate dealer repair cost:		**$70.00**
1 hour labor	70.00	

Hardware affected: AppleColor High-Resolution RGB monitor.

Symptoms: The entire display is tinted blue. Everything looks cold!

Probable diagnosis: The problem is on the B board.

Solution: Carefully adjust variable resistor RV731, labeled *B.BKG*, clockwise until the blue tint just disappears. A *very slight* clockwise turn is generally all that's required.

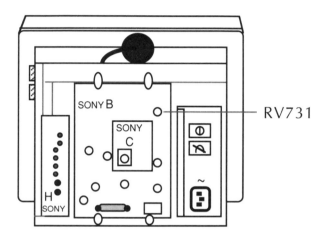

Approximate cost of repairing it yourself:		*1 hour*
Approximate third-party repair cost:		**$65.00**
1 hour labor	65.00	
Approximate dealer repair cost:		**$70.00**
1 hour labor	70.00	

Hardware affected: AppleColor High-Resolution RGB monitor.

Symptoms: After a short while, the monitor dies—the display collapses, and the green power LED goes out. Without a display, the whole computer becomes unusable.

Probable diagnosis: The problem is on the H board, located under the control cover plate at the back of the monitor.

Solution: Carefully turn variable resistor RV 702, labeled *CUT-OFF*, counterclockwise for a darker picture. If this fails to solve the problem, see the next entry.

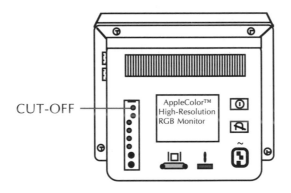

Approximate cost of repairing it yourself:		*1 min.*
Approximate third-party repair cost:		**$65.00**
1 hour labor	65.00	
Approximate dealer repair cost:		**$70.00**
1 hour labor	70.00	

Hardware affected: AppleColor High-Resolution RGB monitor.

Symptoms: After a short while, the monitor dies—the display collapses and the green power LED goes out. Without a display, the whole computer becomes unusable.

Typical history: Adjusting the *CUT-OFF* control (counterclockwise) did not solve the problem.

Probable diagnosis: The problem is in the high-voltage circuit.

Solution: Replace the red, high-voltage resistor (Sony part 1-230-666-12) located inside the monitor. Also see the prior entry.

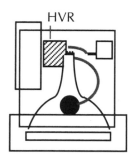

Approximate cost of repairing it yourself:		**$42.94**
1 HVR (Sony 1-230-666-12)	42.94	**1 hour**
Approximate third-party repair cost:		**$151.00**
1 HVR (Sony 1-230-666-12)	86.00	
1 hour labor	65.00	
Approximate dealer repair cost:		**$242.00**
1 HVC (Apple 910-0058)	172.00	
1 hour labor	70.00	

Hardware affected: AppleColor High-Resolution RGB monitor.

Symptoms: On powerup, the monitor clicks and the green light comes on, but there's no video.

Probable diagnosis: The brightness and contrast controls (located on the right side of the cabinet) have been inadvertently turned down.

Solution: Adjust the brightness and contrast controls. If that's not it, see the next entry.

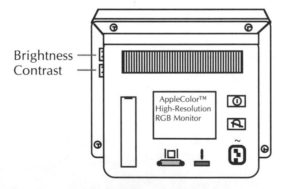

Approximate cost of repairing it yourself:		***1 min.***
Approximate third-party repair cost:		**$65.00**
1 hour labor	65.00	
Approximate dealer repair cost:		**$70.00**
1 hour labor	70.00	

Hardware affected: AppleColor High-Resolution RGB monitor.

Symptoms: On powerup, the monitor clicks and the green light comes on, but there's no video.

Typical history: Adjusting the brightness and contrast controls (located on the right side of the cabinet) had no effect.

Probable diagnosis: The problem is on the D board.

Solution: Check/replace the HZ3983 zener diode (39V) at board reference D504.

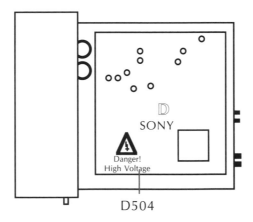

D504

Approximate cost of repairing it yourself:		
1 39V zener diode	1.00	*1 hour*
Approximate third-party repair cost:		*$70.00*
1 39V zener diode	5.00	
1 hour labor	65.00	
Approximate dealer repair cost:		*$316.67*
1 main logic board	246.67	
1 hour labor	70.00	

Hardware affected: AppleColor High-Resolution RGB monitor.

Symptoms: The display is noticeably off center. Otherwise, the monitor seems OK.

Probable diagnosis: The problem is on the H board.

Solution: Carefully turn the variable resistors labeled *H.CENT* and *V.CENT* until the display is centered on the screen.

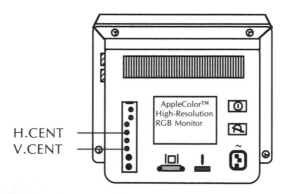

Approximate cost of repairing it yourself:		*5 min.*
Approximate third-party repair cost:		**$65.00**
1 hour labor	65.00	
Approximate dealer repair cost:		**$70.00**
1 hour labor	70.00	

Hardware affected: AppleColor High-Resolution RGB monitor.

Symptoms: The display is horizontally compressed. It lacks width.

Probable diagnosis: The problem is on the H board.

Solution: To restore the factory specified width based on 640 x 480 at 69 ppi, carefully turn the variable resistor labeled *WIDTH* until the display measures 9.28 inches wide.

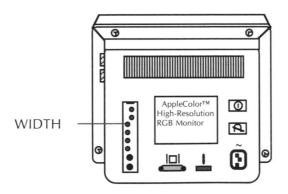

Approximate cost of repairing it yourself:	*5 min.*
Approximate third-party repair cost:	*$65.00*
1 hour labor 65.00	
Approximate dealer repair cost:	*$70.00*
1 hour labor 70.00	

Hardware affected: AppleColor High-Resolution RGB monitor.

Symptoms: The display is vertically compressed. It lacks height.

Probable diagnosis: The problem is on the H board.

Solution: To restore the factory specified height based on 640 x 480 at 69 ppi, carefully turn the variable resistor labeled *HEIGHT* until the display measures 6.96 inches high.

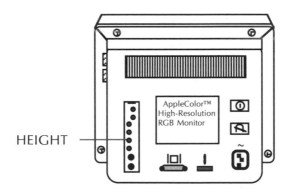

Approximate cost of repairing it yourself:		*5 min.*
Approximate third-party repair cost:		*$65.00*
1 hour labor	65.00	
Approximate dealer repair cost:		*$70.00*
1 hour labor	70.00	

Hardware affected: Apple High-Resolution Monochrome monitor.

Symptoms: The display is fine at 640 x 480, but when expanded to 672 x 512 or 704 x 512 using MaxAppleZoom (MAZ), it rolls from top to bottom (no vertical hold).

Probable diagnosis: The problem is on the H board, located under the control cover plate at the back of the monitor.

Solution: Carefully adjust the variable resistor labeled *V.HOLD* for a stable picture.

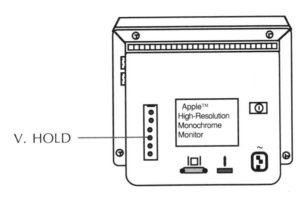

Approximate cost of repairing it yourself:		*1 min.*
Approximate third-party repair cost:		*$65.00*
1 hour labor	65.00	
Approximate dealer repair cost:		*$70.00*
1 hour labor	70.00	

Hardware affected: Apple High-Resolution Monochrome monitor.

Symptoms: The display is always out of focus.

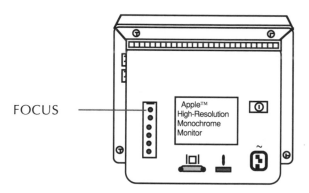

Probable diagnosis: The problem is on the H board, located under the control cover plate at the back of the monitor.

Solution: Carefully adjust the variable resistor, labeled *FOCUS*, for a sharp, clear picture.

FOCUS

Approximate cost of repairing it yourself:		*5 min.*
Approximate third-party repair cost:		**$65.00**
1 hour labor	65.00	
Approximate dealer repair cost:		**$70.00**
1 hour labor	70.00	

Hardware affected: Apple High-Resolution Monochrome monitor.

Symptoms: After a short while, the monitor dies—the display collapses and the green power LED goes out. Without a display, the whole computer becomes unusable.

Probable diagnosis: The problem is on the H board, located under the control cover plate at the back of the monitor.

Solution: Carefully turn the variable resistor labeled *CUT-OFF* counterclockwise for a darker picture.

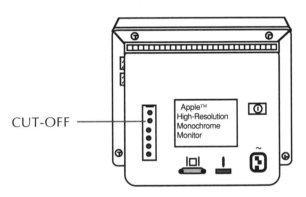

Approximate cost of repairing it yourself:		*1 min.*
Approximate third-party repair cost:		**$65.00**
1 hour labor	65.00	
Approximate dealer repair cost:		**$70.00**
1 hour labor	70.00	

Hardware affected: Apple High-Resolution Monochrome monitor.

Symptoms: On powerup, the monitor clicks and the green light comes on, but there's no video.

on

Probable diagnosis: The brightness and contrast controls (located on the right side of the cabinet) have been inadvertently turned down.

Solution: Adjust the brightness and contrast controls.

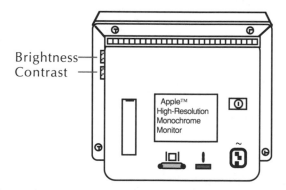

Approximate cost of repairing it yourself:	*1 min.*
Approximate third-party repair cost:	*$65.00*
1 hour labor	65.00
Approximate dealer repair cost:	*$70.00*
1 hour labor	70.00

Hardware affected: Apple High-Resolution Monochrome monitor.

Symptoms: The display is noticeably off center. Otherwise, the monitor seems OK.

Probable diagnosis: The problem is on the H board.

Solution: Carefully turn the variable resistor labeled *H.HOLD* until the display is centered on the screen.

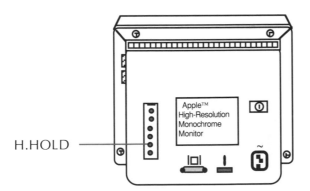

Approximate cost of repairing it yourself:	***5 min.***
Approximate third-party repair cost:	***$65.00***
1 hour labor 65.00	
Approximate dealer repair cost:	***$70.00***
1 hour labor 70.00	

Hardware affected: Apple High-Resolution Monochrome monitor.

Symptoms: The display is dark and horizontally compressed. It's dingy looking and it lacks width.

Probable diagnosis: The problem is on the H board.

Solution: To restore the factory specified width and appearance based on 640 x 480 at 76 ppi, carefully turn the variable resistor labeled *WIDTH* until the display measures 8.42 inches wide. Also see the next entry.

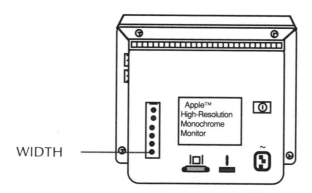

WIDTH

Approximate cost of repairing it yourself:		*5 min.*
Approximate third-party repair cost:		*$65.00*
1 hour labor	65.00	
Approximate dealer repair cost:		*$70.00*
1 hour labor	70.00	

Hardware affected: Apple High-Resolution Monochrome monitor.

Symptoms: The display is vertically compressed. It lacks height.

Probable diagnosis: The problem is on the H board, located under the control cover plate at the back of the monitor.

Solution: To restore the factory specified height based on 640 x 480 at 76 ppi, carefully turn the variable resistor labeled *HEIGHT* until the display measures 6.32 inches wide. Also see the prior entry.

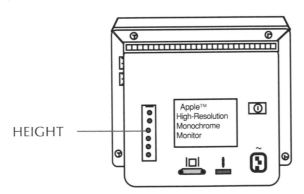

HEIGHT

Approximate cost of repairing it yourself:		*5 min.*
Approximate third-party repair cost:		**$65.00**
1 hour labor	65.00	
Approximate dealer repair cost:		**$70.00**
1 hour labor	70.00	

Hardware affected: Any external monitor connected to a Macintosh Plus, SE or SE/30.

Symptoms: There is a black line rippling through the display on the external monitor.

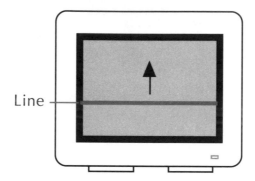

Line

Probable diagnosis: Radio frequency interference (RFI) emanating from the Macintosh analog board (located on the left side of the Mac's cabinet) is causing the line.

Solution: Relocate the external monitor to the right of the Macintosh. If the rippling line persists, separate the two by an additional twelve to eighteen inches.

Approximate cost of repairing it yourself:		***15 min.***
Approximate third-party repair cost:		***$65.00***
1 hour labor	65.00	
Approximate dealer repair cost:		***$70.00***
1 hour labor	70.00	

Hardware affected: Any primary or secondary monitor connected to a Macintosh II.

Symptoms: There is a black line rippling through the display on one or both of the monitors.

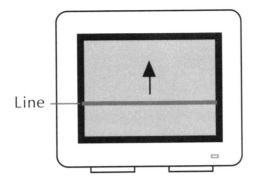

Line

Probable diagnosis: Radio frequency interference (RFI) emanating from one or both of the monitors is causing the line(s).

Solution: Reverse the location of the monitors. If the rippling persists, separate the two by an additional twelve to eighteen inches.

Approximate cost of repairing it yourself:		*15 min.*
Approximate third-party repair cost:		*$65.00*
1 hour labor	65.00	
Approximate dealer repair cost:		*$70.00*
1 hour labor	70.00	

Hardware affected: Any VGA monitor.

Symptoms: The supplied video cable does not mate with the 15-pin video connector built into a Macintosh L

Probable diagnosis: The monitor was supplied with a standard VGA cable for PC use. VGA cables have high-density 15-pin connectors.

Solution: Construct a Mac LC to VGA monitor adapter as shown. *In addition, jumper pin 7 to pin 10 on the Apple end.*

VGA End (DB15HD-S)	Apple End (DB15-P)
1 Red	2 Red
2 Green	5 Green
3 Blue	9 Blue
6 Ground	1 Red return
7 Ground	6 Green return
8 Ground	13 Blue return
10 Ground	14 Hsync return
13 Hsync	15 Hsync
14 Vsync	12 Vsync

Approximate cost of repairing it yourself:		**$3.16**
1 DB15-P (plug)	0.55	**1 hour**
1 DB15-H (hood)	0.39	
1 DB15HD-S (socket)	1.50	
1 DB9-H/15HD-H (hood)	0.39	
1 foot of 10-conductor cable	0.33	
Approximate third-party repair cost:		**$38.50**
miscellaneous materials	6.00	
½ hour labor (flat rate)	32.50	
Approximate dealer repair cost:		**$500.00**
1 12-inch Apple RGB monitor	500.00	

Hardware affected: Goldstar 1450 Plus Multiscan monitor.

Symptoms: The supplied cable does not mate with an Apple Macintosh II video card. The 15-pin connector is too small.

Probable diagnosis: The monitor was supplied with a standard VGA cable for PC use. VGA cables have high-density 15-pin connectors.

Solution: Cut off the supplied DB15-HDP (D-sub, 15-pin, high-density, plug) and rewire the Apple end of the cable as shown (or make a DB15HD-S to DB15-P adapter).

Goldstar End (DB15HD-S)		Apple End (DB15-P)	
1	Red	2	Red
2	Green	5	Green
3	Blue	9	Blue
6	Ground	1	Red return
7	Ground	6	Green return
8	Ground	13	Blue return
S	Shell (Ground)	4	Csync return

Approximate cost of repairing it yourself:		**94¢**
1 DB15-P (D-sub, 15-pin, plug)	0.55	**1 hour**
1 DB15-H (D-sub, 15-pin, hood)	0.39	
Approximate third-party repair cost:		**$34.50**
1 DB15-P (D-sub, 15-pin, plug)	1.00	
1 DB15-H (D-sub, 15-pin, hood)	1.00	
½ hour labor (flat rate)	32.50	
Approximate dealer repair cost:		**$995.00**
1 AppleColor RGB monitor	995.00	

Hardware affected: Packard Bell PB 1272A, Samsung MG 2565 and other 12-inch TTL monitors built on the MG 2565 chassis.

Symptoms: Does not work properly (no horizontal sync) with the TTL video card described in *Macintosh Repair & Upgrade Secrets.*

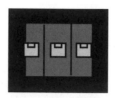

Typical history: The same monitor works fine when connected to a PC-compatible TTL video card.

Probable diagnosis: The PCB has to be modified for Macintosh use.

Solution: Replace OEM resistor R606 (10K, ¼-watt, 5%) with a 6.8K, ¼-watt, 5% resistor. Replace OEM resistor R602 (10K, ¼-watt, 5%) labeled *H-POSIT* with a 10K vertical-style trimmer potentiometer (RS 271-218). Adjust the *H-HOLD, V-HOLD, V-SIZE, H-WIDTH, H-POSIT* and *LINEARITY* controls for a stable, full-screen picture.

Approximate cost of repairing it yourself:		*78¢*
1 10K vertical trimmer potentiometer	.69	*30 min.*
1 6.8K ¼-watt, 5% resistor	.09	
Approximate third-party repair cost:		*$75.00*
miscellaneous small parts	10.00	
1 hour labor	65.00	
Approximate dealer repair cost:		*$470.00*
1 new Mac monitor upgrade	400.00	
1 hour labor	70.00	

Hardware affected: Princeton Max 15 Multiscan monitor.

Symptoms: The supplied cable does not mate with an Apple Macintosh II Video Card. The 15-pin connector is too small.

Probable diagnosis: The monitor was supplied with a standard VGA cable for PC use. VGA cables have high-density 15-pin connectors.

Solution: Cut off the supplied DB15-HDP (D-sub, 15-pin, high-density, plug) and rewire the Apple end of the cable as shown (or make a new DB25-P to DB15-P cable).

Princeton End (DB25-P)	Apple End (DB15-P)
11 Red	2 Red
12 Green	5 Green
13 Blue	9 Blue
16 Ground	1 Red return
17 Ground	6 Green return
18 Ground	13 Blue return
20 Ground	4 Csync return

Approximate cost of repairing it yourself:		**94¢**
1 DB15-P (D-sub, 15-pin, plug)	0.55	**1 hour**
1 DB15-H (D-sub, 15-pin, hood)	0.39	
Approximate third-party repair cost:		**$34.50**
1 DB15-P (D-sub, 15-pin, plug)	1.00	
1 DB15-H (D-sub, 15-pin, hood)	1.00	
½ hour labor (flat rate)	32.50	
Approximate dealer repair cost:		**$300.00**
1 12-inch Apple		
Monochrome monitor	300.00	

Hardware affected: Samsung MG 2525 12-inch TTL monitor.

Symptoms: Does not work properly (no horizontal sync) with the build-it-yourself TTL video card described in *Macintosh Repair & Upgrade Secrets.*

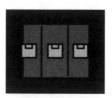

Typical history: The same monitor works fine when connected to a PC-compatible TTL video card.

Probable diagnosis: The PCB at the bottom of the Samsung monitor has to be modified for Macintosh use.

Solution: Replace OEM resistor R304 with a 10K, ¼-watt, 5% resistor. Readjust the H-HOLD and V-HOLD controls for a stable picture.

Approximate cost of repairing it yourself:		*09¢*
1 10K ¼-watt, 5% resistor	.09	*30 min.*
Approximate third-party repair cost:		*$70.00*
1 10K ¼-watt, 5% resistor	5.00	
1 hour labor	65.00	
Approximate dealer repair cost:		*$470.00*
1 new Mac monitor upgrade	400.00	
1 hour labor	70.00	

Hardware affected: Sony CPD 1302 Multiscan monitor.

Symptoms: The sides of the video display curve inward (showing pincushion distortion).

Probable diagnosis: The problem is on the D board.

Solution: Adjust variable resistor RV504, labeled *PINAMP*, for a square picture.

Approximate cost of repairing it yourself:		*1 hour*
Approximate third-party repair cost:		*$65.00*
1 hour labor	65.00	
Approximate dealer repair cost:		*$70.00*
1 hour labor	70.00	

Hardware affected: Sony CPD 1302 Multiscan monitor.

Symptoms: After a while, the vertical height collapses to approximately 66% of normal size. Tapping the cabinet may or may not restore the full height.

Probable diagnosis: The problem is on the H board.

Solution: Clean/replace variable resistor RV 804, Sony part 1-237-359-11 (res. var. carbon 5K).

Approximate cost of repairing it yourself:		**$1.46**
1 Sony part 1-237-359-11	1.46	**30 min.**
Approximate third-party repair cost:		**$70.00**
1 Sony part 1-237-359-11	5.00	
1 hour labor	65.00	
Approximate dealer repair cost:		**$120.00**
1 new H board	50.00	
1 hour labor	70.00	

Hardware affected: Sony CPD 1302 Multiscan monitor.

Symptoms: The monitor will not switch off.

Probable diagnosis: The SPDT power switch is broken.

Solution: Rewire/replace S901, Sony part 1-572-599-11 (switch seesaw AC power) .

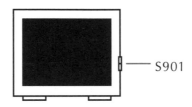

S901

Approximate cost of repairing it yourself:		*$12.36*
1 Sony part 1-572-599-11	12.36	*30 min.*
Approximate third-party repair cost:		*$90.00*
1 Sony part 1-572-599-11	25.00	
1 hour labor	65.00	
Approximate dealer repair cost:		*$120.00*
1 Sony part 1-572-599-11	50.00	
1 hour labor	70.00	

Hardware affected: Sony CPD 1302 Multiscan monitor.

Symptoms: The supplied cable does not mate with an Apple Macintosh II Video Card. The 15-pin connector is too small. The monitor is useless.

Probable diagnosis: The monitor was supplied with a standard VGA cable for PC use. VGA cables have high-density 15-pin connectors.

Solution: Cut off the supplied DB15-HDP (D-sub, 15-pin, high-density, plug). Rewire the Apple end of the cable as shown. Set the monitor's RGB input-selector switch (located under the service panel at the back of the monitor) to analog, *not* digital.

Sony End (DB9-P)	Apple End (DB15-P)
1 Ground	1 Red return
1 Ground	4 Csync return
3 Red	2 Red
4 Green	5 Green
5 Blue	9 Blue

Approximate cost of repairing it yourself:		**94¢**
1 DB15-P (D-sub, 15-pin, plug)	0.55	**1 hour**
1 DB15-H (D-sub, 15-pin, hood)	0.39	
Approximate third-party repair cost:		**$34.50**
1 DB15-P (D-sub, 15-pin, plug)	1.00	
1 DB15-H (D-sub, 15-pin, hood)	1.00	
1 ½ hour labor (flat rate)	32.50	
Approximate dealer repair cost:		**$995.00**
1 AppleColor RGB monitor	995.00	

Hardware affected: Sony CPD 1302 Multiscan monitor.

Symptoms: The existing Mac II cable does not work on a Mac SE equipped with an Orchid ColorVue SE video card.

Typical history: This same monitor and cable combination works fine on a Macintosh II equipped with an Apple Mac II Video Card.

Probable diagnosis: The composite-synch lines were never connected in the Sony CPD 1302 to Mac II cable.

Solution: Use a ready-made Sony CPD 1302 to VGA cable (and hook up to the VGA connector on the ColorVue SE card) or rewire the existing Mac II cable as shown (italics indicate where changes are to be made).

Sony End (DB9-P)	Apple End (DB15-P)
1 Ground	1 Red return
1 Ground	4 Csync return
1 Ground	*6 Green return*
1 Ground	*13 Blue return*
3 Red	2 Red
4 Green	5 Green
5 Blue	9 Blue
8 Csync	*3 Csync*

Approximate cost of repairing it yourself:		***30 min.***
Approximate third-party repair cost:		***$32.50***
½ hour labor (flat rate)	32.50	
Approximate dealer repair cost:		***$995.00***
1 AppleColor RGB monitor	995.00	

CHAPTER 7

IMAGEWRITER I (STANDARD & WIDE)

Symptoms: The Select lamp lights and the printer is properly selected in the Chooser, but it doesn't respond to *Print...* commands. The built-in self-test *does* work.

Typical history: This same printer works fine on an Apple II, II+ or IIe and/or on a Mac 128K, 512K or 512Ke, but it doesn't work when connected to a Mac Plus, SE, II, Classic or LC.

Probable diagnosis: The DIP switches are incorrectly set for all-around Mac use.

Solution: Position the DIP switches inside the ImageWriter exactly as shown. If that doesn't do it, see the next entry.

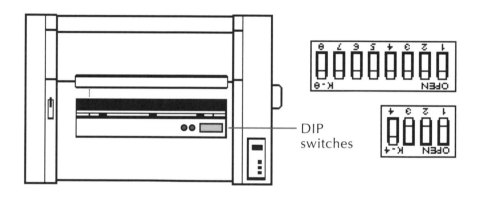

DIP switches

Approximate cost of repairing it yourself:		5 min.
Approximate third-party repair cost:		**$65.00**
1 hour labor	65.00	
Approximate dealer repair cost:		**$70.00**
1 hour labor	70.00	

Symptoms: The Select lamp lights and the printer is properly selected in the Chooser, but it doesn't respond to *Print...* commands. The built-in self-test *does* work.

Typical history: The DIP switch settings agree with the prior entry.

Probable diagnosis: The miniDIN8-P to DB25-P serial cable is wired for Mac-to-modem use (not Mac-to-printer use).

Solution: Check/rewire the existing miniDIN8-P to DB25-P cable as shown or (if available) substitute a Mac-to-serial printer cable that you know works. If that still doesn't do it, see the next entry.

Mac End (miniDIN8-P)	ImageWriter End (DB25-P)
2 DSR	20 DTR
3 TXD-	3 RxD
4 SG	7 SG
5 RXD-	2 TxD
8 RXD+	7 SG
F Ground	F Ground

Approximate cost of repairing it yourself:		***$10.00***
1 Mac-to-serial printer cable	10.00	***5 min.***
Approximate third-party repair cost:		***$65.00***
1 hour labor	65.00	
Approximate dealer repair cost:		***$110.00***
1 Mac-to-serial printer cable	40.00	
1 hour labor	70.00	

Symptoms: The Select lamp lights and the printer is properly selected in the Chooser, but it doesn't respond to *Print...* commands. The built-in self-test *does* work.

Typical history: The Mac and the miniDIN8-P to DB25-P cable are known to be OK because both work fine with other ImageWriter printers. The current ImageWriter DIP switch settings are correct.

Probable diagnosis: The problem is on the ImageWriter logic board.

Solution: Replace the 74LS393N IC (14-pin DIP, dual 4-bit binary ripple counter) at board reference IC12. Also see the prior entry.

Approximate cost of repairing it yourself:		79¢
1 74LS393N IC	.79	*1 hour*
Approximate third-party repair cost:		**$70.00**
1 74LS393N IC	5.00	
1 hour labor	65.00	
Approximate dealer repair cost:		**$315.00**
1 new main logic board	245.00	
1 hour labor	70.00	

Symptoms: The Select lamp *does not* light, the printer *does not* respond to *Print...* commands and the built-in self-test *does not* work.

Probable diagnosis: The carrier cover is incorrectly positioned, or the safety magnet (underneath the carrier cover) is missing.

Solution: Check/reposition the carrier cover. Check the safety magnet. Verify the operation of the reed switch (normally activated by the carrier cover magnet) with a small crafts magnet. If everything under the carrier cover checks OK, see the next entry.

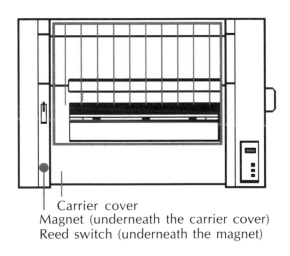

Carrier cover
Magnet (underneath the carrier cover)
Reed switch (underneath the magnet)

Approximate cost of repairing it yourself:		***49¢***
1 crafts magnet	.49	***10 min.***
Approximate third-party repair cost:		***$70.00***
1 safety magnet	5.00	
1 hour labor	65.00	
Approximate dealer repair cost:		***$115.00***
1 new carrier cover	45.00	
1 hour labor	70.00	

Symptoms: The Select lamp *does not* light, the Printer *does not* respond to *Print...* commands and the built-in self-test *does not* work.

Typical history: The carrier cover is on the printer. The carrier cover magnet is present. The reed switch seems to work.

Probable diagnosis: The problem is on the ImageWriter logic board.

Solution: Check for loose metallic objects (coins, hair pins, paper clips) inside the printer. Check/replace the 5 A glass fuse (AGC 5) at board reference FU3. If that still doesn't do it, see the next entry.

Approximate cost of repairing it yourself:		49¢
1 5A fuse (AGC 5)	.49	*1 hour*
Approximate third-party repair cost:		**$70.00**
1 5A fuse (AGC 5)	5.00	
1 hour labor	65.00	
Approximate dealer repair cost:		**$315.00**
1 new main logic board	245.00	
1 hour labor	70.00	

Symptoms: The Select lamp *does not* light, the printer *does not* respond to *Print...* commands. The built-in self-test *does not* work.

Typical history: The carrier cover is on the printer. The carrier-cover magnet is present. The reed switch seems to work. No metallic objects were found inside the printer. The fuses have been tested, and they all check good.

Probable diagnosis: The problem is on the ImageWriter logic board.

Solution: Check/replace the 8085A-2 IC (40-pin CPU, 8-bit, N-channel, 5MHz) at board reference IC10. Also see the prior entry.

Approximate cost of repairing it yourself:		*$3.59*
1 8085A-2 IC	3.59	*1 hour*
Approximate third-party repair cost:		*$72.18*
1 8085A-2 IC	7.18	
1 hour labor	65.00	
Approximate dealer repair cost:		*$315.00*
1 new main logic board	245.00	
1 hour labor	70.00	

Symptoms: The Select lamp *does* light and the printer responds to *Print...* commands, but there is no line feed. The carrier motor works, the typehead fires and the ribbon deck goes back and forth, but every line prints on top of the prior line. The Form Feed button *does* work, but the Line Feed button *does not* work. Except for the line-feed problem, the built-in self-test also works.

Probable diagnosis: The problem is on the ImageWriter logic board.

Solution: Check/replace the SN 7406 IC (14-pin DIP, hex inverter buffer/driver, open collector, high voltage) at board reference IC4.

Approximate cost of repairing it yourself:		*39¢*
1 SN 7406 IC	.39	*1 hour*
Approximate third-party repair cost:		**$70.00**
1 SN 7406 IC	5.00	
1 hour labor	65.00	
Approximate dealer repair cost:		**$315.00**
1 new main logic board	245.00	
1 hour labor	70.00	

Symptoms: The printer makes a horrible grinding noise. It prints a few lines, stutters and then stalls.

Probable diagnosis: The carrier shaft and the carriage guide rail are so dry and gritty that the carriage return motor can barely move the ribbon deck back and forth.

Solution: Clean and lubricate the carrier shaft and the carriage guide rail.

Shaft—————

Rail —————
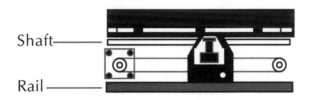

Approximate cost of repairing it yourself:	*30 min.*
Approximate third-party repair cost:	*$65.00*
1 hour labor 65.00	
Approximate dealer repair cost:	*$70.00*
1 hour labor 70.00	

Symptoms: The unit makes an unusually loud *clunk..., clunk..., clunk...* noise when printing. Other than the loud, rhythmic clunking, the printer works OK.

Probable diagnosis: Torque resulting from the carriage return is causing a loose carrier motor to rap against the printer cabinet.

Solution: Loosen the carrier motor screws, and reposition the carrier motor. If that doesn't work, lift up the printer and place a small foam pad (made from scrap packing material) between the carrier motor and the printer table. When the pad is compressed by the weight of the printer, it will lift the motor and dampen the clunking noise.

Motor———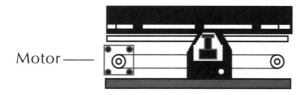

Approximate cost of repairing it yourself:		*30 min.*
Approximate third-party repair cost:		**$65.00**
1 hour labor	65.00	
Approximate dealer repair cost:		**$47.04**
1 new carrier motor	47.04	
1 hour labor	70.00	

Symptoms: The ribbon cartridge deck makes a scraping noise as it moves from side to side. Printed pages contain regularly spaced horizontal scratch marks (even in the white spaces).

abcdefghijklmnopqrstuvwxyzabcdefghijklmnopqrstuvwxyz

abcdefghijklmnopqrstuvwxyz

abcdefghijklmnopqrstuvwxyz

Probable diagnosis: The ribbon guide plate (on the typehead) is torn. A metal hangnail is catching on the paper stock.

Solution: Replace the ribbon guide plate (C. Itoh CLA20-13801).

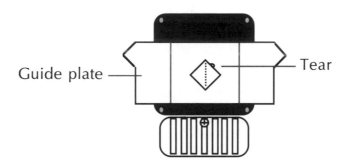

Guide plate ——   —— Tear

Approximate cost of repairing it yourself:		*$1.00*
1 ribbon guide plate	1.00	*30 min.*
Approximate third-party repair cost:		*$70.00*
1 ribbon guide plate	5.00	
1 hour labor	65.00	
Approximate dealer repair cost:		*$243.33*
1 new printhead assembly	173.33	
1 hour labor	70.00	

Symptoms: The first line printed on every page is squashed.

The first line printed on every page is squashed.
The second and every other line printed is fine.

Probable diagnosis: The roller shaft assembly is so dry and gritty that it's causing the paper to buckle.

Solution: Clean and lubricate the roller shaft. If that doesn't do it, see the next entry.

Roller shaft —

Approximate cost of repairing it yourself:		*30 min.*
Approximate third-party repair cost:		**$65.00**
1 hour labor	65.00	
Approximate dealer repair cost:		**$70.00**
1 hour labor	70.00	

Symptoms: The first line printed on every page is squashed.

The first line printed on every page is squashed.
The second and every other line printed is fine.

Typical history: Servicing the roller shaft didn't fix the problem.

Probable diagnosis: The clear plastic noise cover is warped. The weight of the bent plastic is pressing on the paper.

Solution: Lift the weight by sticking a small foam pad between the noise cover and the carrier cover. Also see the prior entry.

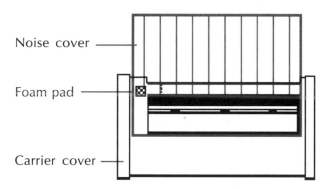

Noise cover

Foam pad

Carrier cover

Approximate cost of repairing it yourself:		*5 min.*
Approximate third-party repair cost:		*$65.00*
1 hour labor	65.00	
Approximate dealer repair cost:		*$115.00*
1 new noise cover	45.00	
1 hour labor	70.00	

Symptoms: There are regularly spaced missing dots in the printout.

There are regularly spaced missing dots in the printout.
There are regularly spaced missing dots in the printout.

Probable diagnosis: The contacts on the typehead PCB are dirty.

Solution: Clean the contacts with a pencil eraser. If that doesn't do it, see the next entry.

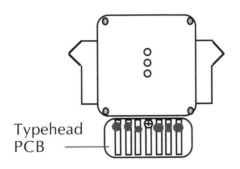

Typehead
PCB

Approximate cost of repairing it yourself:		5 min.
Approximate third-party repair cost:		**$65.00**
1 hour labor	65.00	
Approximate dealer repair cost:		**$243.33**
1 new printhead assembly	173.33	
1 hour labor	70.00	

Symptoms: There are regularly spaced missing dots in the printout.

There are regularly spaced missing dots in the printout.
There are regularly spaced missing dots in the printout.

Typical history: Cleaning the typehead PCB made no difference.

Probable diagnosis: One of the striker wires in the typehead is rusty. The wire is hanging on the plastic ribbon guide (instead of slipping through and onto the paper).

Solution: Spray the ribbon guide with a drop or two of WD-40. Let it soak in for several hours (preferably overnight) before reinstalling the typehead. If that still doesn't do it, see the next entry.

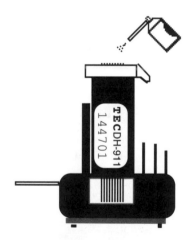

Approximate cost of repairing it yourself:		**5 min.**
Approximate third-party repair cost:		**$65.00**
1 hour labor	65.00	
Approximate dealer repair cost:		**$243.33**
1 new printhead assembly	173.33	
1 hour labor	70.00	

Symptoms: There are regularly spaced missing dots in the printout.

Typical history: Cleaning the contacts on the typehead made no difference. Lubricating the ribbon guide didn't help.

There are regularly spaced missing dots in the printout.
There are regularly spaced missing dots in the printout.

Probable diagnosis: One of the striker wires in the typehead is bent or broken, and/or one of the return springs is weak.

Solution: Send out the typehead (not the whole printer) to a service depot for repair. Also see the prior entry.

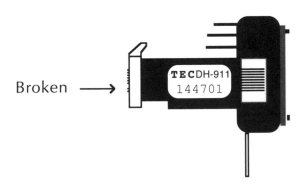

Broken ⟶

TECDH-911
144701

Approximate cost of repairing it yourself:		**$38.00**
1 typehead repair	38.00	**5 min.**
Approximate third-party repair cost:		**$141.00**
1 rebuilt typehead	76.00	
1 hour labor	65.00	
Approximate dealer repair cost:		**$243.33**
1 new printhead assembly	173.33	
1 hour labor	70.00	

Symptoms: Best quality printing is wavy. Vertical lines are uneven.

Best quality printing is wavy. Vertical lines are uneven.
Best quality printing is wavy. Vertical lines are uneven.

Probable diagnosis: The character deviation is out of adjustment.

Solution: Adjust variable resistor VR1 (located under the carrier cover) for best linearity. If that doesn't do it, see the next entry.

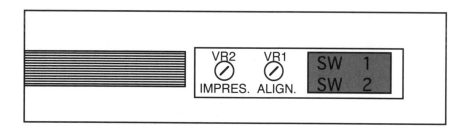

Approximate cost of repairing it yourself:		*10 min.*
Approximate third-party repair cost:		*$65.00*
1 hour labor	65.00	
Approximate dealer repair cost:		*$70.00*
1 hour labor	70.00	

Symptoms: Best quality printing is wavy. Vertical lines are uneven.

Best quality printing is wavy. Vertical lines are uneven.
Best quality printing is wavy. Vertical lines are uneven.

Typical history: Adjusting VR1 (see previous entry) did not completely eliminate the problem.

Probable diagnosis: The carrier-wire tension is too loose.

Solution: Adjust the carrier-wire tension lever (located under the cabinet top), then readjust VR1 (see previous entry). If that still doesn't do it, see the next entry.

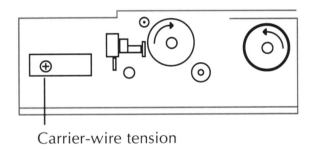

Carrier-wire tension

Approximate cost of repairing it yourself:		*1 hour*
Approximate third-party repair cost:		*$65.00*
1 hour labor	65.00	
Approximate dealer repair cost:		*$70.00*
1 hour labor	70.00	

Symptoms: Best quality printing is wavy. Vertical lines are uneven.

Best quality printing is wavy. Vertical lines are uneven.
Best quality printing is wavy. Vertical lines are uneven.

Typical history: Adjusting the carrier tension and readjusting VR1 didn't seem to make any difference.

Probable diagnosis: The striker wires in the typehead are out of vertical alignment.

Solution: Send out the typehead (not the whole printer) to a service depot for repair.

Striker wires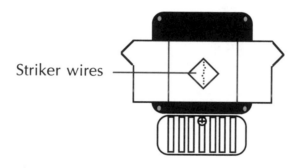

Approximate cost of repairing it yourself:		**$38.00**
1 typehead repair	38.00	**5 min.**
Approximate third-party repair cost:		**$141.00**
1 rebuilt typehead	76.00	
1 hour labor	65.00	
Approximate dealer repair cost:		**$243.33**
1 new printhead assembly	173.33	
1 hour labor	70.00	

Symptoms: The printout is too light.

The printout is too light. The printout is too light. The printout is too light. The printout is too light.

Probable diagnosis: The paper thickness lever is too far back.

Solution: Move the paper thickness lever closer to the platen. If that doesn't do it, see the next entry.

Paper thickness lever

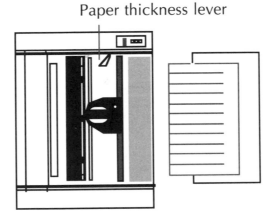

Approximate cost of repairing it yourself:		*1 min.*
Approximate third-party repair cost:		*$65.00*
1 hour labor	65.00	
Approximate dealer repair cost:		*$70.00*
1 hour labor	70.00	

Symptoms: The printout is too light.

The printout is too light. The printout is too light. The printout is too light. The printout is too light.

Typical history: The paper thickness lever has been checked and it's correctly positioned.

Probable diagnosis: The ribbon cassette is dry or worn out. (Many ImageWriters are still equipped with their original ribbons!)

Solution: Replace the ribbon cassette, C. Itoh part CLABK-12802. Also see the prior entry.

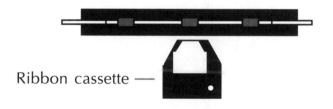

Ribbon cassette —

Approximate cost of repairing it yourself:		*$1.69*
1 ribbon cassette	1.69	*1 min.*
Approximate third-party repair cost:		*$70.00*
1 ribbon cassette	5.00	
1 hour labor	65.00	
Approximate dealer repair cost:		*$82.00*
1 ribbon cassette	12.00	
1 hour labor	70.00	

Symptoms: There are intermittent dropouts in the printout. Some areas are dark, and some areas are light.

There are intermittent dropouts in the printout.
Some areas are dark, and some areas are light.

Probable diagnosis: The ribbon cassette is worn or defective.

Solution: Replace the ribbon cassette.

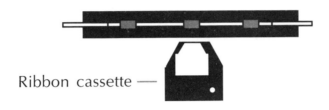

Ribbon cassette —

Approximate cost of repairing it yourself:		$1.69
1 ribbon cassette	1.69	1 min.
Approximate third-party repair cost:		$70.00
1 ribbon cassette	5.00	
1 hour labor	65.00	
Approximate dealer repair cost:		$82.00
1 ribbon cassette	12.00	
1 hour labor	70.00	

Symptoms: After a few pages, the pin-feed paper derails and the printer jams.

Probable diagnosis: The release lever is positioned for friction-feed paper (not pin-feed).

Solution: Push the release lever toward the pin-feed icon.

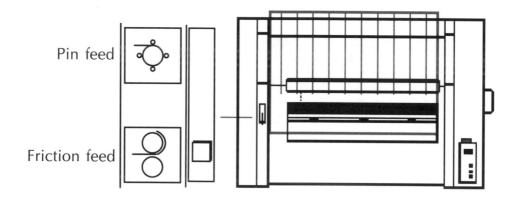

Approximate cost of repairing it yourself:	*1 min.*
Approximate third-party repair cost:	**$65.00**
1 hour labor 65.00	
Approximate dealer repair cost:	**$70.00**
1 hour labor 70.00	

Symptoms: Printing doesn't stop when the paper runs out. Instead, it continues right across the platen.

This printer does not stop when the paper runs out.

It continues printing, right across the platen.

Probable diagnosis: The paper error detector is malfunctioning. Most likely, a mailing label got stuck under the platen and the detector arm is jammed by a piece that's still in there.

Solution: Remove the platen. Clear the stuck mailing label. Check/reposition the paper error detector.

—— Paper error detector

Label remains

Approximate cost of repairing it yourself:	*1 hour*
Approximate third-party repair cost:	*$65.00*
1 hour labor 65.00	
Approximate dealer repair cost:	*$70.00*
1 hour labor 70.00	

Symptoms: It's hard to load paper. Something seems to be blocking the paper path.

Probable diagnosis: Most likely, a mailing label is or was stuck under the platen and/or the arm on the paper-error detector is bent.

Solution: Remove the platen. Clear the label jam. Check/reposition the paper-error detector.

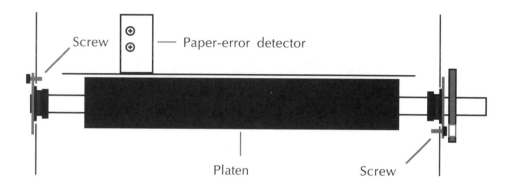

Approximate cost of repairing it yourself:		*1 hour*
Approximate third-party repair cost:		**$65.00**
1 hour labor	65.00	
Approximate dealer repair cost:		**$70.00**
1 hour labor	70.00	

Symptoms: Cut-sheet paper slips and lines overprint in friction-feed mode.

Cut-sheet paper slips and lines overprint in friction feed mode.
Cut-sheet paper slips and lines overprint in friction feed mode.
Cut-sheet paper slips and lines overprint in friction feed mode.
Cut-sheet paper slips and lines overprint in friction feed mode.

Probable diagnosis: The platen is slipping. It's lost its grip!

Solution: Restore the platen grip with liquid tape-recorder rubber cleaner, Teac RC1 or equivalent, and a clean cotton rag.

Platen ———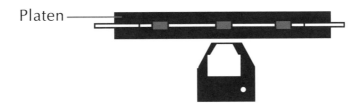

Approximate cost of repairing it yourself:		*15 min.*
Approximate third-party repair cost:		**$65.00**
1 hour labor	65.00	
Approximate dealer repair cost:		**$70.00**
1 hour labor	70.00	

CHAPTER 8
IMAGEWRITER II

Symptoms: The Select lamp *does not* light, the printer *does not* respond to *Print...* commands and the built-in self-test *does not* work.

Probable diagnosis: The front cover is incorrectly positioned, or the safety magnet (underneath the front cover) is missing.

Solution: Check/reposition the front cover. Check the safety magnet. Verify the operation of the reed switch (normally activated by the front cover magnet) with a small crafts magnet. If everything under the front cover checks OK, see the next entry.

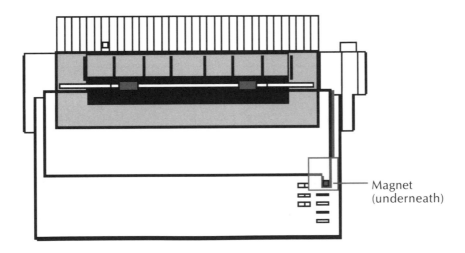

Magnet (underneath)

Approximate cost of repairing it yourself:		49¢
1 crafts magnet	.49	*10 min.*
Approximate third-party repair cost:		**$70.00**
1 safety magnet	5.00	
1 hour labor	65.00	
Approximate dealer repair cost:		**$115.00**
1 new front cover	45.00	
1 hour labor	70.00	

Symptoms: The Select lamp *does not* light and the unit *does not* respond to *Print...* commands. The built-in self-test *does not* work.

Probable diagnosis: The problem is on the ImageWriter II logic board.

Solution: Check/replace the EC-A056 IC (64-pin MOS CPU), C. Itoh part EAO-06-64300, at board reference IC9.

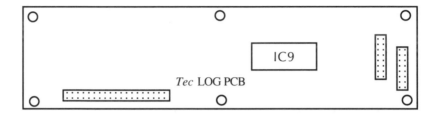

Approximate cost of repairing it yourself:		$21.78
1 EC-A056 IC	21.78	*1 hour*
Approximate third-party repair cost:		$107.00
1 CPU IC	42.00	
1 hour labor	65.00	
Approximate dealer repair cost:		$251.67
1 new main PCB board	181.67	
1 hour labor	70.00	

Symptoms: The Select lamp *does* light, and the unit responds to *Print...* commands, but there's no line feed. The carrier motor works, the print head fires and the ribbon cartridge deck goes back and forth, but every line prints on top of the prior line. The Form Feed button *does* work, but the Line Feed button *does not* work. Except for the line-feed problem, the built-in self-test also works.

Probable diagnosis: The problem is on the ImageWriter II driver PCB.

Solution: Check/replace the 27B1 (25V, 1W) zener diode, ECG5082A, at board reference ZD3, and check/replace the radial electrolytic capacitor (2,200 mfd, 35/44V) Digi-Key part P5262, at board reference C11. If there's still no line feed, see the next entry.

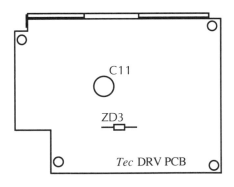

Approximate cost of repairing it yourself:		$3.69
1 25V, 1W zener diode	1.00	*1 hour*
1 2,200 mfd, 35/44V capacitor	2.69	
Approximate third-party repair cost:		**$75.00**
miscellaneous parts	10.00	
1 hour labor	65.00	
Approximate dealer repair cost:		**$206.67**
1 new power supply board	136.67	
1 hour labor	70.00	

Symptoms: The Select lamp *does* light, and the unit responds to *Print...* commands, but there's no line feed. The carrier motor works, the print head fires and the ribbon cartridge deck goes back and forth, but every line prints on top of the prior line. The Form Feed button *does* work, but the Line Feed button *does not* work. Except for the line-feed problem, the built-in self-test also works.

Typical history: Zener diode ZD3 and capacitor C11 on the power supply/driver board have been checked, and they're both OK.

Probable diagnosis: The problem is on the ImageWriter II logic board.

Solution: Check/replace the SN 7406 IC (hex inverter buffer/driver, open collector, high voltage) at board reference IC8. Also see the prior entry.

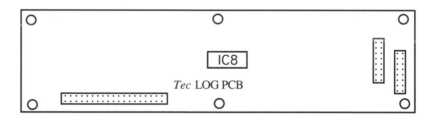

Approximate cost of repairing it yourself:		39¢
1 SN 7406 IC	.39	*1 hour*
Approximate third-party repair cost:		$70.00
1 SN 7406 IC	5.00	
1 hour labor	65.00	
Approximate dealer repair cost:		$251.67
1 new main PCB board	181.67	
1 hour labor	70.00	

Symptoms: An ImageWriter II equipped with an AppleTalk Option Card does not show up in the Chooser or Choose Printer DA.

Probable diagnosis: The problem is on the AppleTalk Option Card (inside the ImageWriter II).

Solution: Check/replace the SN 74LS245N IC (20-pin DIP, octal bus transceiver, noninverting) at board reference U8 (on the AppleTalk Option Card inside the ImageWriter II).

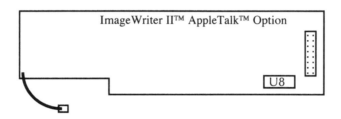

Approximate cost of repairing it yourself:		79¢
1 74LS245N IC	.79	*1 hour*
Approximate third-party repair cost:		**$70.00**
1 74LS245N IC	5.00	
1 hour labor	65.00	
Approximate dealer repair cost:		**$211.67**
1 new LocalTalk Card	141.67	
1 hour labor	70.00	

Symptoms: The red error light on the control panel is lit, even though there's paper in the printer.

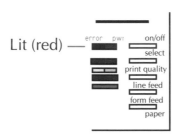

Lit (red) ——

Probable diagnosis: The paper is too far to the right. It's not being detected by the paper error sensor, which is located on the left side of the platen.

Solution: Move the paper to the left. Center it on the platen.

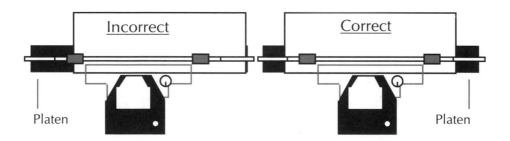

Approximate cost of repairing it yourself:		*1 min.*
Approximate third-party repair cost:		**$65.00**
1 hour labor	65.00	
Approximate dealer repair cost:		**$70.00**
1 hour labor	70.00	

Symptoms: The ribbon carrier makes a scraping noise as it moves from side to side. Printed pages contain regularly spaced horizontal scratch marks (even in the white spaces).

abcdefghijkimnopqrstuvwxyzabcdefghijkimnopqrstuvwxyz

abcdefghijklmnopqrstuvwxyz

abcdefghijklmnopqrstuvwxyz

Probable diagnosis: The edge of the plastic card holder (or paper guide) is melted. Beads of melted plastic are scratching the paper.

Solution: Replace the card holder (C. Itoh CQAAK-10501).

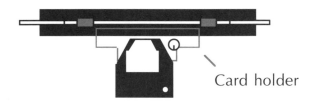

Card holder

Approximate cost of repairing it yourself:		$2.00
1 card holder	2.00	5 min.
Approximate third-party repair cost:		$70.00
1 card holder	5.00	
1 hour labor	65.00	
Approximate dealer repair cost:		$80.00
1 new paper guide	10.00	
1 hour labor	70.00	

Symptoms: When a four-color ribbon is installed, cyan overlaps black at the *top* of every text character.

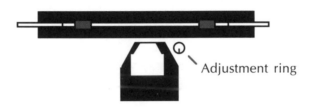

Typical history: Monochrome (black) ribbons seem to work OK.

Probable diagnosis: The ribbon cam is out of adjustment.

Solution: Turn the adjustment ring *counterclockwise* until the colors register correctly.

Approximate cost of repairing it yourself:		*5 min.*
Approximate third-party repair cost:		**$65.00**
1 hour labor	65.00	
Approximate dealer repair cost:		**$90.00**
1 new color ribbon	20.00	
1 hour labor	70.00	

Symptoms: When a four-color ribbon is installed, yellow overlaps black at the *bottom* of every text character.

Typical history: Monochrome (black) ribbons seem to work OK.

Probable diagnosis: The ribbon cam is out of adjustment.

Solution: Turn the adjustment ring *clockwise* until the colors register correctly.

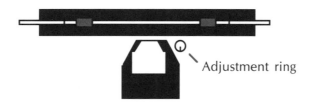

Adjustment ring

Approximate cost of repairing it yourself:	*5 min.*
Approximate third-party repair cost:	*$65.00*
1 hour labor 65.00	
Approximate dealer repair cost:	*$90.00*
1 new color ribbon 20.00	
1 hour labor 70.00	

Symptoms: The on/off button on a late-model (unitized) ImageWriter II (marked *Family number: G0010; Marketing number: C0090LL/A*) is intermittent. Sometimes it works, sometimes it doesn't.

Typical history: The problem occurred after completion of service work (right after you put everything back together).

Probable diagnosis: The extension cable connecting the on/off button on the control panel to the power switch (located on the power supply/driver PCB) is pinched under the printer frame.

Solution: Reposition the extension cable as shown.

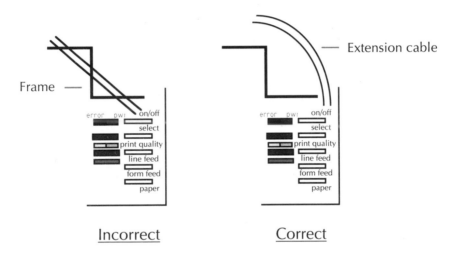

Incorrect   Correct

Approximate cost of repairing it yourself:		*1 hour*
Approximate third-party repair cost:		**$65.00**
1 hour labor	65.00	
Approximate dealer repair cost:		**$70.00**
1 hour labor	70.00	

Symptoms: Whenever you select high-speed *Draft* quality, the text is printed in an ugly, 15-cpi (characters per inch) type with unacceptably large spacing between words. The same thing happens when *Best* quality is selected (printout is ugly), except the type is darker.

```
Gettysburg    Address

Fourscore    and  seven  years  ago  our  fathers    brought
forth  on  this  continent a  new  nation,  conceived  in
liberty   and  dedicated   to  the  proposition  that all
men   are  created  equal.
```

Probable diagnosis: The problem is in the ImageWriter resource, not in the ImageWriter II.

Solution: Replace the ImageWriter resource with the BetterWriter II driver developed by GDT Softworks. Once that's done, *Draft* and *Best* quality will both print perfectly!

```
 BetterWriters                    BetterWriter II v1.0
 ─────────────────────────────────────────────────────
 Quality: ○ Best ○ Fair ○ Fast  ● Draft  ✓Low
                                           Mid
            □ Darker      □ Color         High
```

Approximate cost of repairing it yourself:		***$39.95***
1 BetterWriters package (street price)	39.95	***15 min.***
Approximate third-party repair cost:		***$134.00***
1 BetterWriters package	69.00	
1 hour labor	65.00	
Approximate dealer repair cost:		***$599.00***
1 new StyleWriter	599.00	

Symptoms: The ribbon cartridge deck jams while going to the left. The printout resembles a staircase, ascending to the right.

> The printout resembles a staircase, ascending to the right. The printout resembles a staircase, ascending to the right. The printout resembles a staircase, ascending to the right. The printout resembles a staircase, ascending to the right. The printout resembles a staircase, ascending to

Probable diagnosis: There's too much friction on the carrier shaft and the carriage guide rail.

Solution: Thoroughly clean and lubricate the carrier shaft and the carriage guide rail.

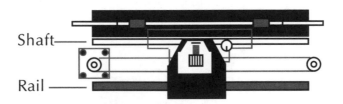

Shaft
Rail

Approximate cost of repairing it yourself:		30 min.
Approximate third-party repair cost:		**$65.00**
1 hour labor	65.00	
Approximate dealer repair cost:		**$70.00**
1 hour labor	70.00	

Symptoms: There are regularly spaced missing dots in the printout.

There are regularly spaced missing dots in the printout.
There are regularly spaced missing dots in the printout.

Probable diagnosis: The contacts on the print head PCB are dirty.

Solution: Clean the contacts with a pencil eraser. If that doesn't do it, see the next entry.

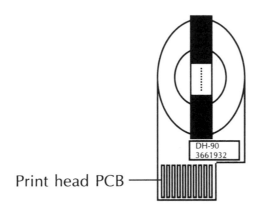

Print head PCB

Approximate cost of repairing it yourself:		5 min.
Approximate third-party repair cost:		**$65.00**
1 hour labor	65.00	
Approximate dealer repair cost:		**$225.00**
1 new print head DDH-90	155.00	
1 hour labor	70.00	

Symptoms: There are regularly spaced missing dots in the printout.

There are regularly spaced missing dots in the printout.
There are regularly spaced missing dots in the printout.

Typical history: Cleaning the print head PCB made no difference.

Probable diagnosis: One of the striker wires in the print head is rusty. The wire is hanging on the ribbon guide (instead of slipping through and onto the paper).

Solution: Spray the ribbon guide with a drop or two of WD-40. Let it soak in for several hours (preferably overnight) before reinstalling the print head. If that still doesn't do it, see the next entry.

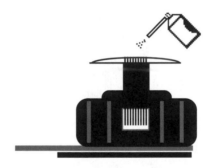

Approximate cost of repairing it yourself:		*5 min.*
Approximate third-party repair cost:		*$65.00*
1 hour labor	65.00	
Approximate dealer repair cost:		*$225.00*
1 new print head DDH-90	155.00	
1 hour labor	70.00	

Symptoms: There are regularly spaced missing dots in the printout.

Typical history: Cleaning the contacts on the print head made no difference. Lubricating the ribbon guide didn't help.

There are regularly spaced missing dots in the printout.
There are regularly spaced missing dots in the printout.

Probable diagnosis: One of the striker wires in the print head is bent or broken, and/or one of the return springs is weak.

Solution: Send out the print head (not the whole printer) to a service depot for repair. Also see the prior entry.

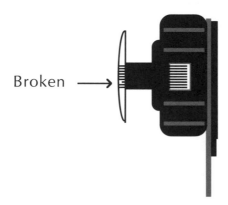

Broken ──→

Approximate cost of repairing it yourself:		$46.00
1 print head repair	46.00	5 min.
Approximate third-party repair cost:		$157.00
1 rebuilt print head	92.00	
1 hour labor	65.00	
Approximate dealer repair cost:		$225.00
1 new print head DDH-90	155.00	
1 hour labor	70.00	

Symptoms: Best quality printing is wavy. Vertical lines are uneven.

Best quality printing is wavy. Vertical lines are uneven.
Best quality printing is wavy. Vertical lines are uneven.

Probable diagnosis: The character deviation is out of adjustment.

Solution: Adjust DIP switches SW2-5 and SW2-6 (located under the front cover) for best linearity. Also see the next entry.

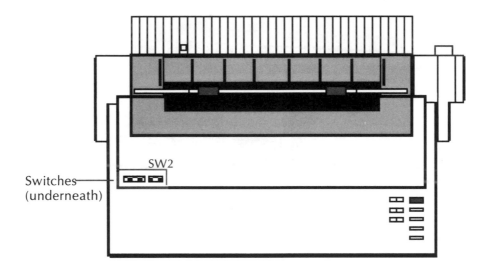

Switches
(underneath)

SW2

Approximate cost of repairing it yourself:		*10 min.*
Approximate third-party repair cost:		*$65.00*
1 hour labor	65.00	
Approximate dealer repair cost:		*$70.00*
1 hour labor	70.00	

Symptoms: Best quality printing is wavy. Vertical lines are uneven.

Best quality printing is wavy. Vertical lines are uneven.
Best quality printing is wavy. Vertical lines are uneven.

Typical history: Adjusting DIP switches SW2-5 and SW2-6 didn't completely eliminate the problem.

Probable diagnosis: There's not enough tension on the carrier belt.

Solution: Adjust the carrier-belt tension lever (located under the front cover) for best linearity. If that doesn't do it, see the next entry.

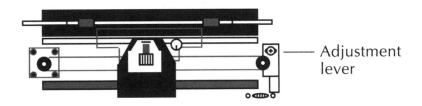

—— Adjustment lever

Approximate cost of repairing it yourself:		*10 min.*
Approximate third-party repair cost:		**$65.00**
1 hour labor	65.00	
Approximate dealer repair cost:		**$70.00**
1 hour labor	70.00	

Symptoms: Best quality printing is wavy. Vertical lines are uneven.

Best quality printing is wavy. Vertical lines are uneven.
Best quality printing is wavy. Vertical lines are uneven.

Typical history: Adjusting DIP switches SW2-5 and SW2-6 and the carrier-belt tension lever didn't seem to make any difference.

Probable diagnosis: The striker wires in the print head are out of vertical alignment.

Solution: Send out the print head (not the whole printer) to a service depot for repair. If that's not it, see the next entry.

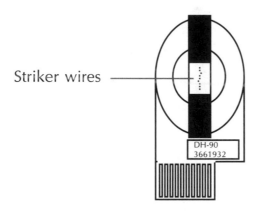

Striker wires

Approximate cost of repairing it yourself:		$46.00
1 print head repair	46.00	5 min.
Approximate third-party repair cost:		**$157.00**
1 rebuilt print head	92.00	
1 hour labor	65.00	
Approximate dealer repair cost:		**$225.00**
1 new print head DDH-90	155.00	
1 hour labor	70.00	

Symptoms: Best quality printing is wavy, blurred and/or almost double-struck. Vertical lines are uneven.

Best quality printing is wavy. Vertical lines are uneven.
Best quality printing is wavy. Vertical lines are uneven.

Typical history: Adjusting DIP switches SW2-5 and SW2-6 and the carrier belt tension lever didn't seem to make any difference. The striker wires in the print head are in perfect alignment.

Probable diagnosis: The problem is on the ImageWriter II driver PCB.

Solution: Check/replace the EC-A051 IC (18-pin, carrier motor driver), C. Itoh part EAT-00-09900, at board reference HIC1.

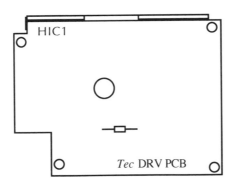

Approximate cost of repairing it yourself:		*$21.78*
1 EC-A051 IC	21.78	*1 hour*
Approximate third-party repair cost:		*$109.00*
1 carrier motor driver IC	44.00	
1 hour labor	65.00	
Approximate dealer repair cost:		*$206.67*
1 new power supply board	136.67	
1 hour labor	70.00	

Symptoms: The printout is too light.

The printout is too light. The printout is too light.
The printout is too light. The printout is too light.

Probable diagnosis: The paper thickness lever is too far back.

Solution: Move the paper thickness lever (located under the front cover) closer to the platen. If that doesn't do it, see the next entry.

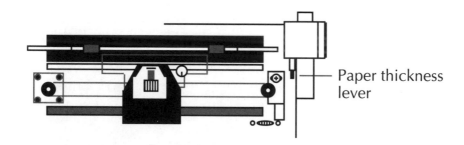

Paper thickness lever

Approximate cost of repairing it yourself:	*1 min.*
Approximate third-party repair cost:	**$65.00**
1 hour labor 65.00	
Approximate dealer repair cost:	**$70.00**
1 hour labor 70.00	

Symptoms: The printout is too light.

The printout is too light. The printout is too light.
The printout is too light. The printout is too light.

Typical history: The paper thickness lever has been checked, and it's correctly positioned.

Probable diagnosis: The ribbon cartridge is dry or worn out.

Solution: Replace the ribbon cartridge, C. Itoh part CLABK-128S2. Also see the prior entry.

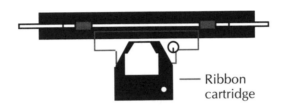

— Ribbon
cartridge

Approximate cost of repairing it yourself:		**$1.69**
1 ribbon cartridge	1.69	**1 min.**
Approximate third-party repair cost:		**$70.00**
1 ribbon cartridge	5.00	
1 hour labor	65.00	
Approximate dealer repair cost:		**$82.00**
1 ribbon cartridge	12.00	
1 hour labor	70.00	

Symptoms: There are intermittent dropouts in the printout. Some areas are dark, and some areas are light.

> There are intermittent dropouts in the printout.
> Some areas are dark, and some areas are light.

Probable diagnosis: The ribbon cartridge is worn or defective.

Solution: Replace the ribbon cartridge, C. Itoh part CLABK-128S2.

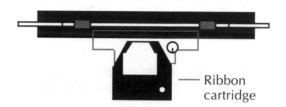

——— Ribbon
cartridge

Approximate cost of repairing it yourself:		*$1.69*
1 ribbon cartridge	1.69	*1 min.*
Approximate third-party repair cost:		*$70.00*
1 ribbon cartridge	5.00	
1 hour labor	65.00	
Approximate dealer repair cost:		*$82.00*
1 ribbon cartridge	12.00	
1 hour labor	70.00	

Symptoms: The printout fades from dark to light (or from light to dark). One side of the printout is darker or lighter than the other.

The printout fades from dark-to-light (or light to dark). One side of the printout is darker or lighter than the other.

Probable diagnosis: The carrier shaft isn't square to the platen.`The side farthest away is where the printing is the lightest.

Solution: Square the carrier shaft to the platen by installing a 0.002-inch, 0.004-inch or 0.008-inch adjust plate (C. Itoh part numbers CBA20-02901, CBA20-02902 and CBA20-02903),on the carrier shaft bush located on the side where printing is the lightest, or by removing a 0.002-inch, 0.004-inch or 0.008-inch adjust plate from the carrier shaft bush located on the side where printing is the darkest.

Carrier shaft bush
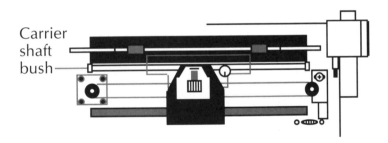

Approximate cost of repairing it yourself:		*$3.00*
1 set of adjust plates	3.00	*1 hour*
Approximate third-party repair cost:		*$71.00*
1 set of adjust plates	6.00	
1 hour labor	65.00	
Approximate dealer repair cost:		*$82.00*
1 shim kit (part 955-0005)	12.00	
1 hour labor	70.00	

Symptoms: After a few pages, the pin-feed paper derails and the printer jams.

Probable diagnosis: The paper feed selector (located on the right leg) is positioned for friction-feed paper (not pin-feed).

Solution: Push the paper feed selector toward the pin-feed icon.

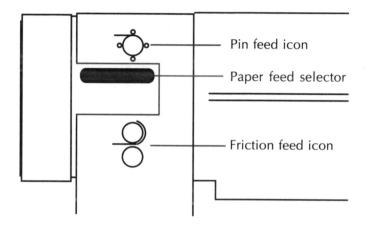

Pin feed icon

Paper feed selector

Friction feed icon

Approximate cost of repairing it yourself:		*1 min.*
Approximate third-party repair cost:		*$65.00*
1 hour labor	65.00	
Approximate dealer repair cost:		*$70.00*
1 hour labor	70.00	

Symptoms: Printing doesn't stop when the paper runs out. Instead, it continues right across the platen.

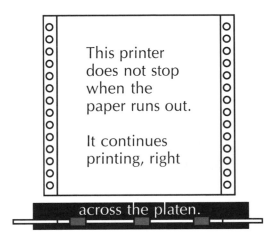

Probable diagnosis: The paper empty sensor is malfunctioning. Most likely, a mailing label is stuck under the platen.

Solution: Remove the platen. Clear the stuck mailing label.

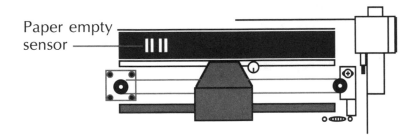

Approximate cost of repairing it yourself:	*1 hour*
Approximate third-party repair cost:	*$65.00*
1 hour labor 65.00	
Approximate dealer repair cost:	*$70.00*
1 hour labor 70.00	

Symptoms: It's hard to load paper. Something seems to be blocking the paper path.

Probable diagnosis: A mailing label is or was stuck under the platen, and/or the arms on the mechanical paper empty sensor are bent.

Solution: Remove the platen. Clear the stuck mailing label, if any, and straighten the arms on the paper empty sensor, if necessary.

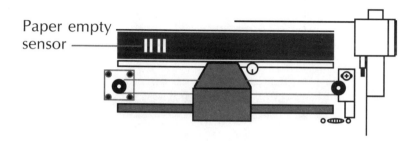

Paper empty sensor

Approximate cost of repairing it yourself:		*1 hour*
Approximate third-party repair cost:		**$65.00**
1 hour labor	65.00	
Approximate dealer repair cost:		**$70.00**
1 hour labor	70.00	

Symptoms: Cut-sheet paper slips and lines overprint in friction-feed mode.

Cut-sheet paper slips and lines overprint in friction feed mode.
Cut-sheet paper slips and lines overprint in friction feed mode.
Cut-sheet paper slips and lines overprint in friction feed mode.
Cut-sheet paper slips and lines overprint in friction feed mode.

Probable diagnosis: The platen is slipping. It's lost its grip!

Solution: Restore the platen grip with liquid tape-recorder rubber cleaner, Teac RC1 or equivalent, and a clean cotton rag.

Platen

Approximate cost of repairing it yourself:		*15 min.*
Approximate third-party repair cost:		*$65.00*
1 hour labor	65.00	
Approximate dealer repair cost:		*$70.00*
1 hour labor	70.00	

CHAPTER 9

LASERWRITER AND LASERWRITER PLUS

Symptoms: On a LaserWriter, there's no test page. The green Test LED on the interface panel comes on and remains on (does not shut off).

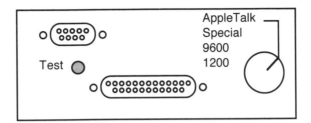

Probable diagnosis: The problem is on the LaserWriter logic board.

Solution: Check/replace the ROMs marked H0 and L0.

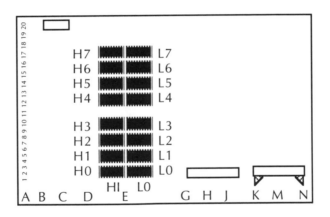

Approximate cost of repairing it yourself:		**$50.00**
1 ROM chip	50.00	**2 hours**
Approximate third-party repair cost:		**$425.00**
1 ROM chip	100.00	
5 hours labor	325.00	
Approximate dealer repair cost:		**$1,043.33**
1 new I/O board with ROMs	693.33	
5 hours labor	350.00	

Symptoms: On a LaserWriter, there's no test page. The green Test LED on the interface panel *never* comes on (doesn't even blink once).

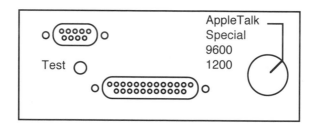

Probable diagnosis: The problem is on the LaserWriter logic board.

Solution: Check/replace the ROMs marked H0, L0, H7 and L7.

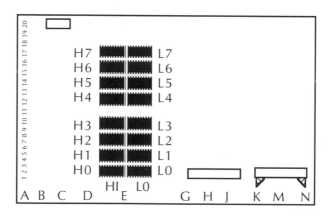

Approximate cost of repairing it yourself:		**$50.00**
1 ROM chip	50.00	**2 hours**
Approximate third-party repair cost:		**$425.00**
1 ROM chip	100.00	
5 hours labor	325.00	
Approximate dealer repair cost:		**$1,043.33**
1 new I/O board with ROMs	693.33	
5 hours labor	350.00	

Symptoms: On a LaserWriter, there's no test page. The green Test LED on the interface panel is blinking.

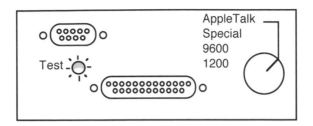

Probable diagnosis: The problem is on the LaserWriter logic board.

Solution: Check/replace the ROMs marked H1–H7 and L1–L7.

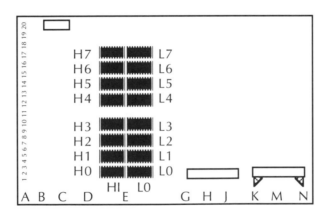

Approximate cost of repairing it yourself:		**$50.00**
1 ROM chip	50.00	**2 hours**
Approximate third-party repair cost:		**$425.00**
1 ROM chip	100.00	
5 hours labor	325.00	
Approximate dealer repair cost:		**$1,043.33**
1 new I/O board with ROMs	693.33	
5 hours labor	350.00	

Symptoms: On a LaserWriter Plus, there's no test page. The green Test LED on the interface panel comes on and remains on (does not shut off). Test Character Generator version 2.0 (on *The Dead Mac Scrolls Disk)* or other diagnostics software reports error code nnnnnn01 (where the value of nnnnnn is insignificant).

```
*APPLE*00010001*APPLE*
```

Probable diagnosis: The problem is on the LaserWriter Plus logic board.

Solution: Check/replace the version-2 ROMs marked H0 and L0.

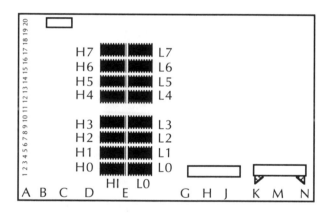

Approximate cost of repairing it yourself:		**$50.00**
1 ROM chip	50.00	**2 hours**
Approximate third-party repair cost:		**$425.00**
1 ROM chip	100.00	
5 hours labor	325.00	
Approximate dealer repair cost:		**$1,043.33**
1 new I/O board with ROMs	693.33	
5 hours labor	350.00	

Symptoms: On a LaserWriter Plus, there's no test page. The green Test LED on the interface panel is blinking. Test Character Generator version 2.0 (on *The Dead Mac Scrolls Disk*) or other diagnostics software reports error code nnnnn02 (where the value of nnnnnn is insignificant).

```
*APPLE*00010002*APPLE*
```

Probable diagnosis: The problem is on the LaserWriter Plus logic board.

Solution: Check/replace the version-2 ROMs marked H1 and L1.

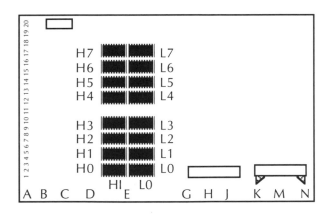

Approximate cost of repairing it yourself:		$50.00
1 ROM chip	50.00	*2 hours*
Approximate third-party repair cost:		**$425.00**
1 ROM chip	100.00	
5 hours labor	325.00	
Approximate dealer repair cost:		**$1,043.33**
1 new I/O board with ROMs	693.33	
5 hours labor	350.00	

Symptoms: On a LaserWriter Plus, there's no test page. The green Test LED on the interface panel is blinking. Test Character Generator version 2.0 (on *The Dead Mac Scrolls Disk)* or other diagnostics software reports error code nnnnnn04 (where the value of nnnnnn is insignificant).

```
*APPLE*00010004*APPLE*
```

Probable diagnosis: The problem is on the LaserWriter Plus logic board.

Solution: Check/replace the version-2 ROMs marked H2 and L2.

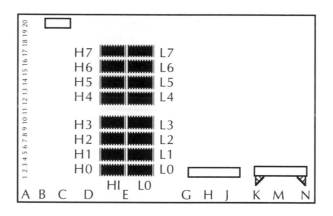

Approximate cost of repairing it yourself:		$50.00
1 ROM chip	50.00	2 hours
Approximate third-party repair cost:		$425.00
1 ROM chip	100.00	
5 hours labor	325.00	
Approximate dealer repair cost:		$1,043.33
1 new I/O board with ROMs	693.33	
5 hours labor	350.00	

Symptoms: On a LaserWriter Plus, there's no test page. The green Test LED on the interface panel is blinking. Test Character Generator version 2.0 (on *The Dead Mac Scrolls Disk*) or other diagnostics software reports error code nnnnn08 (where the value of nnnnnn is insignificant).

`*APPLE*00010008*APPLE*`

Probable diagnosis: The problem is on the LaserWriter Plus logic board.

Solution: Check/replace the version-2 ROMs marked H3 and L3.

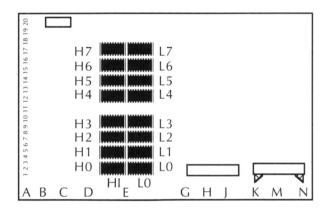

Approximate cost of repairing it yourself:		***$50.00***
1 ROM chip	50.00	***2 hours***
Approximate third-party repair cost:		***$425.00***
1 ROM chip	100.00	
5 hours labor	325.00	
Approximate dealer repair cost:		***$1,043.33***
1 new I/O board with ROMs	693.33	
5 hours labor	350.00	

Symptoms: On a LaserWriter Plus, there's no test page. The green Test LED on the interface panel is blinking. Test Character Generator version 2.0 (on *The Dead Mac Scrolls Disk)* or other diagnostics software reports error code nnnnnn10 (where the value of nnnnnn is insignificant).

```
*APPLE*00010010*APPLE*
```

Probable diagnosis: The problem is on the LaserWriter Plus logic board.

Solution: Check/replace the version-2 ROMs marked H4 and L4.

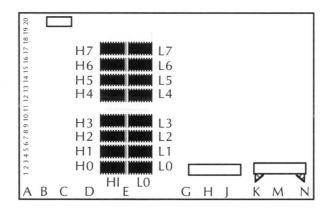

Approximate cost of repairing it yourself:		$50.00
1 ROM chip	50.00	*2 hours*
Approximate third-party repair cost:		$425.00
1 ROM chip	100.00	
5 hours labor	325.00	
Approximate dealer repair cost:		$1,043.33
1 new I/O board with ROMs	693.33	
5 hours labor	350.00	

Symptoms: On a LaserWriter Plus, there's no test page. The green Test LED on the interface panel is blinking. Test Character Generator version 2.0 (on *The Dead Mac Scrolls Disk*) or other diagnostics software reports error code nnnnn20 (where the value of nnnnn is insignificant).

```
*APPLE*00010020*APPLE*
```

Probable diagnosis: The problem is on the LaserWriter Plus logic board.

Solution: Check/replace the version-2 ROMs marked H5 and L5.

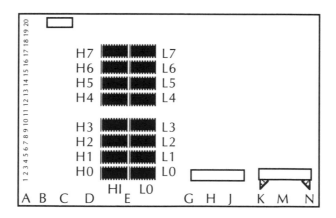

Approximate cost of repairing it yourself:		**$50.00**
1 ROM chip	50.00	**2 hours**
Approximate third-party repair cost:		**$425.00**
1 ROM chip	100.00	
5 hours labor	325.00	
Approximate dealer repair cost:		**$1,043.33**
1 new I/O board with ROMs	693.33	
5 hours labor	350.00	

Symptoms: On a LaserWriter Plus, there's no test page. The green Test LED on the interface panel is blinking. Test Character Generator version 2.0 (on *The Dead Mac Scrolls Disk*) or other diagnostics software reports error code nnnnnn40 (where the value of nnnnnn is insignificant).

```
*APPLE*00010040*APPLE*
```

Probable diagnosis: The problem is on the LaserWriter Plus logic board.

Solution: Check/replace the version-2 ROMs marked H6 and L6.

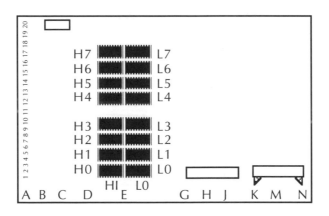

Approximate cost of repairing it yourself:		$50.00
1 ROM chip	50.00	2 hours
Approximate third-party repair cost:		$425.00
1 ROM chip	100.00	
5 hours labor	325.00	
Approximate dealer repair cost:		$1,043.33
1 new I/O board with ROMs	693.33	
5 hours labor	350.00	

Symptoms: On a LaserWriter Plus, there's no test page. The green Test LED on the interface panel is blinking. Test Character Generator version 2.0 (on *The Dead Mac Scrolls Disk*) or other diagnostics software reports error code nnnnn80 (where the value of nnnnnn is insignificant).

```
*APPLE*00010080*APPLE*
```

Probable diagnosis: The problem is on the LaserWriter Plus logic board.

Solution: Check/replace the version-3 ROMs marked H7 and L7.

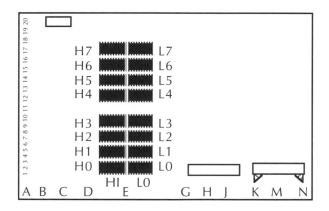

Approximate cost of repairing it yourself:		**$50.00**
1 ROM chip	50.00	***2 hours***
Approximate third-party repair cost:		**$425.00**
1 ROM chip	100.00	
5 hours labor	325.00	
Approximate dealer repair cost:		**$1,043.33**
1 new I/O board with ROMs	693.33	
5 hours labor	350.00	

Symptoms: On a LaserWriter Plus, there's no test page. The green Test LED on the interface panel comes on and remains on (does not shut off). Test Character Generator version 2.0 (on *The Dead Mac Scrolls Disk)* or other LaserWriter Plus diagnostics software reports error code nnnnnn03 (where the value of nnnnnn is insignificant).

```
*APPLE*00010003*APPLE*
```

Probable diagnosis: The problem is on the LaserWriter Plus logic board.

Solution: Check/replace the version-3 ROMs marked H0 and L0.

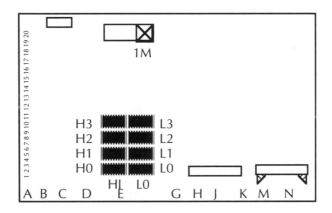

Approximate cost of repairing it yourself:		$100.00
1 ROM chip	100.00	2 hours
Approximate third-party repair cost:		$525.00
1 ROM chip	200.00	
5 hours labor	325.00	
Approximate dealer repair cost:		$1,043.33
1 new I/O board with ROMs	693.33	
5 hours labor	350.00	

Symptoms: On a LaserWriter Plus, there's no test page. The green Test LED on the interface panel is blinking. Test Character Generator version 2.0 (on *The Dead Mac Scrolls Disk)* or other diagnostics software reports error code nnnnnn0C (where the value of nnnnnn is insignificant).

```
*APPLE*0001000C*APPLE*
```

Probable diagnosis: The problem is on the LaserWriter Plus logic board.

Solution: Check/replace the version-3 ROMs marked H1 and L1.

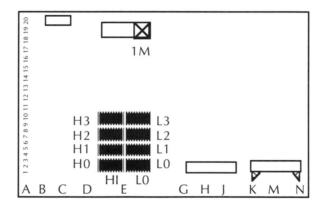

Approximate cost of repairing it yourself:		**$100.00**
1 ROM chip	100.00	**2 hours**
Approximate third-party repair cost:		**$525.00**
1 ROM chip	200.00	
5 hours labor	325.00	
Approximate dealer repair cost:		**$1,043.33**
1 new I/O board with ROMs	693.33	
5 hours labor	350.00	

Symptoms: On a LaserWriter Plus, there's no test page. The green Test LED on the interface panel is blinking. Test Character Generator version 2.0 (on *The Dead Mac Scrolls Disk)* or other diagnostics software reports error code nnnnnn30 (where the value of nnnnnn is insignificant).

```
*APPLE*00010030*APPLE*
```

Probable diagnosis: The problem is on the LaserWriter Plus logic board.

Solution: Check/replace the version-3 ROMs marked H2 and L2.

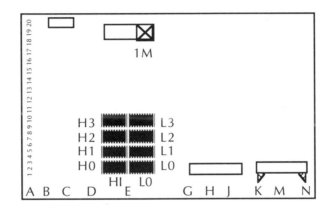

Approximate cost of repairing it yourself:		$100.00
1 ROM chip	100.00	*2 hours*
Approximate third-party repair cost:		**$525.00**
1 ROM chip	200.00	
5 hours labor	325.00	
Approximate dealer repair cost:		**$1,043.33**
1 new I/O board with ROMs	693.33	
5 hours labor	350.00	

Symptoms: On a LaserWriter Plus, there's no test page. The green Test LED on the interface panel is blinking. Test Character Generator version 2.0 (on _The Dead Mac Scrolls Disk)_ or other diagnostics software reports error code nnnnnnC0 (where the value of nnnnnn is insignificant).

```
*APPLE*000100C0*APPLE*
```

Probable diagnosis: The problem is on the LaserWriter Plus logic board.

Solution: Check/replace the version-3 ROMs marked H3 and L3.

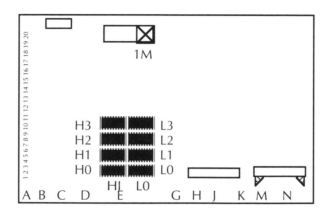

Approximate cost of repairing it yourself:		**$100.00**
1 ROM chip	100.00	**2 hours**
Approximate third-party repair cost:		**$525.00**
1 ROM chip	200.00	
5 hours labor	325.00	
Approximate dealer repair cost:		**$1,043.33**
1 new I/O board with ROMs	693.33	
5 hours labor	350.00	

Symptoms: On powerup, the *ready/wait* light (located on the status panel) blinks for a minute or so, then lights continuously as usual, but there's no test page. The printer *is* recognized in the Chooser, but there's no response to the print command.

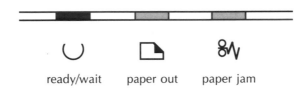

ready/wait   paper out   paper jam

Probable diagnosis: The problem is in the fuser assembly and/or on the upper AC driver PCB (both located in the printer's lower unit).

Solution: Check/replace the quartz-heater bulb (HP part RH7-4007-000CN) in the fuser assembly and check/replace current limiting resistor J107 (47Ω, ¼-watt, 5%) on the upper AC driver PCB. If that doesn't do it, see the next entry.

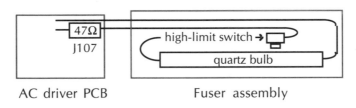

AC driver PCB   Fuser assembly

Approximate cost of repairing it yourself:		**$29.59**
1 quartz-heater bulb	29.50	***1 hour***
1 47Ω, ¼-watt resistor	.09	
Approximate third-party repair cost:		**$385.00**
1 fuser bulb	60.00	
5 hours labor	325.00	
Approximate dealer repair cost		**$448.00**
1 fuser assembly (699-0306)	378.00	
1 hour labor	70.00	

Symptoms: On powerup, the *ready/wait* light (located on the status panel) blinks for a minute or so, then lights continuously as usual, but there's no test page. The printer *is* recognized in the Chooser, but there's no response to the print command.

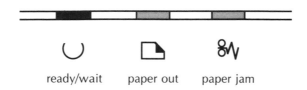

ready/wait   paper out   paper jam

Typical history: Continuity testing has verified that it's not the fuser bulb or the 47Ω resistor on the AC driver PCB.

Probable diagnosis: The problem is in the fuser assembly.

Solution: Check/replace the high-limit switch (HP part FH7-7041-000CN). If that's not it, see the next entry.

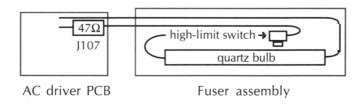

AC driver PCB   Fuser assembly

Approximate cost of repairing it yourself:		$25.00
1 high-limit switch	25.00	1 hour
Approximate third-party repair cost:		$375.00
1 fuser thermoprotector	50.00	
5 hours labor	325.00	
Approximate dealer repair cost		$448.00
1 fuser assembly (699-0306)	378.00	
1 hour labor	70.00	

Symptoms: On powerup, the *ready/wait* light (located on the status panel) blinks for a minute or so, then lights continuously as usual, but there's no test page. The printer *is* recognized in the Chooser, but there's no response to the print command.

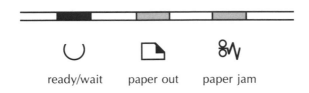

Typical history: Continuity testing has verified that it's not the quartz heater bulb, the high-limit switch or the 47Ω resistor.

Probable diagnosis: The problem is still in the fuser assembly.

Solution: Check/replace the fuser thermostat (HP part RH7-7002-000CN). Also see the prior entry.

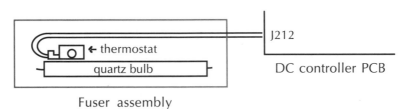

Fuser assembly

Approximate cost of repairing it yourself:		$25.00
1 thermostat assembly	25.00	*1 hour*
Approximate third-party repair cost:		**$375.00**
1 fuser thermistor	50.00	
5 hours labor	325.00	
Approximate dealer repair cost		**$448.00**
1 fuser assembly (699-0306)	378.00	
1 hour labor	70.00	

Symptoms: There are white water spots (dropouts) on the printout.

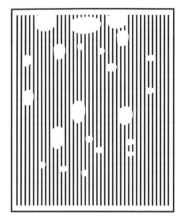

Probable diagnosis: The toner is unevenly distributed.

Solution: Check/replace the toner cartridge (HP part 92285A). Also see the next entry.

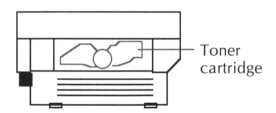

Toner cartridge

Approximate cost of repairing it yourself:		**$89.95**
1 toner cartridge	89.95	**1 min.**
Approximate third-party repair cost:		**$164.95**
1 toner cartridge	99.95	
1 hour labor	65.00	
Approximate dealer repair cost:		**$195.00**
1 toner cartridge	125.00	
1 hour labor	70.00	

Symptoms: There are white water spots (dropouts) on the printout.

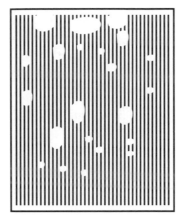

Typical history: The problem occurred right after you blew out the dust buildup with compressed air.

Probable diagnosis: The problem is in the erase lamp assembly (located in the upper unit). Some of the dust blew upward and settled on the red lens.

Solution: Thoroughly clean the red erase-lamp lens (inside and out).

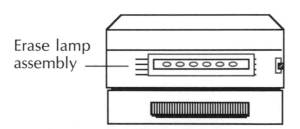

Erase lamp assembly

Approximate cost of repairing it yourself:		*30 min.*
Approximate third-party repair cost:		*$325.00*
5 hours labor	325.00	
Approximate dealer repair cost:		*$350.00*
5 hours labor	350.00	

Symptoms: The printout is generally too light.

LaserWriter

Probable diagnosis: The print density setting is too low.

Solution: Turn the unmarked print-density dial fully counterclockwise. If that doesn't do it, see the next entry.

Print-density dial

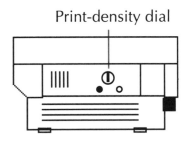

Approximate cost of repairing it yourself:		*1 min.*
Approximate third-party repair cost:		*$65.00*
1 hour labor	65.00	
Approximate dealer repair cost:		*$70.00*
1 hour labor	70.00	

Symptoms: The printout is generally too light.

LaserWriter

Probable diagnosis: The toner cartridge is empty.

Solution: Check/replace the toner cartridge (HP part 92285A). If that still doesn't do it, see the next entry.

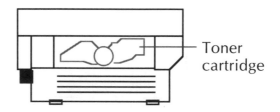

Toner cartridge

Approximate cost of repairing it yourself:		**$89.95**
1 toner cartridge	89.95	**1 min.**
Approximate third-party repair cost:		**$164.95**
1 toner cartridge	99.95	
1 hour labor	65.00	
Approximate dealer repair cost:		**$195.00**
1 toner cartridge	125.00	
1 hour labor	70.00	

Symptoms: Solid blacks appear to have been blotted. The edges are rough, not crisp.

LaserWriter

Probable diagnosis: The problem is in the transfer corona assembly (located in the lower unit).

Solution: Clean/tighten the transfer corona assembly. If that doesn't do it, see the next entry.

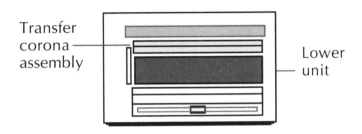

Approximate cost of repairing it yourself:		*10 min.*
Approximate third-party repair cost:		**$325.00**
5 hours labor	325.00	
Approximate dealer repair cost:		**$350.00**
5 hours labor	350.00	

Symptoms: Solid blacks appear to have been blotted. The edges are rough, not crisp.

LaserWriter

Probable diagnosis: The problem is a cracked solder joint in the high-voltage power supply.

Solution: Check/resolder the electrolytic capacitor at board reference C28. Also see the prior entry.

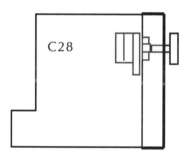

Approximate cost of repairing it yourself:		*1 hour*
Approximate third-party repair cost:		**$325.00**
5 hours labor	325.00	
Approximate dealer repair cost:		**$548.33**
1 new power supply, HV	198.33	
5 hours labor	350.00	

Symptoms: The printout is generally too dark.

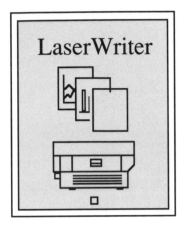

Probable diagnosis: The print density setting is too high.

Solution: Turn the unmarked print-density dial fully clockwise.

Print-density dial

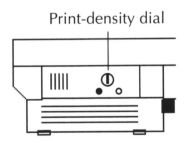

Approximate cost of repairing it yourself:		*1 min.*
Approximate third-party repair cost:		*$65.00*
1 hour labor	65.00	
Approximate dealer repair cost:		*$70.00*
1 hour labor	70.00	

Symptoms: Every printout, including the test page, is solid white.

Typical history: The problem occurred right after you installed a new toner cartridge.

Probable diagnosis: The sealing tape is still on the toner cartridge.

Solution: Check/remove the factory sealing tape.

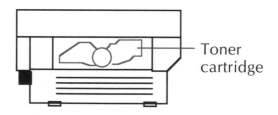

Toner cartridge

Approximate cost of repairing it yourself:		*1 min.*
Approximate third-party repair cost:		*$65.00*
1 hour labor	65.00	
Approximate dealer repair cost:		*$70.00*
1 hour labor	70.00	

Symptoms: Every printout, including the test page, is solid black.

Probable diagnosis: The problem is in the toner cartridge.

Solution: Check/replace the toner cartridge (HP part 92285A).

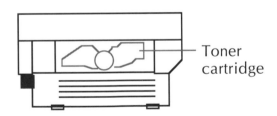

Toner cartridge

Approximate cost of repairing it yourself:		$89.95
1 toner cartridge	89.95	*1 min.*
Approximate third-party repair cost:		**$164.95**
1 toner cartridge	99.95	
1 hour labor	65.00	
Approximate dealer repair cost:		**$195.00**
1 toner cartridge	125.00	
1 hour labor	70.00	

Symptoms: Every printout, including the test page, is solid gray.

Probable diagnosis: The problem is in the toner cartridge.

Solution: Check/replace the toner cartridge (HP part 92285A).

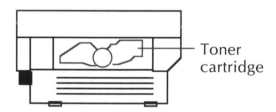
Toner
cartridge

Approximate cost of repairing it yourself:		**$89.95**
1 toner cartridge	89.95	**1 min.**
Approximate third-party repair cost:		**$164.95**
1 toner cartridge	99.95	
1 hour labor	65.00	
Approximate dealer repair cost:		**$195.00**
1 toner cartridge	125.00	
1 hour labor	70.00	

Symptoms: There are stains on the back of every printed page.

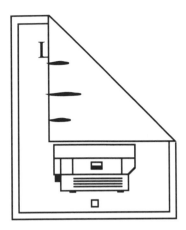

Probable diagnosis: The fuser roller cleaner felt is worn.

Solution: Check/replace the fuser roller cleaner felt (HP part FG1-2377-020). If that doesn't do it, see the next entry.

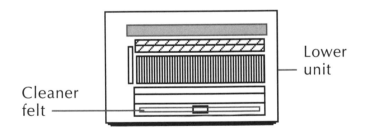

Lower unit

Cleaner felt

Approximate cost of repairing it yourself:		*1 min.*
Approximate third-party repair cost:		**$325.00**
5 hours labor	325.00	
Approximate dealer repair cost:		**$350.00**
5 hours labor	350.00	

Symptoms: There are stains on the back of every printed page.

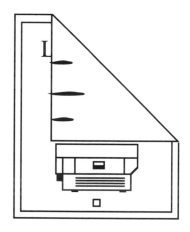

Probable diagnosis: The lower unit is dirty.

Solution: Clean the lower unit, particularly the black plastic feeder guide and brass-color transfer guide. Also see the prior entry.

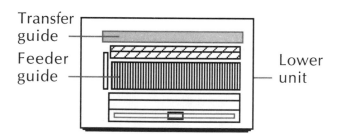

Approximate cost of repairing it yourself:		*30 min.*
Approximate third-party repair cost:		**$325.00**
5 hours labor	325.00	
Approximate dealer repair cost:		**$350.00**
5 hours labor	350.00	

Symptoms: A ¼-inch-wide black stripe (like a tiny tire track) is printed in the right margin of every printed page.

Probable diagnosis: The separation belt is dirty.

Solution: Thoroughly clean the separation belt (HP part RF1-0224-000) and the associated feeder rollers (located in the lower unit). If that doesn't do it, see the next entry.

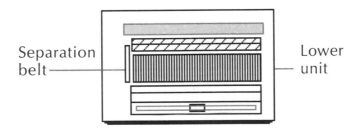

Approximate cost of repairing it yourself:		*10 min.*
Approximate third-party repair cost:		**$325.00**
5 hours labor	325.00	
Approximate dealer repair cost:		**$350.00**
5 hours labor	350.00	

Symptoms: A ¼-inch wide black stripe (like a tiny tire track) is printed in the right margin of every printed page.

Probable diagnosis: The photosensitive drum needs cleaning.

Solution: Clean the affected edge of the photosensitive drum. If the problem recurs, replace the toner cartridge (HP part 92285A).

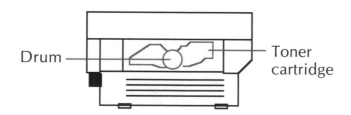

Approximate cost of repairing it yourself:		$89.95
1 toner cartridge	89.95	*10 min.*
Approximate third-party repair cost:		*$164.95*
1 toner cartridge	99.95	
1 hour labor	65.00	
Approximate dealer repair cost:		*$195.00*
1 toner cartridge	125.00	
1 hour labor	70.00	

Symptoms: There are black marks on one side of every page.

Probable diagnosis: The photosensitive drum needs cleaning.

Solution: Clean the affected edge of the photosensitive drum. If the problem recurs, replace the toner cartridge (HP part 92285A).

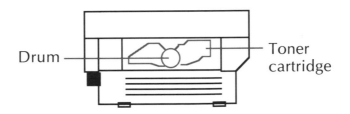

Approximate cost of repairing it yourself:		*$89.95*
1 toner cartridge	89.95	*10 min.*
Approximate third-party repair cost:		*$164.95*
1 toner cartridge	99.95	
1 hour labor	65.00	
Approximate dealer repair cost:		*$195.00*
1 toner cartridge	125.00	
1 hour labor	70.00	

Symptoms: There are regularly spaced horizontal white lines on every page.

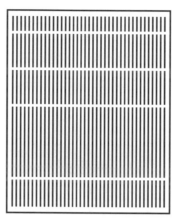

Probable diagnosis: The photosensitive drum is scarred.

Solution: Check/replace the toner cartridge (HP part 92285A).

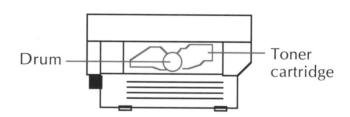

Drum — ... — Toner cartridge

Approximate cost of repairing it yourself:		**$89.95**
1 toner cartridge	89.95	**1 min.**
Approximate third-party repair cost:		**$164.95**
1 toner cartridge	99.95	
1 hour labor	65.00	
Approximate dealer repair cost:		**$195.00**
1 toner cartridge	125.00	
1 hour labor	70.00	

Symptoms: A very thin vertical line appears on every printed page. The line is barely noticeable and extends into the margins.

Probable diagnosis: The problem is in the fuser assembly.

Solution: Check/replace the cleaner felt (HP part FG1-2377-020) and the upper fuser roller (HP part RA1-0697-000).

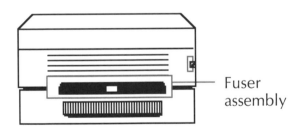

Fuser assembly

Approximate cost of repairing it yourself:		$18.00
1 upper roller	18.00	2 hours
Approximate third-party repair cost:		$361.00
1 upper roller	36.00	
5 hours labor	325.00	
Approximate dealer repair cost		$448.00
1 fuser assembly (699-0306)	378.00	
1 hour labor	70.00	

Symptoms: A black vertical line appears on every printed page. The line is bisected by white water spots (toner dropouts).

Probable diagnosis: The problem is in the fuser assembly.

Solution: Check/replace the upper fuser roller (HP part RA1-0697-000).

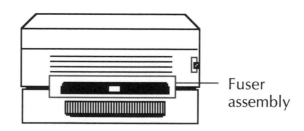

Approximate cost of repairing it yourself:		*$18.00*
1 upper roller	18.00	*2 hours*
Approximate third-party repair cost:		*$361.00*
1 upper roller	36.00	
5 hours labor	325.00	
Approximate dealer repair cost		*$448.00*
1 fuser assembly	378.00	
1 hour labor	70.00	

Symptoms: An ozone (auto-exhaust) smell lingers about the printer. Other than that, it seems to be OK.

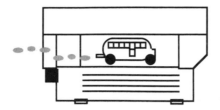

Probable diagnosis: The ozone filter is allowing gas to escape.

Solution: Replace the ozone filter (HP part FA2-5664-020).

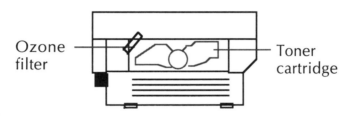

Ozone filter — Toner cartridge

Approximate cost of repairing it yourself:		$10.50
1 ozone filter	10.50	*1 hour*
Approximate third-party repair cost:		***$346.00***
1 ozone filter	21.00	
5 hours labor	325.00	
Approximate dealer repair cost:		***$392.00***
1 ozone filter	42.00	
5 hours labor	350.00	

Symptoms: During every print job, the paper gets caught in the fuser and the paper jam light comes on.

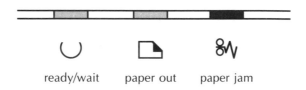

ready/wait   paper out   paper jam

Probable diagnosis: The fuser rollers are clogged with toner.

Solution: Check/replace the toner cartridge (HP part 92285A), clean the lower unit and clean/replace the upper and lower fuser rollers (HP part RA1-0697-000, HP part RA1-0696-000).

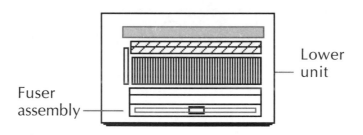

Lower unit

Fuser assembly

Approximate cost of repairing it yourself:		***$47.00***
1 upper roller (RA1-0697-000)	18.00	***2 hours***
1 lower roller (RA1-0696-000)	29.00	
Approximate third-party repair cost:		***$425.00***
1 set of fuser rollers	100.00	
5 hours labor	325.00	
Approximate dealer repair cost		***$448.00***
1 fuser assembly (699-0306)	378.00	
1 hour labor	70.00	

Symptoms: The margin width is irregular.

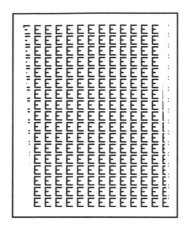

Probable diagnosis: The problem is in the paper tray.

Solution: Realign the paper fence to the side of the paper tray.

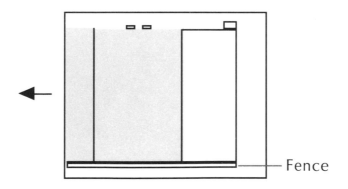

Fence

Approximate cost of repairing it yourself:		*5 min.*
Approximate third-party repair cost:		*$70.00*
1 hour labor	70.00	
Approximate dealer repair cost		*$169.95*
1 new paper cassette	99.95	
1 hour labor	70.00	

CHAPTER 10
LASERWRITER II SC, NT AND NTX

Symptoms: A thin vertical line appears on every printed page. The line is barely noticeable and extends into the margins.

Probable diagnosis: The problem is in the fuser assembly.

Solution: Check/replace the fixing roller cleaner wand (HP part RG1-0966-000) and the upper roller (HP part RA1-3968-000).

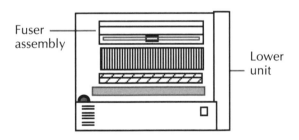

Approximate cost of repairing it yourself:		$26.85
1 fixing roller cleaner wand	1.85	*2 hours*
1 upper roller	25.00	
Approximate third-party repair cost:		**$379.00**
miscellaneous fuser parts	54.00	
5 hours labor	325.00	
Approximate dealer repair cost:		**$595.00**
1 new LaserWriter II fuser 661-0440	525.00	
1 hour labor	70.00	

Symptoms: A black vertical line appears on every printed page. The line is bisected by white water spots (toner dropouts).

Probable diagnosis: The problem is in the fuser assembly (HP part RG1-0939-000) located in the printer's lower unit.

Solution: Check/replace the upper roller (HP part RA1-3968-000).

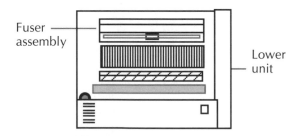

Approximate cost of repairing it yourself:		**$25.00**
1 upper roller	25.00	**2 hours**
Approximate third-party repair cost:		**$375.00**
1 upper roller	50.00	
5 hours labor	325.00	
Approximate dealer repair cost:		**$595.00**
1 new LaserWriter II fuser (661-0440)	525.00	
1 hour labor	70.00	

Symptoms: There's no test page. The *paper out* and *paper jam* lights (located on the status panel) are both blinking (red). The inside of the printer *doesn't* warm up.

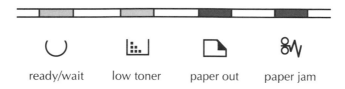

| ready/wait | low toner | paper out | paper jam |

Probable diagnosis: The problem is in the fuser assembly (HP part RG1-0939-000) located in the printer's lower unit.

Solution: Check/replace the quartz heater bulb (HP part RH7-4024-000). Also see the next entry.

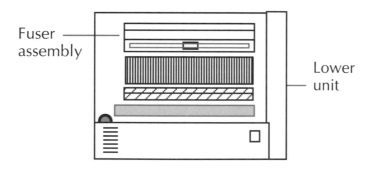

Fuser assembly — Lower unit

Approximate cost of repairing it yourself:		**$32.00**
1 quartz heater bulb	32.00	**2 hours**
Approximate third-party repair cost:		**$389.00**
1 quartz heater lamp	64.00	
5 hours labor	325.00	
Approximate dealer repair cost:		**$595.00**
1 new LaserWriter II fuser (661-0440)	525.00	
1 hour labor	70.00	

Symptoms: There's no test page. The *paper out* and *paper jam* lights (located on the status panel) are both blinking (red). The inside of the printer *doesn't* warm up.

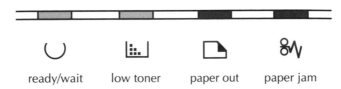

| ready/wait | low toner | paper out | paper jam |

Probable diagnosis: The problem is in the fuser assembly (HP part RG1-0939-000) located in the printer's lower unit.

Solution: Check/replace the high-limit switch (HP part RF1-0842-000). If that's not it, see the next entry.

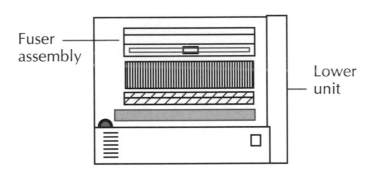

Approximate cost of repairing it yourself:		*$25.00*
1 high-limit switch	25.00	*2 hours*
Approximate third-party repair cost:		*$375.00*
1 fuser thermoswitch	50.00	
5 hours labor	325.00	
Approximate dealer repair cost:		*$595.00*
1 new LaserWriter II fuser (661-0440)	525.00	
1 hour labor	70.00	

Symptoms: There's no test page. The *paper out* and *paper jam* lights (located on the status panel) are both blinking (red). The inside of the printer *doesn't* warm up.

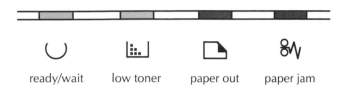

| ready/wait | low toner | paper out | paper jam |

Probable diagnosis: The problem is in the fuser assembly.

Solution: Check/replace the fuser thermostat (HP part RG1-0719-000). Also see the prior entry.

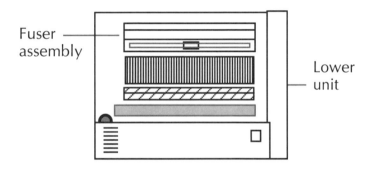

Approximate cost of repairing it yourself:		**$25.00**
1 thermostat assembly	25.00	**2 hours**
Approximate third-party repair cost:		**$375.00**
1 fixing PCB assembly/thermistor	50.00	
5 hours labor	325.00	
Approximate dealer repair cost:		**$595.00**
1 new LaserWriter II fuser (661-0440)	525.00	
1 hour labor	70.00	

Symptoms: There's no test page on a LaserWriter II NTX. On the status panel, the red *paper jam* light, (but not the red *paper out* light), the orange *low toner* light and the green *ready/wait* light are blinking from right to left (red-skip-orange-green, red-skip-orange-green…).

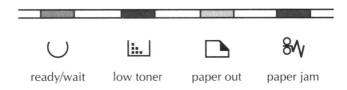

| ready/wait | low toner | paper out | paper jam |

Probable diagnosis: The problem is on the LaserWriter II NTX I/O board.

Solution: Check/replace the SIMMs in banks A, B and C.

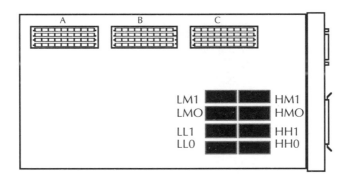

Approximate cost of repairing it yourself:		**$40.00**
1 LaserWriter II FX/II NTX SIMM	40.00	**1 hour**
Approximate third-party repair cost:		**$405.00**
1 LaserWriter II FX/II NTX SIMM	80.00	
5 hours labor	325.00	
Approximate dealer repair cost:		**$1,101.67**
1 new LaserWriter NTX I/O board	1031.67	
1 hour labor	70.00	

Symptoms: There's no test page on a LaserWriter II NT. The *paper jam* light is blinking red, but there's no paper jam. The self-test (print engine test) works OK.

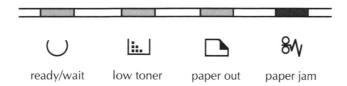

ready/wait	low toner	paper out	paper jam

Probable diagnosis: The problem is on the LaserWriter II NT logic board.

Solution: Check/replace the ROMs marked H2/L2 and H1/L1.

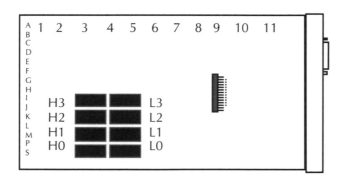

Approximate cost of repairing it yourself:		**$50.00**
1 ROM chip	50.00	**2 hours**
Approximate third-party repair cost:		**$375.00**
1 ROM chip	50.00	
5 hours labor	325.00	
Approximate dealer repair cost:		**$851.67**
1 new LaserWriter II NT I/O board	781.67	
1 hour labor	70.00	

Symptoms: There's no test page on a LaserWriter II NT. The status panel never lights up, but the self-test (print engine) works OK.

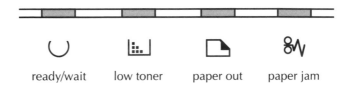

ready/wait   low toner   paper out   paper jam

Probable diagnosis: The problem is on the LaserWriter II NT logic board.

Solution: Check/replace the ROMs marked H3/L3 and H0/L0.

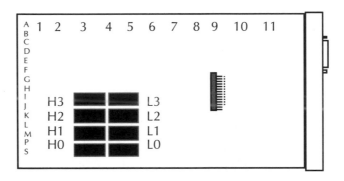

Approximate cost of repairing it yourself:		$50.00
1 ROM chip	50.00	2 hours
Approximate third-party repair cost:		$375.00
1 ROM chip	50.00	
5 hours labor	325.00	
Approximate dealer repair cost:		$851.67
1 new LaserWriter II NT I/O board	781.67	
1 hour labor	70.00	

Symptoms: The green *ready* light on a LaserWriter II SC is on and steady, but there is no response to the *Print...* command. Under Backgrounder, you get a dialog box indicating *Print Error: 258*.

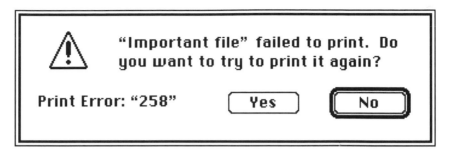

> ⚠ **"Important file" failed to print. Do you want to try to print it again?**
>
> **Print Error: "258"**   [**Yes**]   [**No**]

Probable diagnosis: The problem is on the LaserWriter II SC logic board.

Solution: Check/replace the SIMMs at board references D1 to J1.

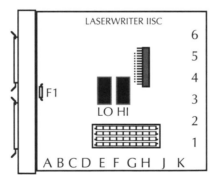

Approximate cost of repairing it yourself:		$32.00
1 256K LaserWriter II SC SIMM	32.00	*1 hour*
Approximate third-party repair cost:		**$389.00**
1 256K LaserWriter II SC SIMM	64.00	
5 hours labor	325.00	
Approximate dealer repair cost:		**$361.67**
1 new LaserWriter II SC I/O board	291.67	
1 hour labor	70.00	

Symptoms: When printing 8-bit frame captures on a LaserWriter II SC, everything prints in black and white (not in grayscale). When printing object drawings, special effects like flips and rotations generally fail to print.

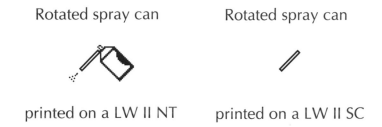

Rotated spray can   Rotated spray can

printed on a LW II NT   printed on a LW II SC

Probable diagnosis: Unlike the LaserWriter II NT and II NTX, the LaserWriter II SC doesn't have PostScript in ROM.

Solution: Install a software PostScript interpreter, like TScript Basic (published by TeleTypesetting) on your hard drive (you'll need at least 2 MB of RAM to use it).

T-Script Basic v3.0   T-Script® Fonts

Approximate cost of repairing it yourself:		***$55.00***
1 TScript Basic (street price)	55.00	***1 hour***
Approximate third-party repair cost:		***$1,565.00***
1 LaserWriter II NT I/O board	1,495.00	
1 hour labor	70.00	
Approximate dealer repair cost:		***$2,331.67***
1 LaserWriter II NT I/O board	2,261.67	
1 hour labor	70.00	

Symptoms: There are irregularly spaced white spots on every page.

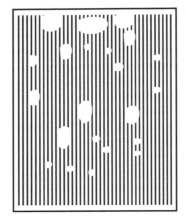

Probable diagnosis: The toner is unevenly distributed.

Solution: Check/replace the toner cartridge (HP part 92295A).

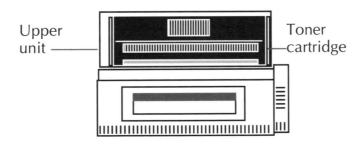

Upper unit ———— Toner cartridge

Approximate cost of repairing it yourself:		**$89.95**
1 toner cartridge	89.95	**1 min.**
Approximate third-party repair cost:		**$164.95**
1 toner cartridge	99.95	
1 hour labor	65.00	
Approximate dealer repair cost:		**$195.00**
1 toner cartridge	125.00	
1 hour labor	70.00	

Symptoms: The printout is generally too light.

Probable diagnosis: The print-density dial is set too high. The higher the setting, the lighter the printout.
Solution: Turn the print-density dial to a lower number or fully counterclockwise for the darkest possible printout.

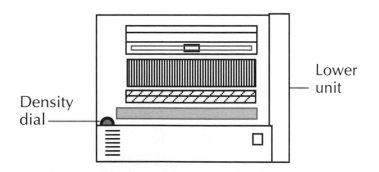

Approximate cost of repairing it yourself:		*1 min.*
Approximate third-party repair cost:		**$65.00**
1 hour labor	65.00	
Approximate dealer repair cost:		**$70.00**
1 hour labor	70.00	

Symptoms: The printout is generally too light. The *low toner* light on the status panel is blinking (orange).

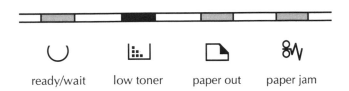

ready/wait   low toner   paper out   paper jam

Probable diagnosis: The toner cartridge is empty.

Solution: Check/replace the toner cartridge (HP part 92295A) located in the printer's upper unit.

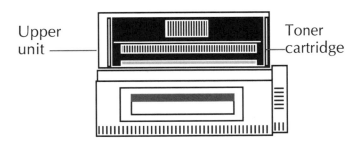

Approximate cost of repairing it yourself:		*$89.95*
1 toner cartridge	89.95	*1 min.*
Approximate third-party repair cost:		*$164.95*
1 toner cartridge	99.95	
1 hour labor	65.00	
Approximate dealer repair cost:		*$195.00*
1 toner cartridge	125.00	
1 hour labor	70.00	

Symptoms: Solid blacks appear to have been blotted. The edges are rough, not crisp.

LaserWriter II NT

Probable diagnosis: The problem is in the transfer corona assembly (located in the lower unit).

Solution: Clean/tighten the transfer corona assembly.

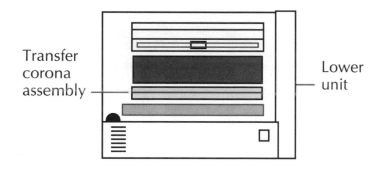

Transfer corona assembly —   Lower unit

Approximate cost of repairing it yourself:		*10 min.*
Approximate third-party repair cost:		**$325.00**
5 hours labor	325.00	
Approximate dealer repair cost:		**$350.00**
5 hours labor	350.00	

Symptoms: The printout is generally too dark.

Probable diagnosis: The print-density dial is set too low. The lower the setting, the darker the printout.

Solution: Turn the print-density dial to a higher number or fully clockwise for the lightest possible printout.

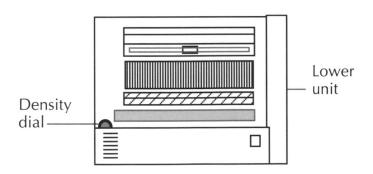

Approximate cost of repairing it yourself:		*1 min.*
Approximate third-party repair cost:		**$65.00**
1 hour labor	65.00	
Approximate dealer repair cost:		**$70.00**
1 hour labor	70.00	

Symptoms: Every printout, including the test page, is solid white.

Typical history: The problem occurred right after you installed a new toner cartridge.

Probable diagnosis: The sealing tape is still in the toner cartridge.

Solution: Check/remove the factory sealing tape.

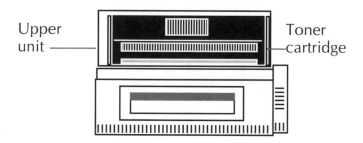

Approximate cost of repairing it yourself:		*1 min.*
Approximate third-party repair cost:		*$65.00*
1 hour labor	65.00	
Approximate dealer repair cost:		*$70.00*
1 hour labor	70.00	

Symptoms: Every printout, including the test page, is solid black.

Probable diagnosis: The problem is in the toner cartridge.

Solution: Check/replace the toner cartridge (HP part 92295A).

Upper unit —— 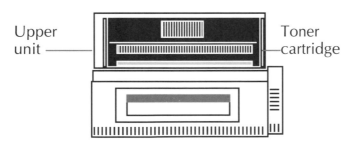 ——Toner cartridge

Approximate cost of repairing it yourself:		**$89.95**
1 toner cartridge	89.95	***1 min.***
Approximate third-party repair cost:		**$164.95**
1 toner cartridge	99.95	
1 hour labor	65.00	
Approximate dealer repair cost:		**$195.00**
1 toner cartridge	125.00	
1 hour labor	70.00	

Symptoms: Every printout, including the test page, is solid gray.

Probable diagnosis: The problem is in the toner cartridge.

Solution: Check/replace the toner cartridge (HP part 92295A).

Upper unit ——— 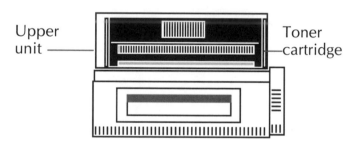 ———Toner cartridge

Approximate cost of repairing it yourself:		**$89.95**
1 toner cartridge	89.95	**1 min.**
Approximate third-party repair cost:		**$164.95**
1 toner cartridge	99.95	
1 hour labor	65.00	
Approximate dealer repair cost:		**$195.00**
1 toner cartridge	125.00	
1 hour labor	70.00	

Symptoms: There are stains on the back of every printed page.

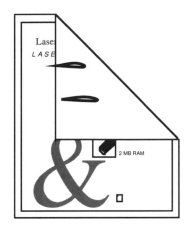

Probable diagnosis: The problem is in the fuser assembly.

Solution: Check/replace the fixing roller cleaner wand (HP part RG1-0966-000).

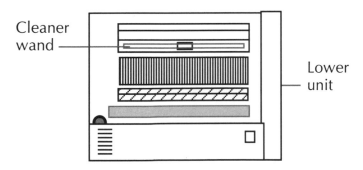

Approximate cost of repairing it yourself:		*$1.85*
1 fixing roller cleaner wand	1.85	*1 min.*
Approximate third-party repair cost:		*$325.00*
5 hours labor	325.00	
Approximate dealer repair cost:		*$350.00*
5 hours labor	350.00	

Symptoms: There are stains on the back of every printed page.

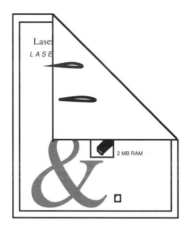

Probable diagnosis: The lower unit is dirty.

Solution: Clean the lower unit, particularly the black plastic feeder guide and brass-color transfer guide.

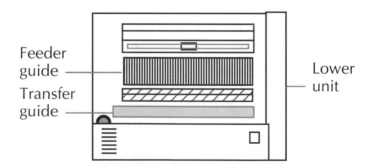

Approximate cost of repairing it yourself:	***30 min.***
Approximate third-party repair cost:	**$325.00**
5 hours labor 325.00	
Approximate dealer repair cost:	**$350.00**
5 hours labor 350.00	

Symptoms: There are black marks on one side of every page.

Probable diagnosis: The photosensitive drum needs cleaning.

Solution: Clean the affected edge of the photosensitive drum. If the problem recurs, replace the toner cartridge (HP part 92295A).

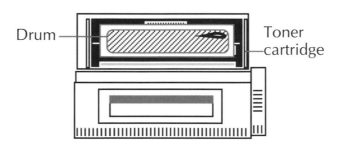

Approximate cost of repairing it yourself:		***$89.95***
1 toner cartridge	89.95	***10 min.***
Approximate third-party repair cost:		***$164.95***
1 toner cartridge	99.95	
1 hour labor	65.00	
Approximate dealer repair cost:		***$195.00***
1 toner cartridge	125.00	
1 hour labor	70.00	

Symptoms: There are regularly spaced horizontal white lines on every page.

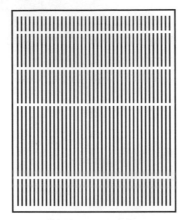

Probable diagnosis: The photosensitive drum is scarred.

Solution: Check/replace the toner cartridge (HP part 92295A).

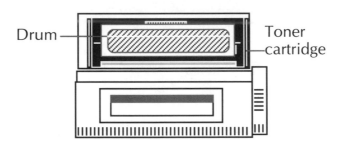

Drum — Toner cartridge

Approximate cost of repairing it yourself:		$89.95
1 toner cartridge	89.95	*1 min.*
Approximate third-party repair cost:		$164.95
1 toner cartridge	99.95	
1 hour labor	65.00	
Approximate dealer repair cost:		$195.00
1 toner cartridge	125.00	
1 hour labor	70.00	

Symptoms: An ozone (auto-exhaust) smell lingers about the printer. Other than that, it seems OK.

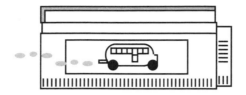

Probable diagnosis: The ozone filter is allowing gas to escape.

Solution: Check/replace the ozone filter.

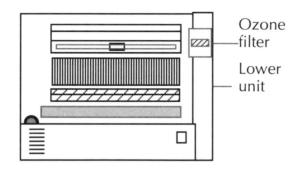

Ozone filter

Lower unit

Approximate cost of repairing it yourself:		$10.50
1 ozone filter	10.50	*1 hour*
Approximate third-party repair cost:		*$346.00*
1 ozone filter	21.00	
5 hours labor	325.00	
Approximate dealer repair cost:		*$392.00*
1 ozone filter	42.00	
5 hours labor	350.00	

PARTS VENDORS
AND
SERVICE PROVIDERS

American Educational Services

7611 Allman Drive
Annandale VA 22003
703/256-5315

component-level repairs on 800K disk drives
replacement heads for 800K disk drives

Digi-Key

701 Brooks Avenue S
Box 677
Thief River Falls MN 56701-0677
800/344-4539

miscellaneous ICs and other small parts

GDT Softworks

Box 1865
Point Roberts WA 98281
604/291-9121

BetterWriter printer drivers

Impact Printhead Services

8701 Cross Park Drive #101
Austin TX 78754
800/777-4323

OEM (C-Tech, formerly C. Itoh) printheads for ImageWriter printers
component-level repair of ImageWriter printheads

JDR Microdevices

2233 Samaritan Drive
San Jose CA 95124
800/538-5000

miscellaneous ICs and other small parts

MCM Electronics
650 E Congress Park Drive
Centerville OH 45459-4072
800/543-4330

miscellaneous ICs and other small parts

MEI/Micro Center
1100 Steelwood Road
Columbus OH 43212
800/634-3478

ribbon cassettes for ImageWriter printers
OEM (HP) toner cartridges for LaserWriter printers

National Parts
Box 573
Chester NY 10918
914/469-4800

OEM (C-Tech, formerly C. Itoh) parts for ImageWriter printers

On-Time Mac Service
830 Woodside Road
Redwood City CA 94061
415/367-6263

component-level repairs on Macintosh analog boards, logic
boards and power supplies, ImageWriters and LaserWriters

Ontrack Computer Systems
6321 Bury Drive, #5-19
Eden Prairie MN 55346
800/752-1333

DiskManager Mac SCSI formatting software

Parts Now

810 Stewart Street
Madison WI 53704
800/421-0967

OEM (HP) parts for LaserWriter printers
component-level repairs on LaserWriter fusers and LaserWriter
  power supplies

Soft Solutions

907 River Road #98
Eugene OR 97404
503/461-1136

OEM parts for Macintosh analog boards and logic boards
component-level repairs on Macintosh analog boards, logic
  boards, and power supplies
Macintosh Repair & Upgrade Secrets
Macintosh Printer (Repair & Upgrade) Secrets
Macintosh II Repair and Upgrade Secrets

Sony Service Company, Parts Division, Publications Department

8281 NW 107th Terrace
Kansas City MO 64153
816/891-7550

service manuals for Sony CPD-1302 and CPD-1304 monitors
OEM parts for Sony monitors

TeleTypesetting

311 Harvard Street
Brookline, MA 02146
617/734-9700

TScript Basic (PostScript interpreter) for LaserWriter IISC

Symptom index

Symptoms are grouped according to the hardware they affect, following the book's chapter organization. For problems with an Apple CD SC or Scanner, Hayes Smartmodem or Hewlett Packard DeskJet Plus or DeskWriter, check the hard drive section.

For more information on Macintosh Bible products, or to order copies, see the following pages.

Macintosh® Bible products

The Mac Bible, Third Edition. It's the best-selling Mac book ever, with 565,000 copies in print (including six foreign translations). The Third Edition has **1,115 pages**, with a 90-page index and a 68-page glossary. At 2½¢ a page for the best—and most clearly written—Mac information available, how can you go wrong? **$28.**

The Mac Bible Guide to FileMaker Pro. "A must for every FileMaker Pro user," as Dennis Marshall, Claris's FileMaker Pro product manager put it, this is the first comprehensive guide to the Mac's leading database program. With dozens of step-by-step procedures, shortcuts and troubleshooting tips, it will save hours of your time. **$18.**

The Mac Bible Guide to System 7. System 7 represents the most dramatic changes ever made to the Mac's basic system software, and sets the stage for all future system improvements. Our crystal-clear, accessible and affordable guide, by veteran Mac author Charles Rubin, gets you up to speed with System 7 in no time. **$12.**

The Mac Bible Software Disks, Third Edition. This companion to *The Mac Bible* is full of great public-domain software, shareware, templates, fonts and art. Painstakingly gleaned from literally thousands of programs, these disks offer you *la crème de la crème*. Over 1.5 megabytes of software on two 800K disks. **$20.**

The Mac Bible "What Do I Do Now?" Book, Second Edition. Completely updated through System 7, this bestseller covers just about every sort of basic problem a Mac user can encounter—from the wrong fonts appearing in a printout to the mouse not responding. Easy to understand, it's an essential resource for beginners and experienced users alike. **$15.**

The Dead Mac Scrolls. Now any Mac owner—from the novice to the expert—can keep repair costs down. In this unique and encyclopedic guide, Macintosh guru Larry Pina diagnoses hundreds of hardware problems, shows you the simplest and cheapest way to fix them, and tells you how much the repairs should cost. **$32.**

T*he Dead Mac Scrolls Disk.* Align, diagnose and evaluate monitors and Apple printers with the latest versions of Larry Pina's Color Test Pattern Generator and Laser Test Character Generator programs. Important logic board tests are also included on this invaluable disk. **$32.**

System 7 package. Save $5 when you buy *The Mac Bible* and our *Guide to System 7* together. **$35.**
Bible/software combo. Save $10 when you buy *The Mac Bible* and the *Bible* disks together. **$38.**
Super combo. Save $13 by buying *The Mac Bible,* the *Bible* disks and *"What Do I Do Now?" Book*. **$50.**
Ultra combo. Save $15 by buying *The Mac Bible* with the *Bible* disks, *the "What Do I Do Now?" Book* and the *Guide to System 7*. **$60.**

***The Macintosh Bible* T-shirt.** Our T-shirts are striking—bright magenta lettering on your choice of black or white. Here's a little picture of the front. The back says: **Easy is hard** *(The second commandment from The Macintosh Bible)*. These are high-quality, preshrunk, 100% cotton shirts; they're thick, well-made and run large. **$9.**

To order any of these products, just fill out the form on the next page and send it with your payment to **Goldstein & Blair, Box 7635, Berkeley CA 94707**. You can also order by phone with Visa or MasterCard. Call us at 510/524-4000 between 10 and 5, Pacific Time, Mon–Fri (or leave your phone number on our answering machine). If you order three or more products (except the T-shirts), we'll give you the same quantity deal as the stores we sell to—call for details.

All our products have a 30-day money-back guarantee. If you're not *completely satisfied*, just return your order within 30 days, with your receipt, in resellable condition (i.e. not damaged) and get all your money back, including what we charged to ship your order and what you spent to return it (by UPS ground or parcel post).

Order form for Macintosh® Bible products

Please send me:

_____ copies of *The Macintosh Bible, 3 ed.*	@ $28 =	$_____
_____ copies of *The Macintosh Bible Guide to FileMaker Pro*	@ $18 =	$_____
_____ copies of *The Macintosh Bible Guide to System 7*	@ $12 =	$_____
_____ copies of *The Macintosh Bible Software Disks, 3 ed.*	@ $20 =	$_____
_____ copies of *The Macintosh Bible "What Do I Do Now?" Book, 2 ed.*	@ $15 =	$_____
_____ copies of *The Dead Mac Scrolls*	@ $32 =	$_____
_____ copies of *The Dead Mac Scrolls disk*	@ $32 =	$_____
_____ copies of the System 7 package	@ $35 =	$_____
_____ copies of the *Bible*/software combination	@ $38 =	$_____
_____ copies of the super combo	@ $50 =	$_____
_____ copies of the ultra combo	@ $60 =	$_____
_____ *Macintosh Bible* T-shirts	@ $ 9 =	$_____

(in black:___S ___M ___L ___XL; in white:___S ___M ___L ___XL)

shipping, handling and tax (if any): $_____
[$4 total per order in the US; see following page for other rates]

TOTAL: $_____

☐ I'm enclosing a check for the total shown above. *(Customers outside the US: checks must be in US funds and payable through a US bank. You can also pay with an international postal money order, but not a Eurocheque. It's easiest if you pay by credit card.)*

☐ Please charge my charge card for the total amount shown above:

VISA/MasterCard # _____ exp. date _____

cardholder signature _____

Ship this order to: *(PLEASE PRINT CLEARLY)*

_____
name

_____
address (please give us a street address so we can ship via UPS)

_____
city, state, zip (or city, postal code, country)

_____
daytime phone number (with area code)

Enclose this order form with your payment in an envelope and send it to:
Goldstein & Blair, Box 7635, Berkeley CA 94707
Thanks.   DMS

Just tear this page out of the book. (It should come out cleanly and won't hurt the book.)

Shipping Information

Anywhere in the US:

Shipping and handling costs $4 for up to three items, and that includes tax (if any). Each combo counts as one item. If you're buying three or more of our products, call us at 510/524-4000 to get shipping costs and find out about our quantity discounts.

Outside the US:

These prices cover *airmail* to Canada and Mexico and *surface* to everywhere else. (Surface and air rates to Canada and Mexico are nearly identical, so we automatically ship by air.)

$7 per copy of *The Macintosh Bible* or *Dead Mac Scolls;* $3 per set of software disks or the T-shirt (T-shirts are shipped free when ordered with other products); $5 per copy of the *Guide to FileMaker Pro* or *Guide to System 7;* $6 per *The "What Do I Do Now?" Book;* $10 per System 7 package, *Bible*/software or super combo; $12 per ultra combo.

International airmail shipping rates

These rates apply *only* to products shipped by *airmail* to countries *other than* the US, Canada & Mexico.

Colombia, Venezuela, Central America and the Caribbean:

$11 per *Macintosh Bible;* $5 per *Guide to System 7,* software disks or T-shirt; $7 per *Guide to FileMaker Pro* or *"What Do I Do Now?" Book;* $9 per *Dead Mac Scrolls;* $15 per System 7 package, *Bible*/software or super combo; $18 per ultra combo.

South America (except Colombia & Venezuela), Europe (except the USSR), Morocco, Algeria, Libya, Egypt & Tunisia:

$18 per *Macintosh Bible;* $6 per software disks or T-shirt; $8 per *Guide to System 7;* $12 per *"What Do I Do Now?" Book;* $10 per *Guide to FileMaker Pro;* $15 per *Dead Mac Scrolls;* $23 per System 7 package or *Bible*/software combo; $25 per super combo; $30 per ultra combo.

Everywhere else:

$24 per *Macintosh Bible;* $8 per software disks or T-shirt; $11 per *Guide to System 7;* $16 per *"What Do I Do Now?" Book;* $13 per *Guide to FileMaker Pro;* $20 per *Dead Mac Scrolls;* $31 per System 7 package or *Bible*/software combo; $35 per super combo; $42 per ultra combo.